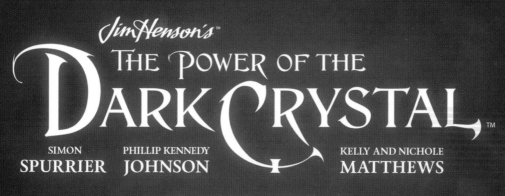

Jim Henson's™
THE POWER OF THE
DARK CRYSTAL™

SIMON
SPURRIER

PHILLIP KENNEDY
JOHNSON

KELLY AND NICHOLE
MATTHEWS

VOLUME THREE

Published by
ARCHAIA™

Jim Henson's
THE POWER OF THE
DARK CRYSTAL ™

Based on screenplays by
Craig Pearce
And
Annette Duffy and **David Odell**

Written by **Simon Spurrier** and
Phillip Kennedy Johnson
Illustrated by **Kelly** and **Nichole Matthews**
Lettered by **Jim Campbell**

Cover by **Jae Lee** and **June Chung**
Chapter Break Art by **Sana Takeda**

Series Designer **Marie Krupina**
Collection Designer **Scott Newman**
Associate Editor **Gavin Gronenthal**
Editors **Cameron Chittock** and **Sierra Hahn**

Special Thanks to **Brian Henson**, **Lisa Henson**,
Jim Formanek, **Nicole Goldman**, **Maryanne Pittman**,
Carla DellaVedova, **Justin Hilden**, **Karen Falk**, **Blanca
Lista**, **Wendy Froud**, **Brian Froud**, **Kelsey Dieterich**,
and the entire **Jim Henson Company** team.

Ross Richie CEO & Founder
Joy Huffman CFO
Matt Gagnon Editor-in-Chief
Filip Sablik President, Publishing & Marketing
Stephen Christy President, Development
Lance Kreiter Vice President, Licensing & Merchandising
Arune Singh Vice President, Marketing
Bryce Carlson Vice President, Editorial & Creative Strategy
Scott Newman Manager, Production Design
Kate Henning Manager, Operations
Spencer Simpson Manager, Sales
Elyse Strandberg Manager, Finance
Sierra Hahn Executive Editor
Jeanine Schaefer Executive Editor
Dafna Pleban Senior Editor
Shannon Watters Senior Editor
Eric Harburn Senior Editor
Chris Rosa Editor
Matthew Levine Editor
Sophie Philips-Roberts Associate Editor
Amanda LaFranco Associate Editor
Jonathan Manning Associate Editor
Gavin Gronenthal Assistant Editor
Gwen Waller Assistant Editor
Allyson Gronowitz Assistant Editor
Jillian Crab Design Coordinator
Michelle Ankley Design Coordinator
Kara Leopard Production Designer
Marie Krupina Production Designer
Grace Park Production Designer
Chelsea Roberts Production Design Assistant
Samantha Knapp Production Design Assistant
José Meza Live Events Lead
Stephanie Hocutt Digital Marketing Lead
Esther Kim Marketing Coordinator
Cat O'Grady Digital Marketing Coordinator
Amanda Lawson Marketing Assistant
Holly Aitchison Digital Sales Coordinator
Morgan Perry Retail Sales Coordinator
Megan Christopher Operations Coordinator
Rodrigo Hernandez Mailroom Assistant
Zipporah Smith Operations Assistant
Sabrina Lesin Accounting Assistant
Breanna Sarpy Executive Assistant

JIM HENSON'S THE POWER OF THE DARK CRYSTAL
Volume Three, March 2020. Published by Archaia, a
division of Boom Entertainment, Inc. © 2020 The Jim
Henson Company. JIM HENSON's mark & logo, THE
POWER OF THE DARK CRYSTAL, mark & logo, and all
related characters and elements are trademarks of The Jim
Henson Company. Originally published in single magazine
form as THE POWER OF THE DARK CRYSTAL No. 9-12.
™ & © 2017, 2018 The Jim Henson Company. All rights
reserved. Archaia™ and the Archaia logo are trademarks of
Boom Entertainment, Inc., registered in various countries
and categories. All characters, events, and institutions
depicted herein are fictional. Any similarity between any of
the names, characters, persons, events, and/or institutions
in this publication to actual names, characters, and persons,
whether living or dead, events, and/or institutions is
unintended and purely coincidental.

BOOM! Studios, 5670 Wilshire Boulevard, Suite 400, Los
Angeles, CA 90036-5679. Printed in China. First Printing.

ISBN: 978-1-68415-493-7, eISBN: 978-1-64144-651-8

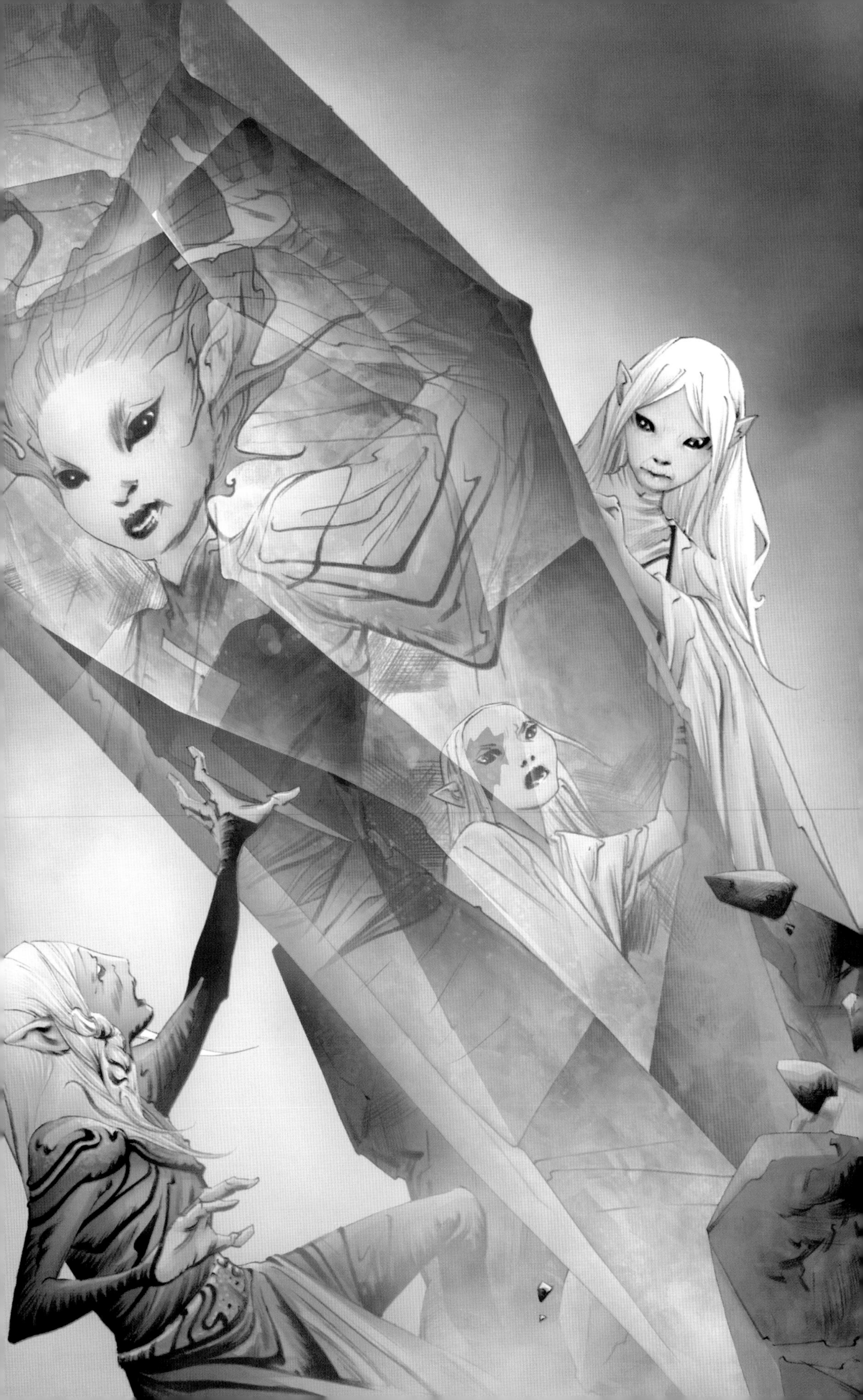

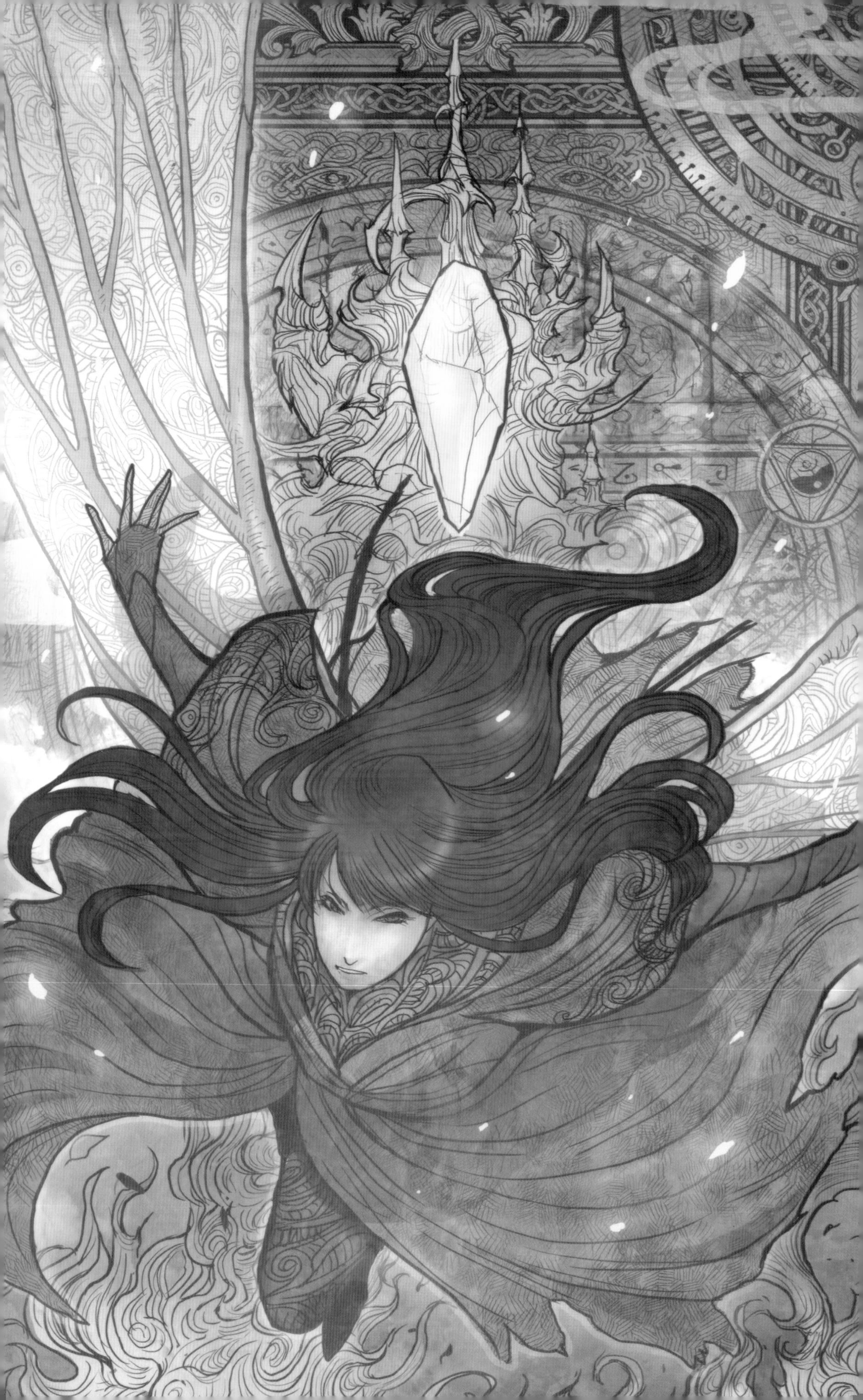

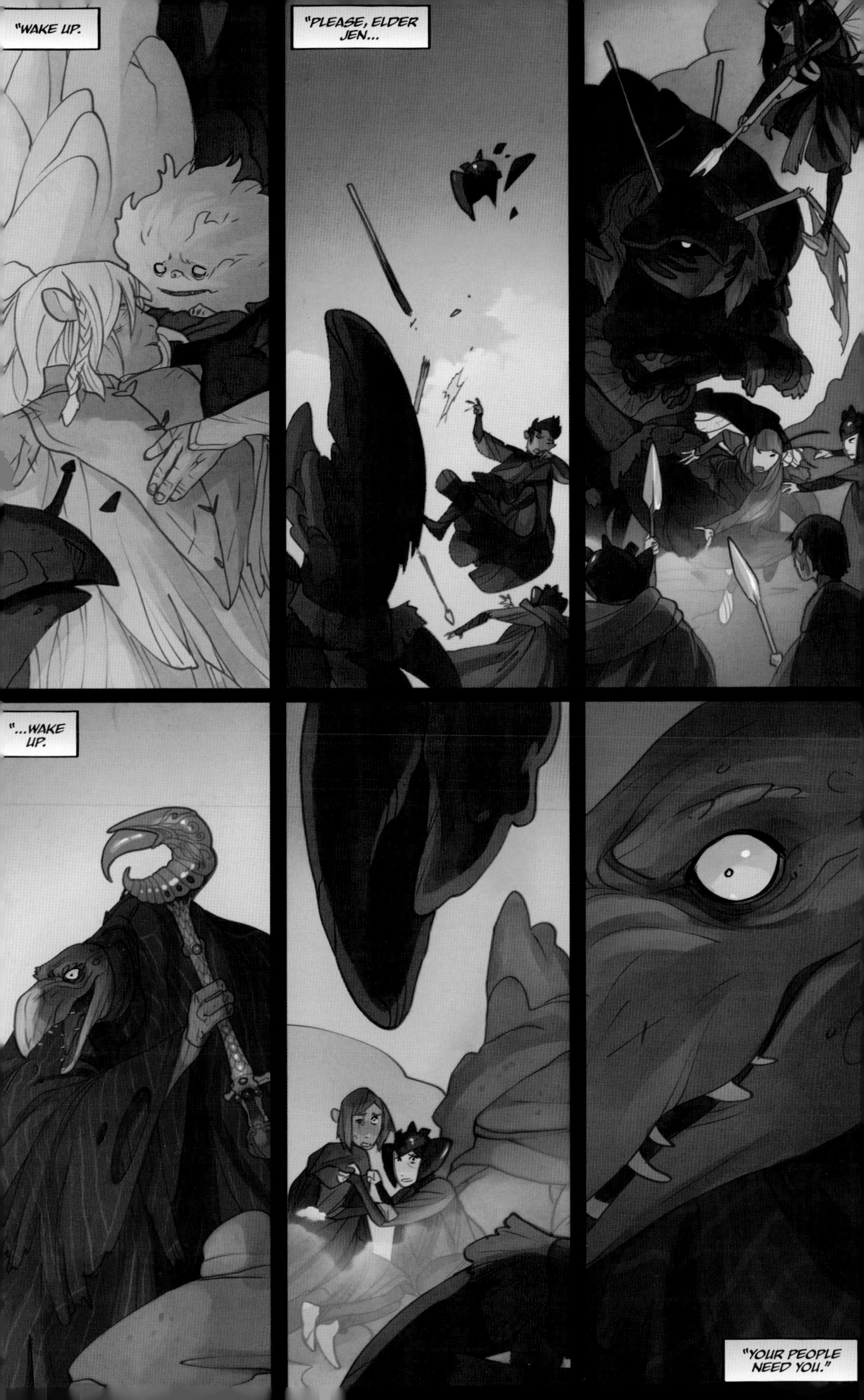
"WAKE UP.
"PLEASE, ELDER JEN...
"...WAKE UP.
"YOUR PEOPLE NEED YOU."

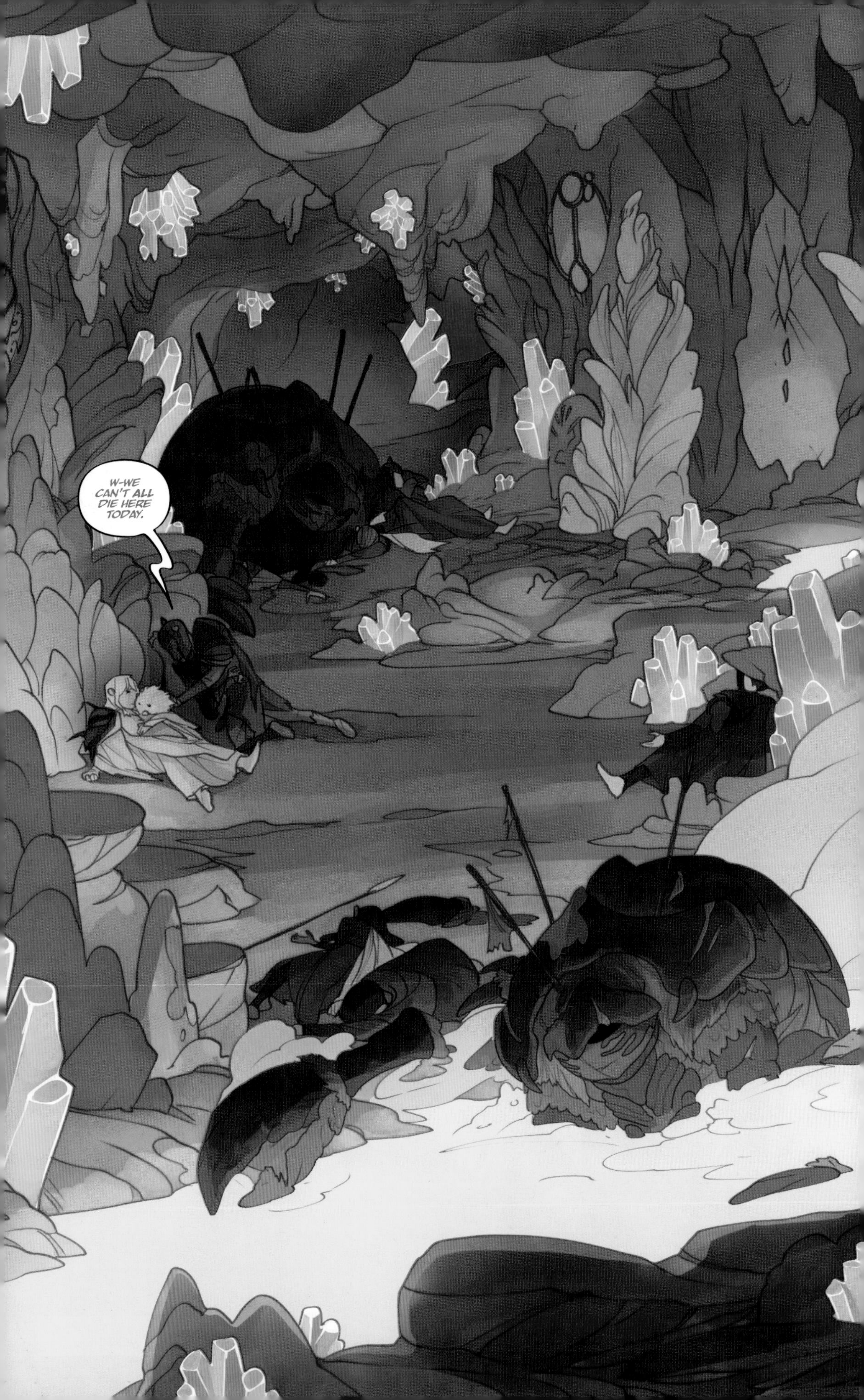
W-WE CAN'T ALL DIE HERE TODAY.

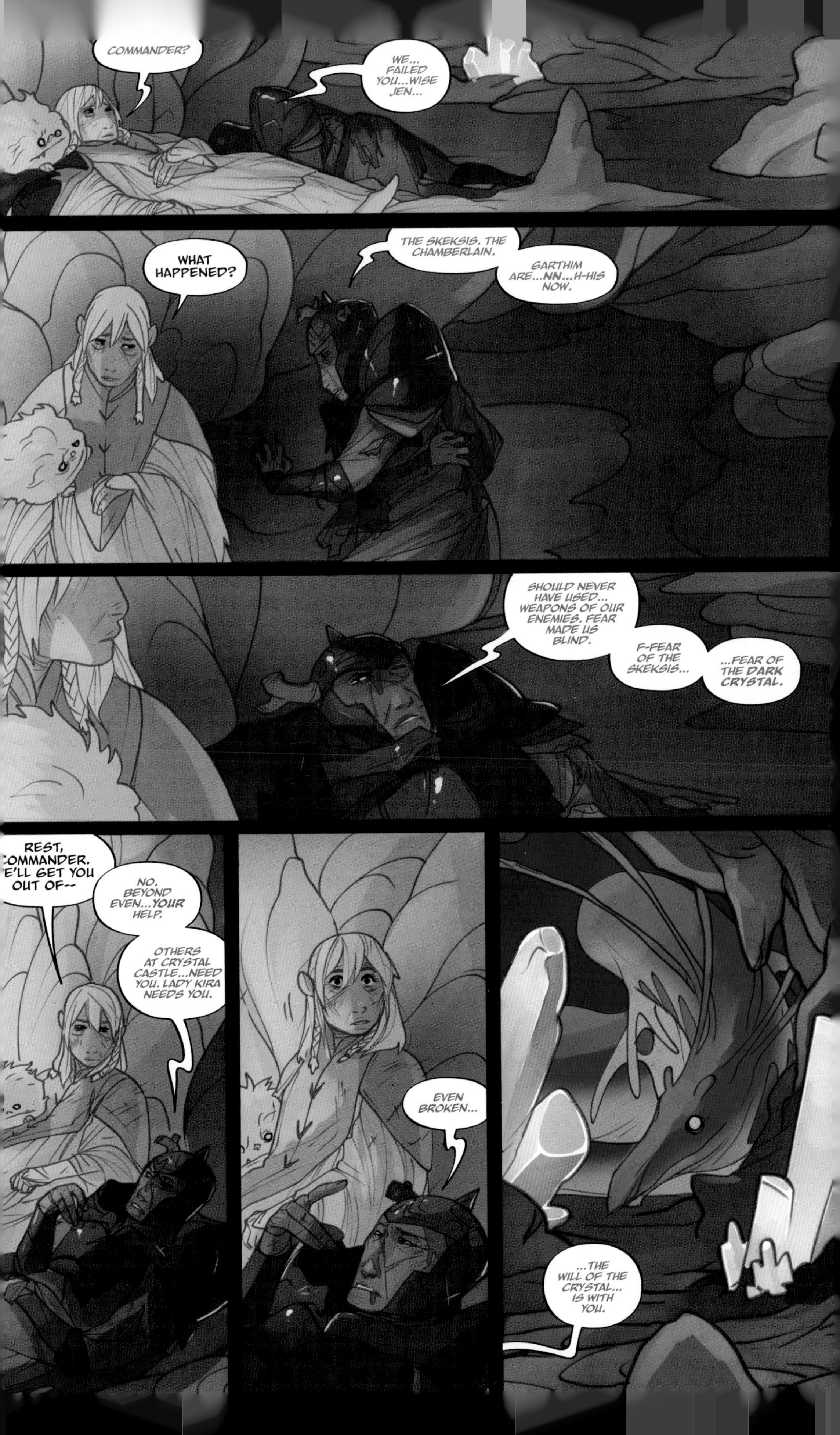
COMMANDER?
WE... FAILED YOU...WISE JEN...
WHAT HAPPENED?
THE SKEKSIS. THE CHAMBERLAIN.
GARTHIM ARE...NN...H-HIS NOW.
SHOULD NEVER HAVE USED... WEAPONS OF OUR ENEMIES. FEAR MADE US BLIND.
F-FEAR OF THE SKEKSIS...
...FEAR OF THE DARK CRYSTAL.
REST, COMMANDER. WE'LL GET YOU OUT OF--
NO. BEYOND EVEN...YOUR HELP.
OTHERS AT CRYSTAL CASTLE...NEED YOU. LADY KIRA NEEDS YOU.
EVEN BROKEN...
...THE WILL OF THE CRYSTAL... IS WITH YOU.

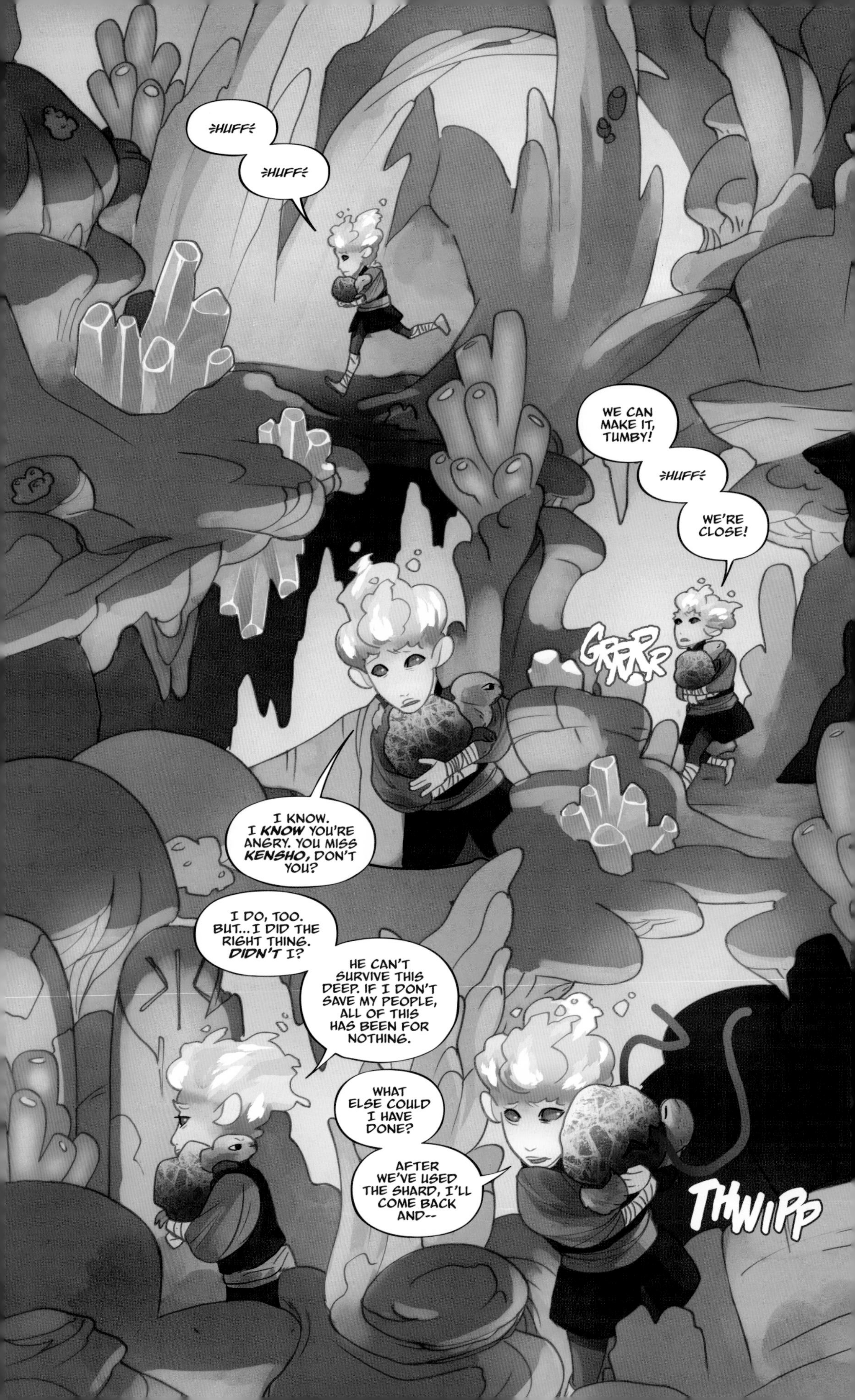

HUFF
HUFF
WE CAN MAKE IT, TUMBY!
HUFF
WE'RE CLOSE!
GRRRR
I KNOW. I **KNOW** YOU'RE ANGRY. YOU MISS **KENSHO**, DON'T YOU?
I DO, TOO. BUT... I DID THE RIGHT THING. ***DIDN'T*** I?
HE CAN'T SURVIVE THIS DEEP. IF I DON'T SAVE MY PEOPLE, ALL OF THIS HAS BEEN FOR NOTHING.
WHAT ELSE COULD I HAVE DONE?
AFTER WE'VE USED THE SHARD, I'LL COME BACK AND--
THWIPP

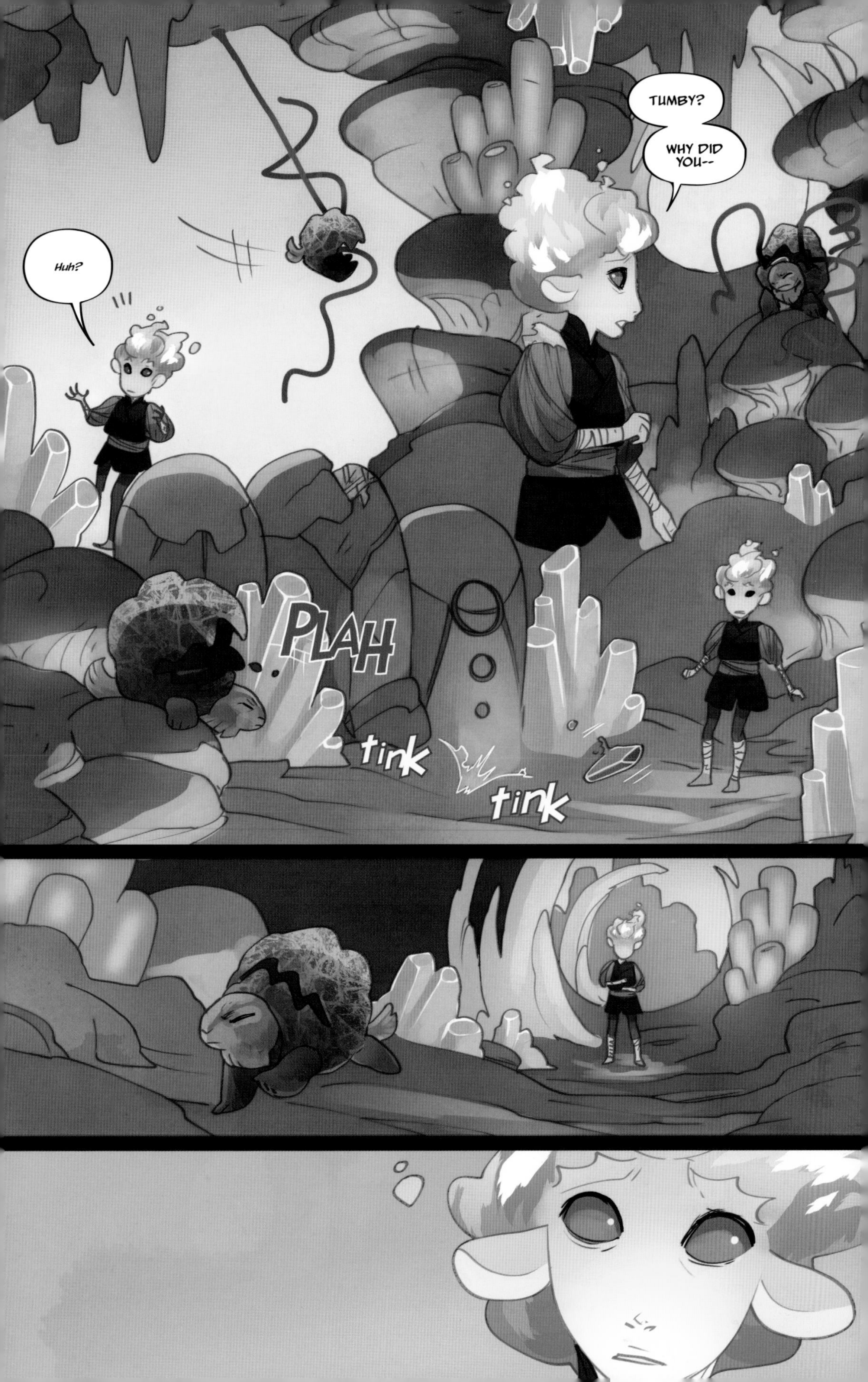
TUMBY?
WHY DID YOU--
Huh?
PLAH
tink
tink

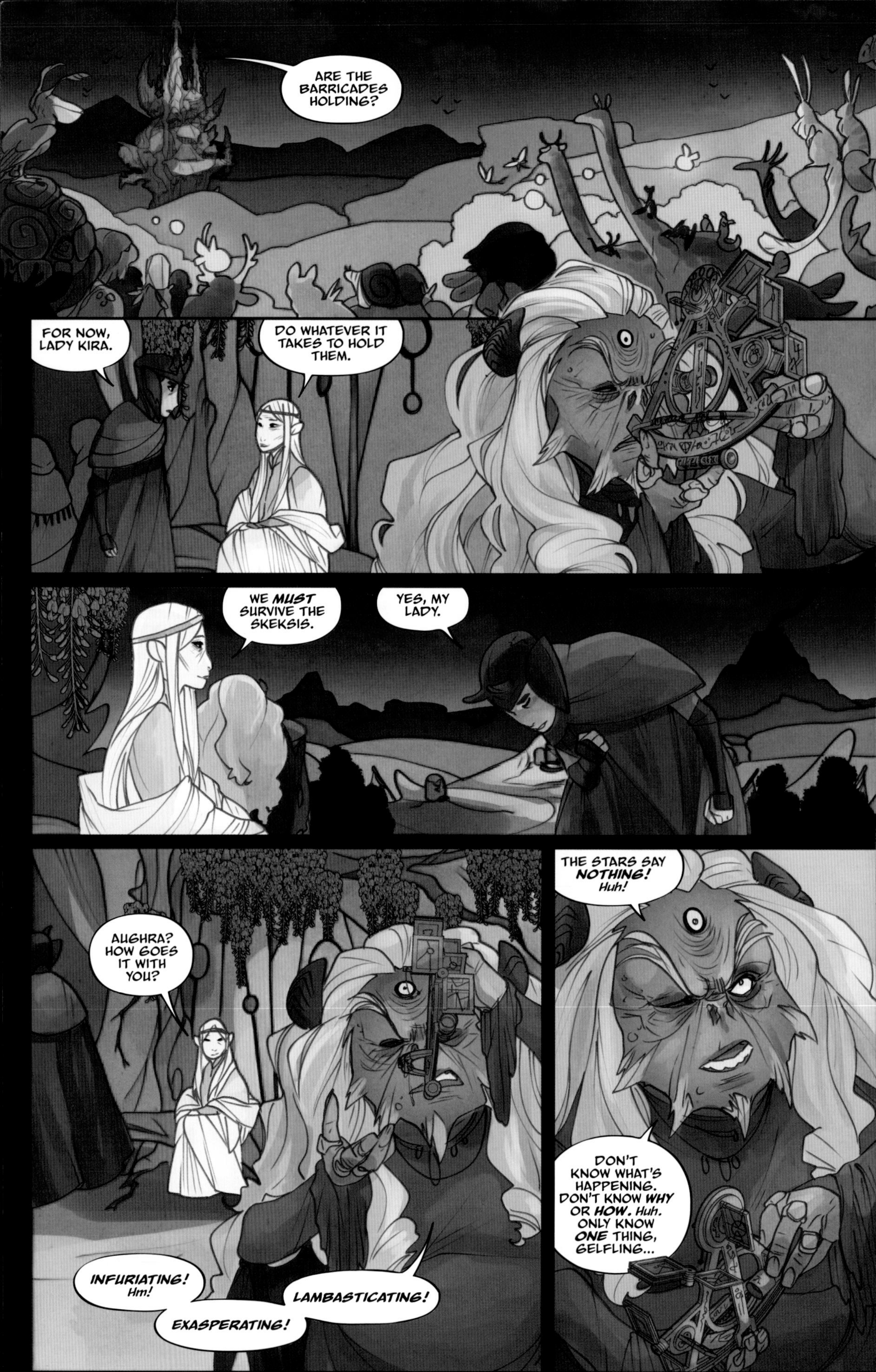
ARE THE BARRICADES HOLDING?
FOR NOW, LADY KIRA.
DO WHATEVER IT TAKES TO HOLD THEM.
WE **MUST** SURVIVE THE SKEKSIS.
YES, MY LADY.
AUGHRA? HOW GOES IT WITH YOU?
INFURIATING! Hm!
EXASPERATING!
LAMBASTICATING!
THE STARS SAY **NOTHING!** *Huh!*
DON'T KNOW WHAT'S HAPPENING. DON'T KNOW **WHY** OR **HOW**. Huh. ONLY KNOW **ONE** THING, GELFLING...

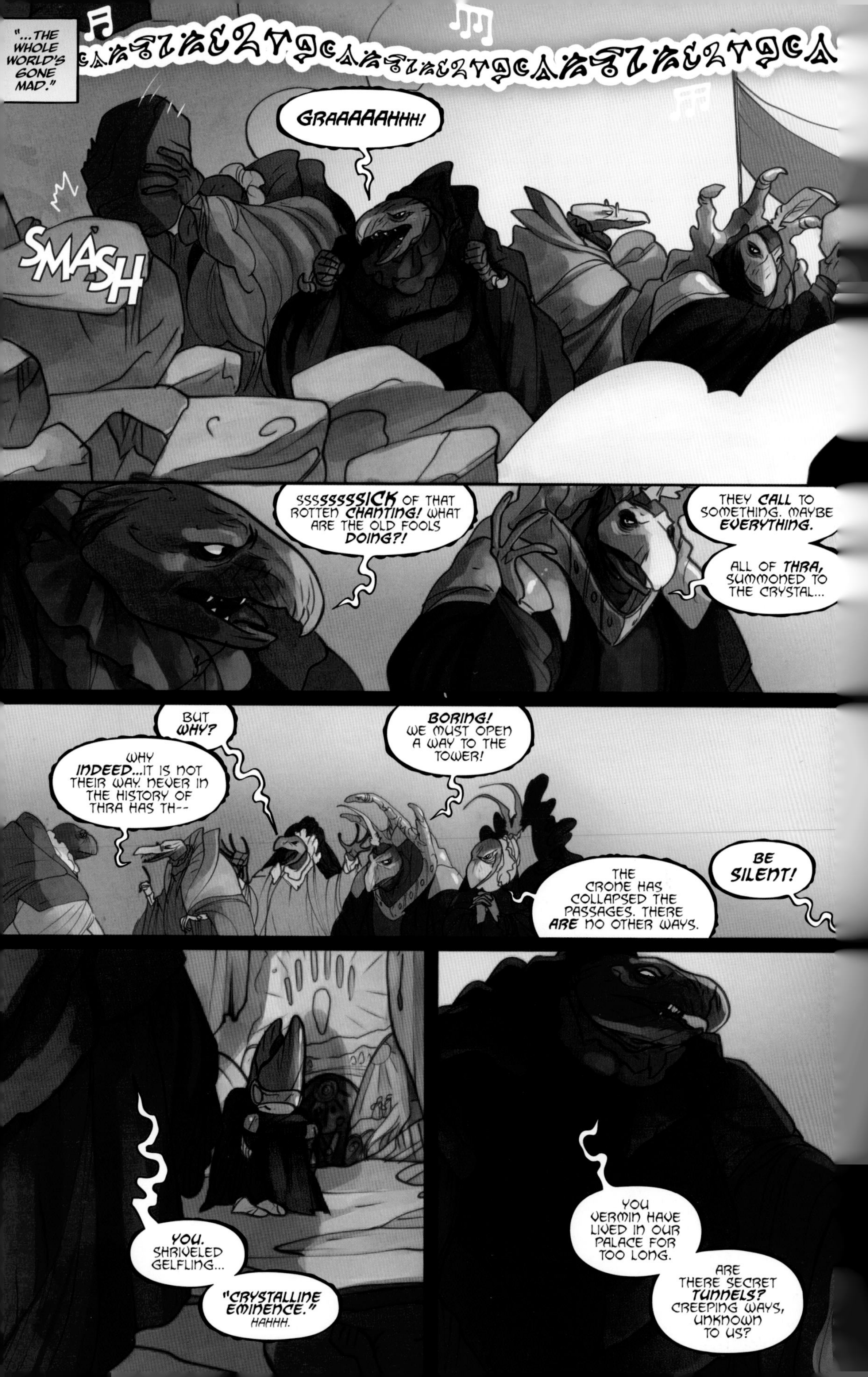
"...THE WHOLE WORLD'S GONE MAD."
SMASH
GRAAAAAHHH!
SSSSSSSSICK OF THAT ROTTEN CHANTING! WHAT ARE THE OLD FOOLS DOING?!
THEY CALL TO SOMETHING. MAYBE EVERYTHING.
ALL OF THRA, SUMMONED TO THE CRYSTAL...
BUT WHY?
WHY INDEED...IT IS NOT THEIR WAY. NEVER IN THE HISTORY OF THRA HAS TH--
BORING! WE MUST OPEN A WAY TO THE TOWER!
THE CRONE HAS COLLAPSED THE PASSAGES. THERE ARE NO OTHER WAYS.
BE SILENT!
YOU. SHRIVELED GELFLING...
"CRYSTALLINE EMINENCE." HAHHH.
YOU VERMIN HAVE LIVED IN OUR PALACE FOR TOO LONG.
ARE THERE SECRET TUNNELS? CREEPING WAYS, UNKNOWN TO US?

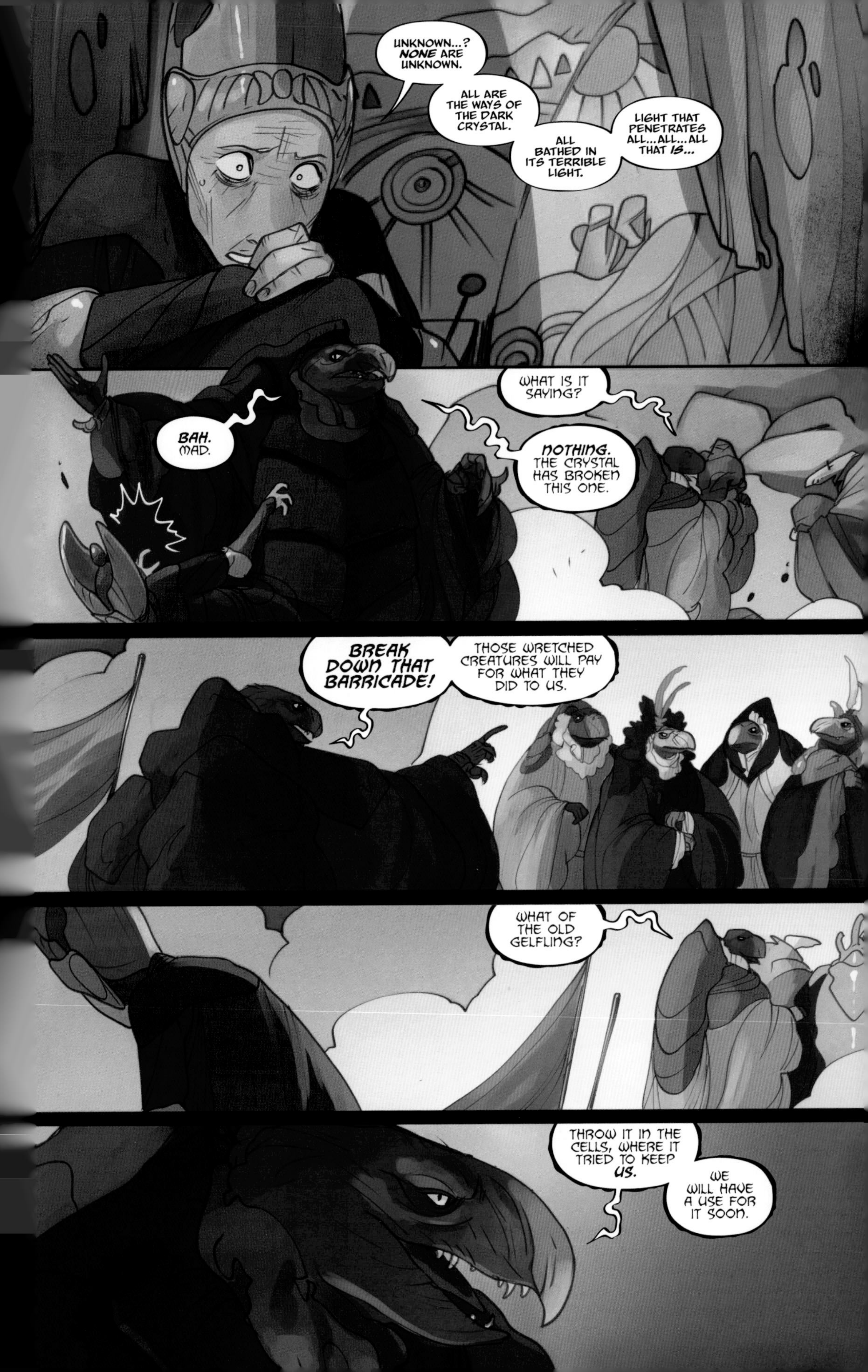
UNKNOWN...? NONE ARE UNKNOWN.
ALL ARE THE WAYS OF THE DARK CRYSTAL.
ALL BATHED IN ITS TERRIBLE LIGHT.
LIGHT THAT PENETRATES ALL...ALL...ALL THAT IS...
WHAT IS IT SAYING?
BAH. MAD.
NOTHING. THE CRYSTAL HAS BROKEN THIS ONE.
BREAK DOWN THAT BARRICADE!
THOSE WRETCHED CREATURES WILL PAY FOR WHAT THEY DID TO US.
WHAT OF THE OLD GELFLING?
THROW IT IN THE CELLS, WHERE IT TRIED TO KEEP US.
WE WILL HAVE A USE FOR IT SOON.

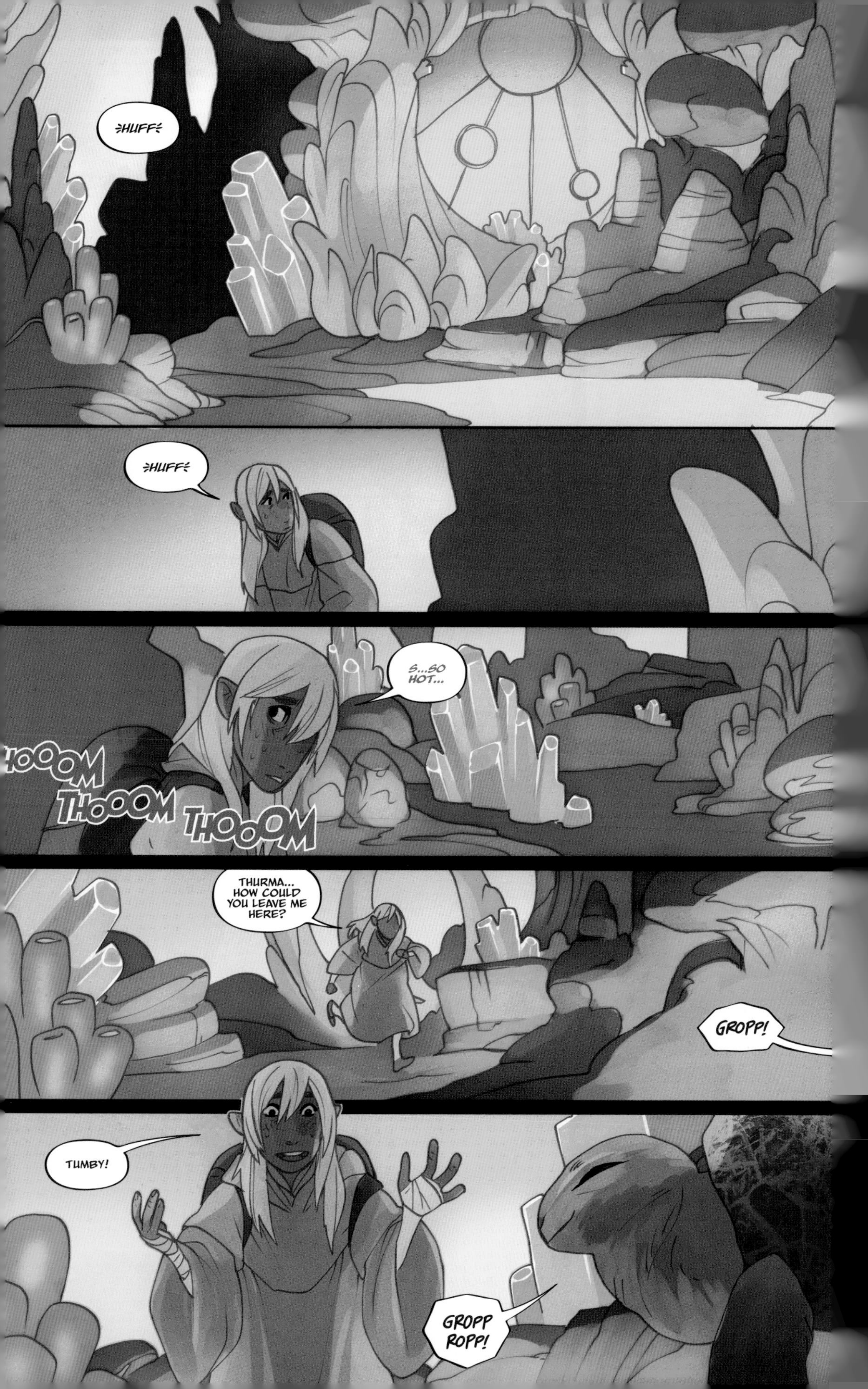
≠HUFF≠
≠HUFF≠
S...SO HOT...
THOOOM THOOOM THOOOM
THURMA... HOW COULD YOU LEAVE ME HERE?
GROPP!
TUMBY!
GROPP ROPP!

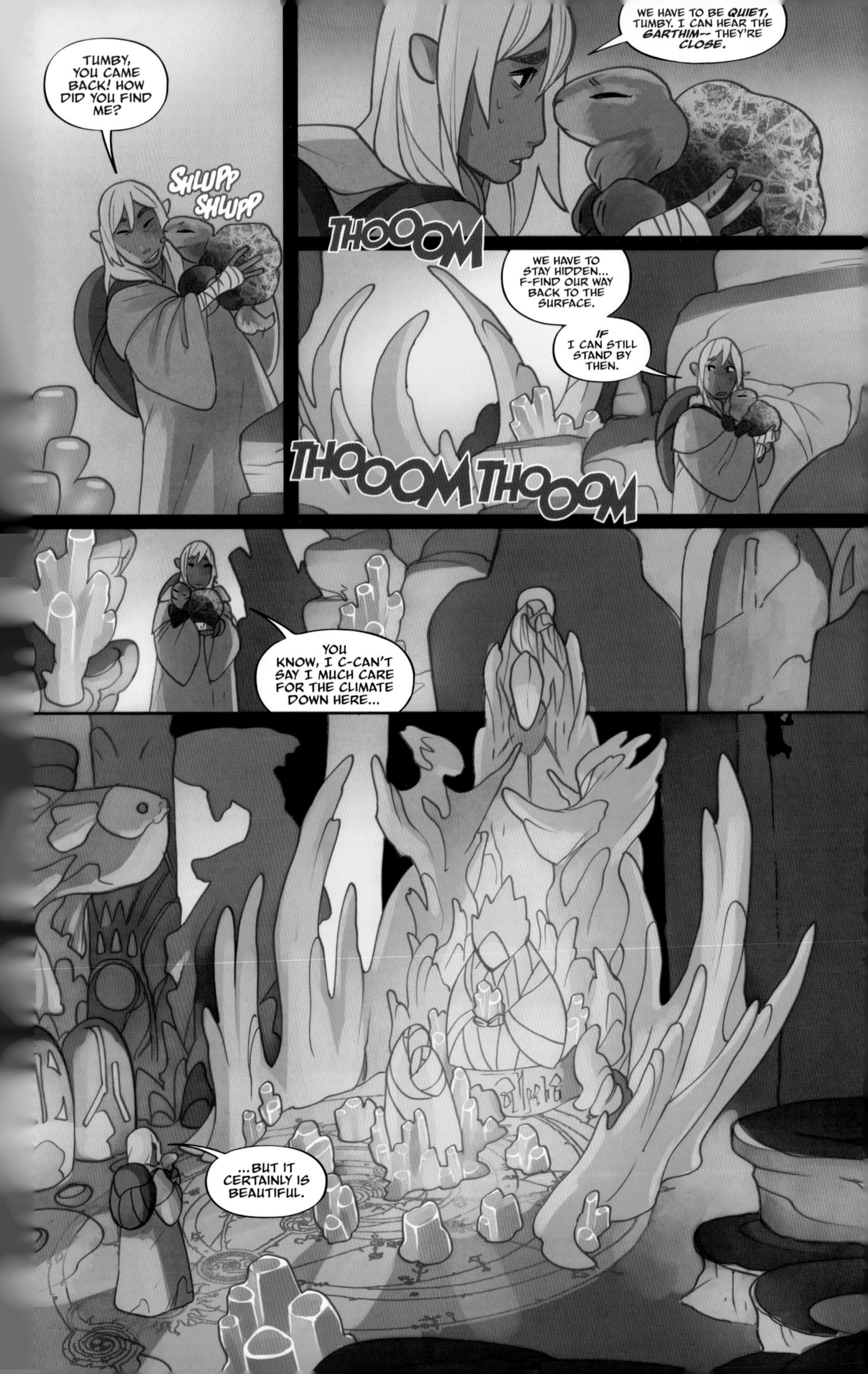
TUMBY, YOU CAME BACK! HOW DID YOU FIND ME?
SHLUPP SHLUPP
WE HAVE TO BE QUIET, TUMBY. I CAN HEAR THE GARTHIM-- THEY'RE CLOSE.
THOOOM
WE HAVE TO STAY HIDDEN... F-FIND OUR WAY BACK TO THE SURFACE.
IF I CAN STILL STAND BY THEN.
THOOOM THOOOM
YOU KNOW, I C-CAN'T SAY I MUCH CARE FOR THE CLIMATE DOWN HERE...
...BUT IT CERTAINLY IS BEAUTIFUL.

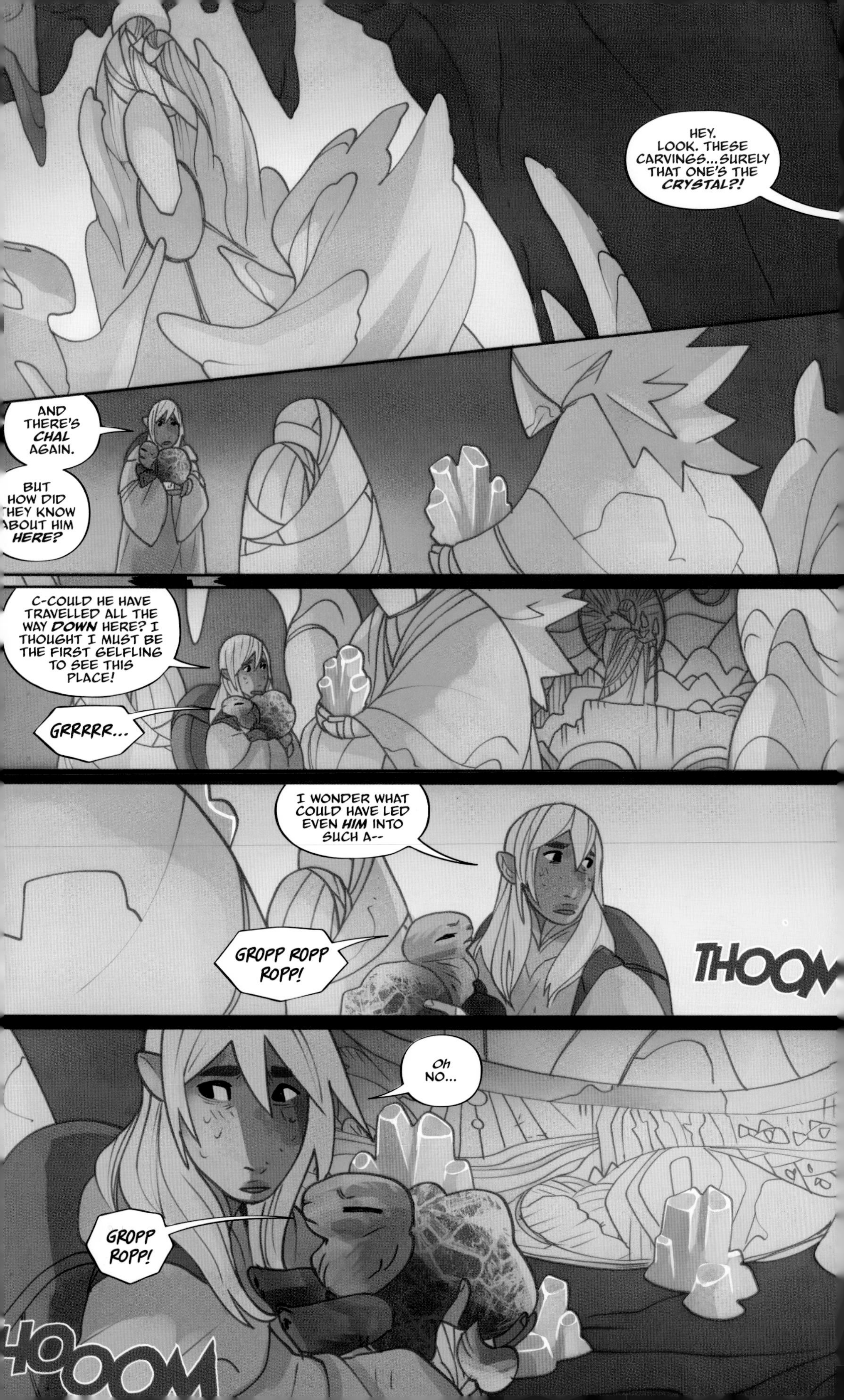
HEY. LOOK. THESE CARVINGS...SURELY THAT ONE'S THE CRYSTAL?!
AND THERE'S CHAL AGAIN.
BUT HOW DID THEY KNOW ABOUT HIM HERE?
C-COULD HE HAVE TRAVELLED ALL THE WAY DOWN HERE? I THOUGHT I MUST BE THE FIRST GELFLING TO SEE THIS PLACE!
GRRRRR...
I WONDER WHAT COULD HAVE LED EVEN HIM INTO SUCH A--
GROPP ROPP ROPP!
THOOM
Oh NO...
GROPP ROPP!
HOOOM

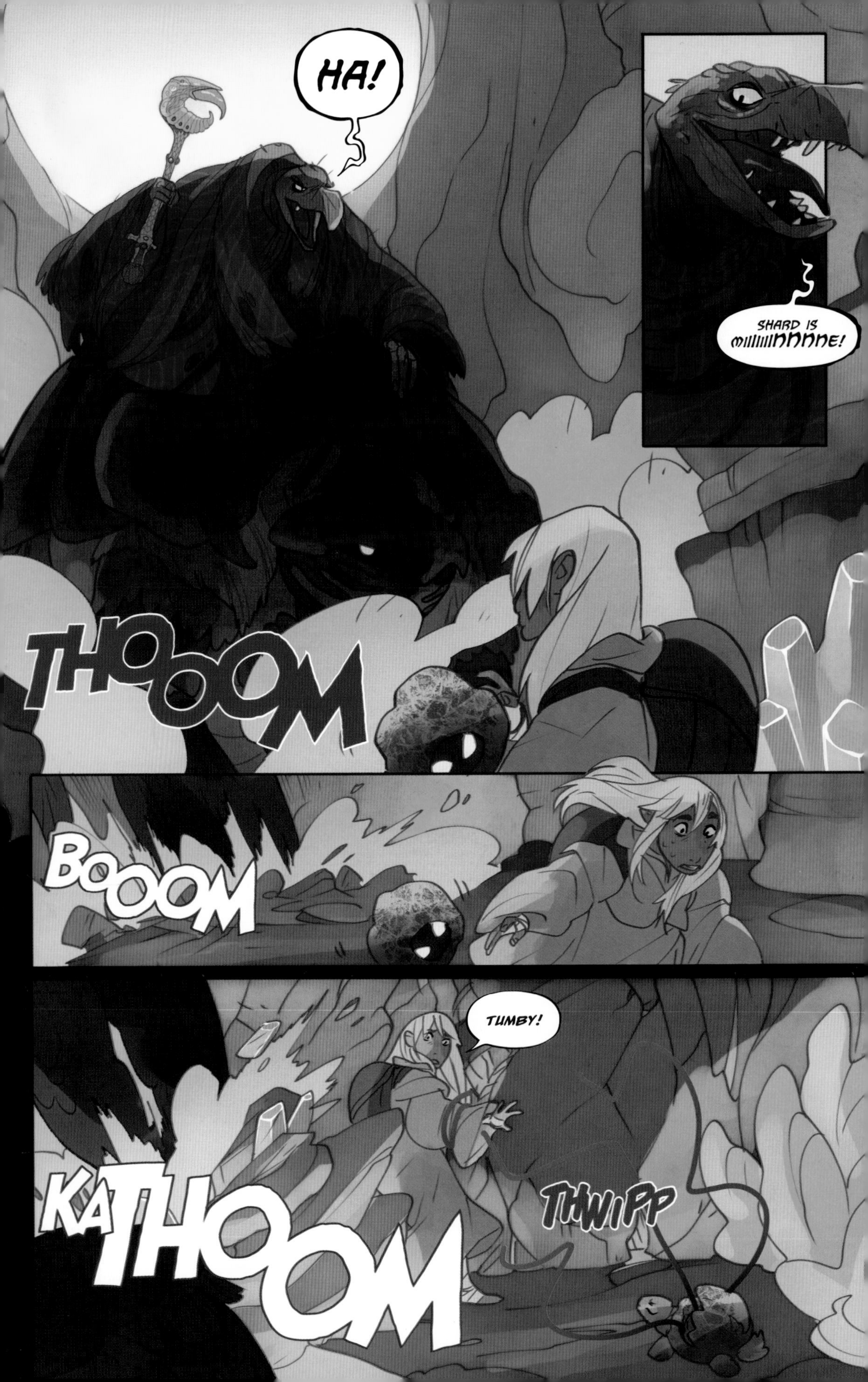
HA!
SHARD IS MIIIIIINNNNE!
THOOOM
BOOOM
TUMBY!
KATHOOOM
THWIPP

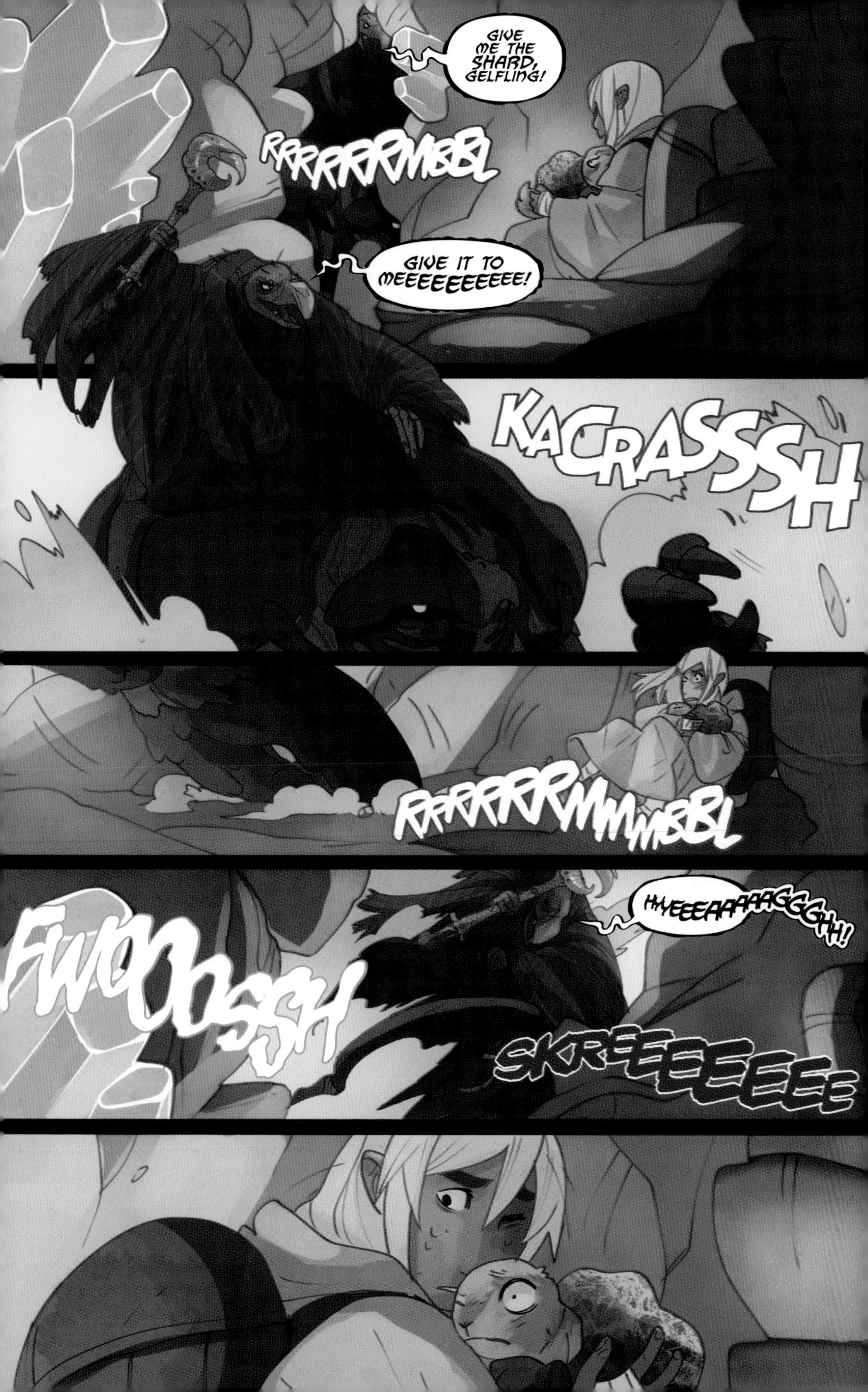
GIVE ME THE SHARD, GELFLING!
RRRRRRRMBBL
GIVE IT TO MEEEEEEEEEE!
KACRASSSH
RRRRRRRMMMBBL
FWOOOSSH
HYYEEEAAAAAAGGGHH!
SKREEEEEEEEEE

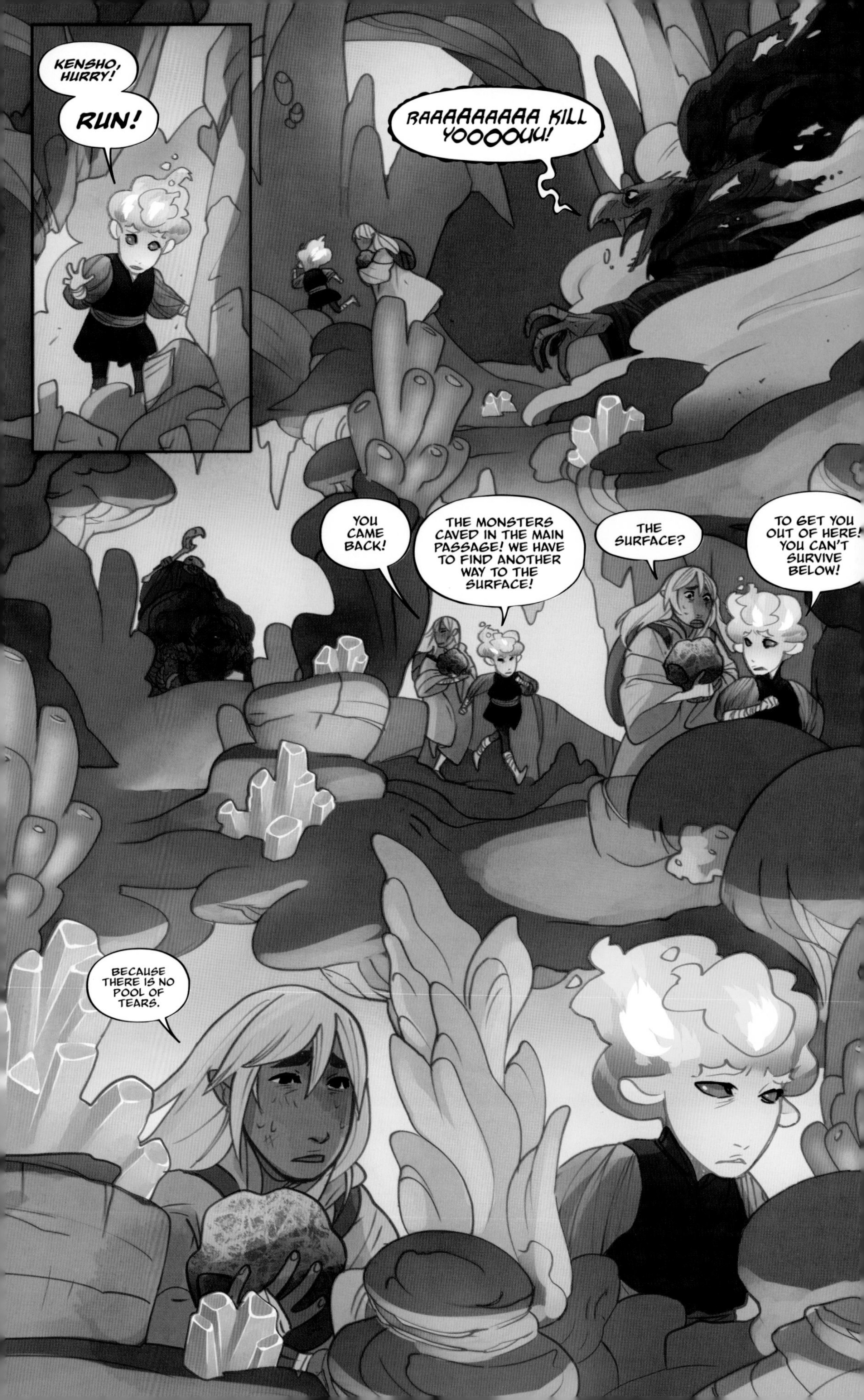
KENSHO, HURRY!
RUN!
RAAAAAAAAA KILL YOOOOUU!
YOU CAME BACK!
THE MONSTERS CAVED IN THE MAIN PASSAGE! WE HAVE TO FIND ANOTHER WAY TO THE SURFACE!
THE SURFACE?
TO GET YOU OUT OF HERE! YOU CAN'T SURVIVE BELOW!
BECAUSE THERE IS NO POOL OF TEARS.

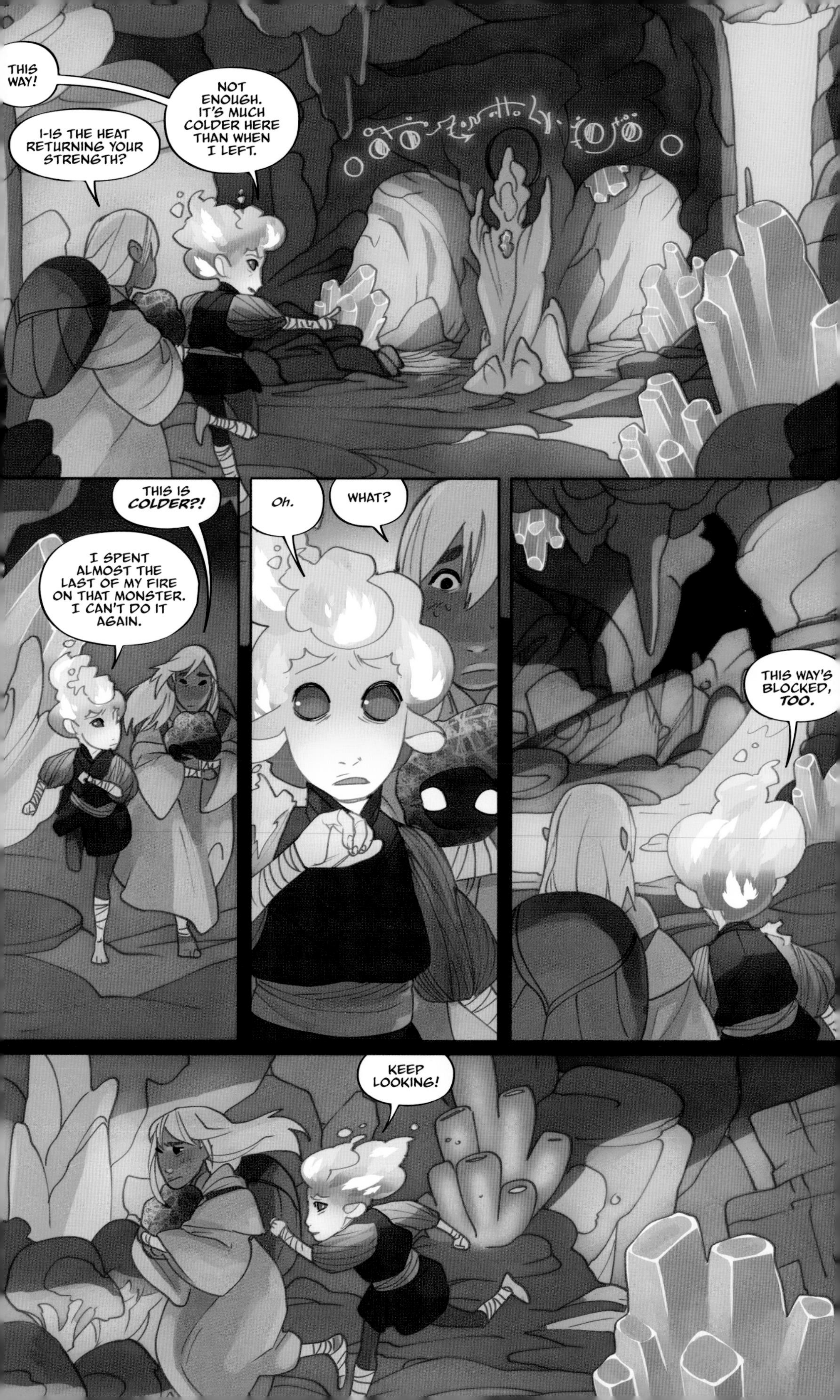
THIS WAY!
I-IS THE HEAT RETURNING YOUR STRENGTH?
NOT ENOUGH. IT'S MUCH COLDER HERE THAN WHEN I LEFT.
THIS IS COLDER?!
I SPENT ALMOST THE LAST OF MY FIRE ON THAT MONSTER. I CAN'T DO IT AGAIN.
Oh.
WHAT?
THIS WAY'S BLOCKED, TOO.
KEEP LOOKING!

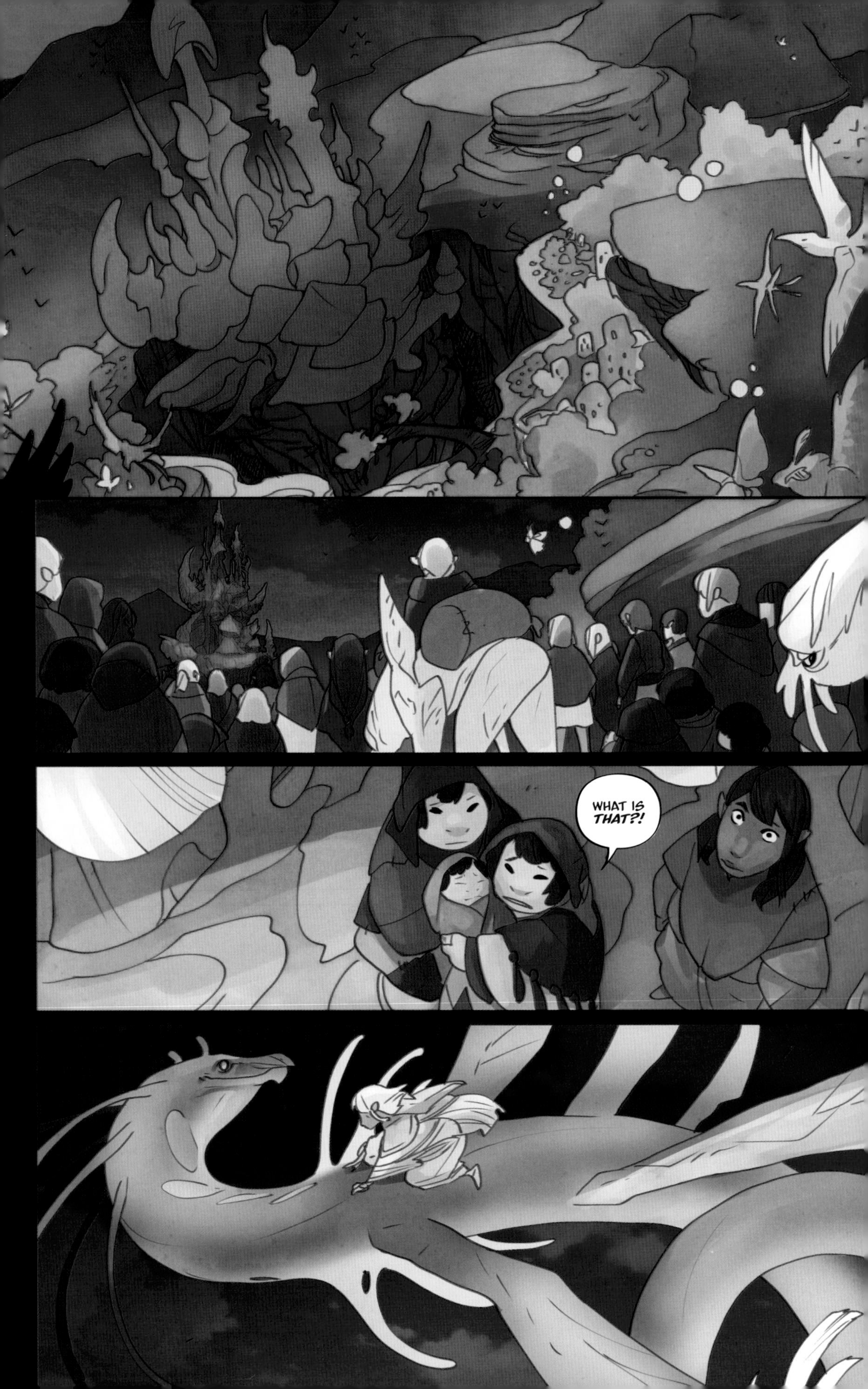
WHAT IS THAT?!

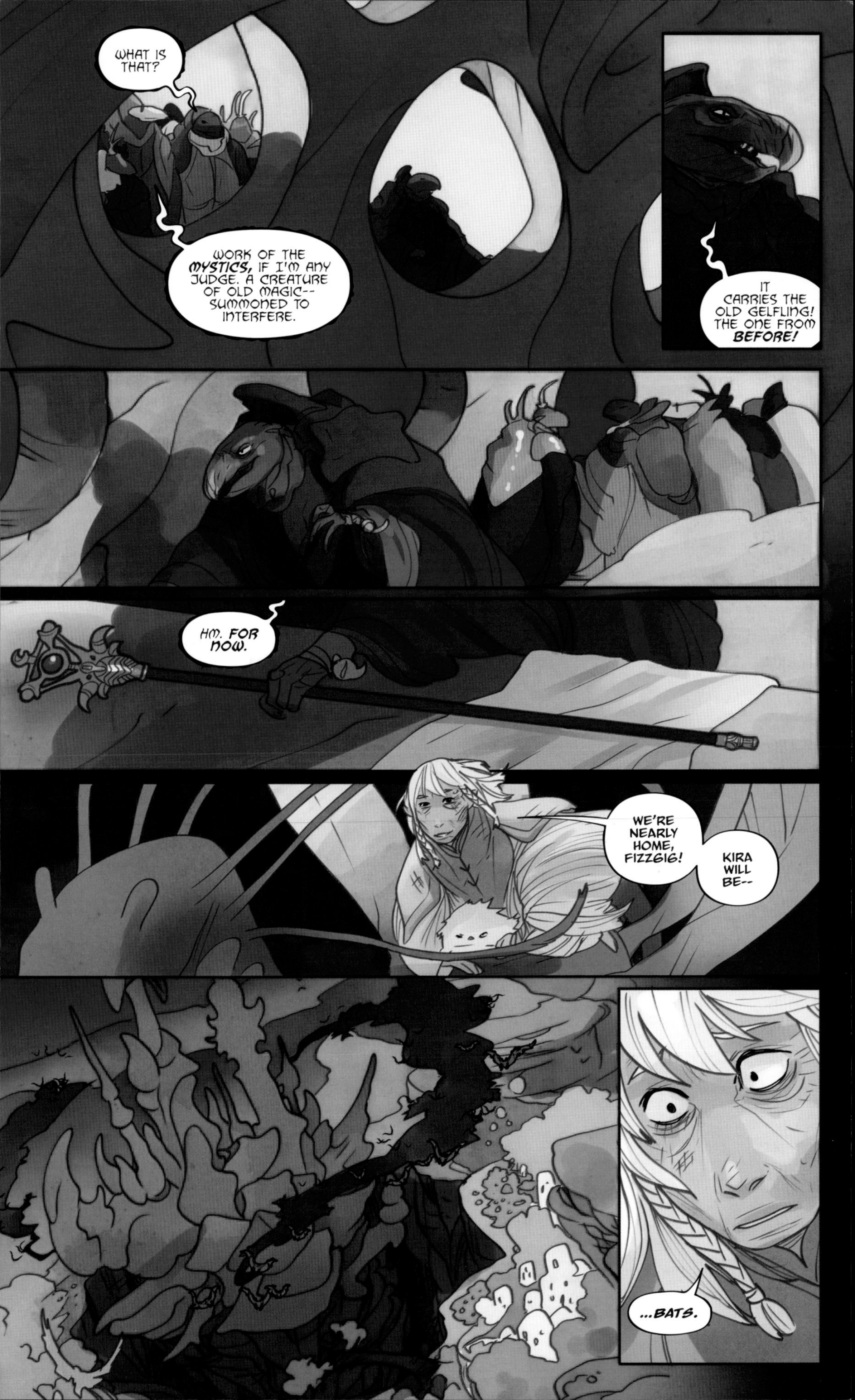
WHAT IS THAT?
WORK OF THE **MYSTICS,** IF I'M ANY JUDGE. A CREATURE OF OLD MAGIC-- SUMMONED TO INTERFERE.
IT CARRIES THE OLD GELFLING! THE ONE FROM ***BEFORE!***
HM. **FOR NOW.**
WE'RE NEARLY HOME, FIZZGIG!
KIRA WILL BE--
...BATS.

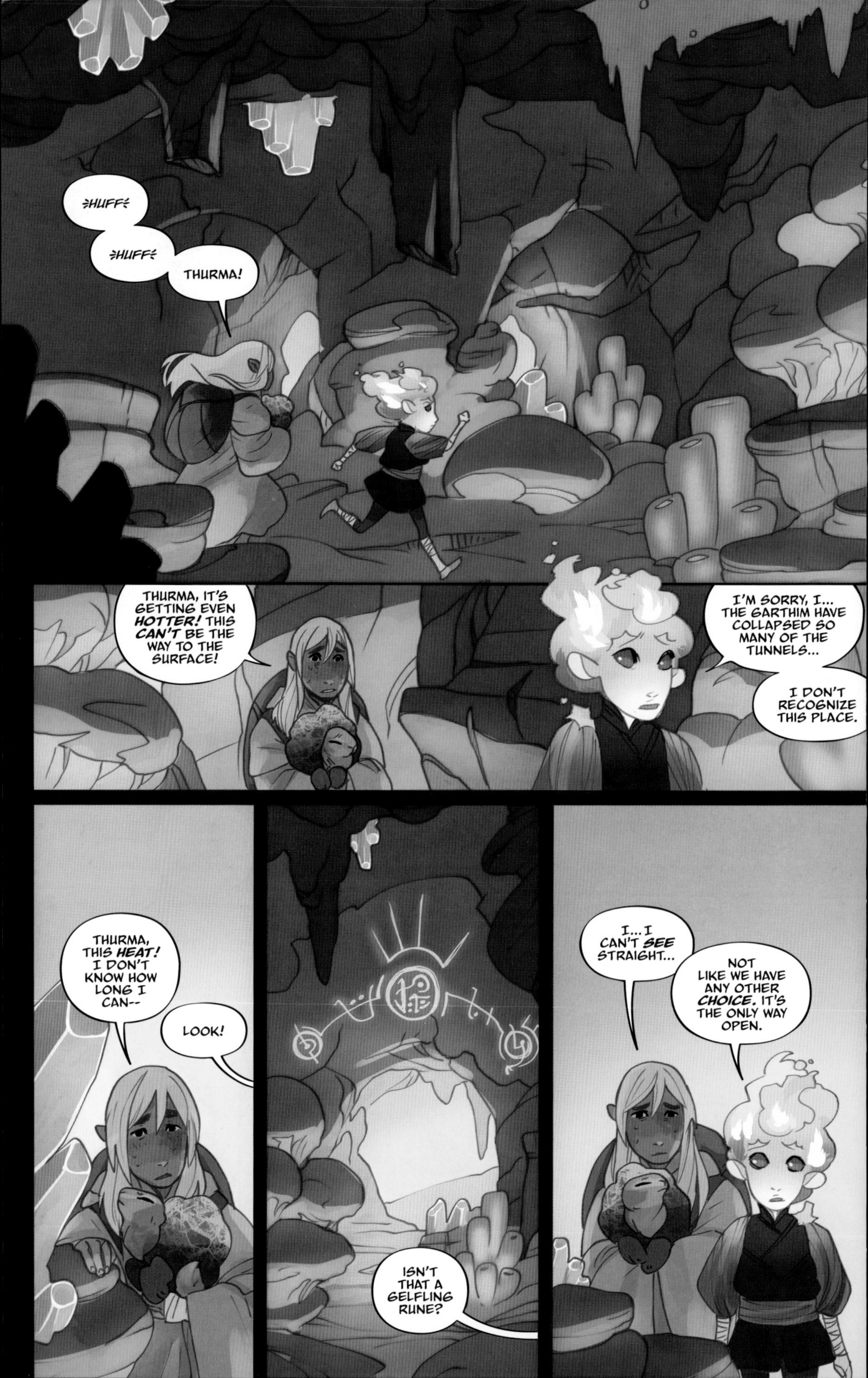

≠HUFF≠
≠HUFF≠
THURMA!
THURMA, IT'S GETTING EVEN **HOTTER!** THIS **CAN'T** BE THE WAY TO THE SURFACE!
I'M SORRY, I... THE GARTHIM HAVE COLLAPSED SO MANY OF THE TUNNELS...
I DON'T RECOGNIZE THIS PLACE.
THURMA, THIS **HEAT!** I DON'T KNOW HOW LONG I CAN--
LOOK!
ISN'T THAT A GELFLING RUNE?
I... I CAN'T **SEE** STRAIGHT...
NOT LIKE WE HAVE ANY OTHER **CHOICE.** IT'S THE ONLY WAY OPEN.

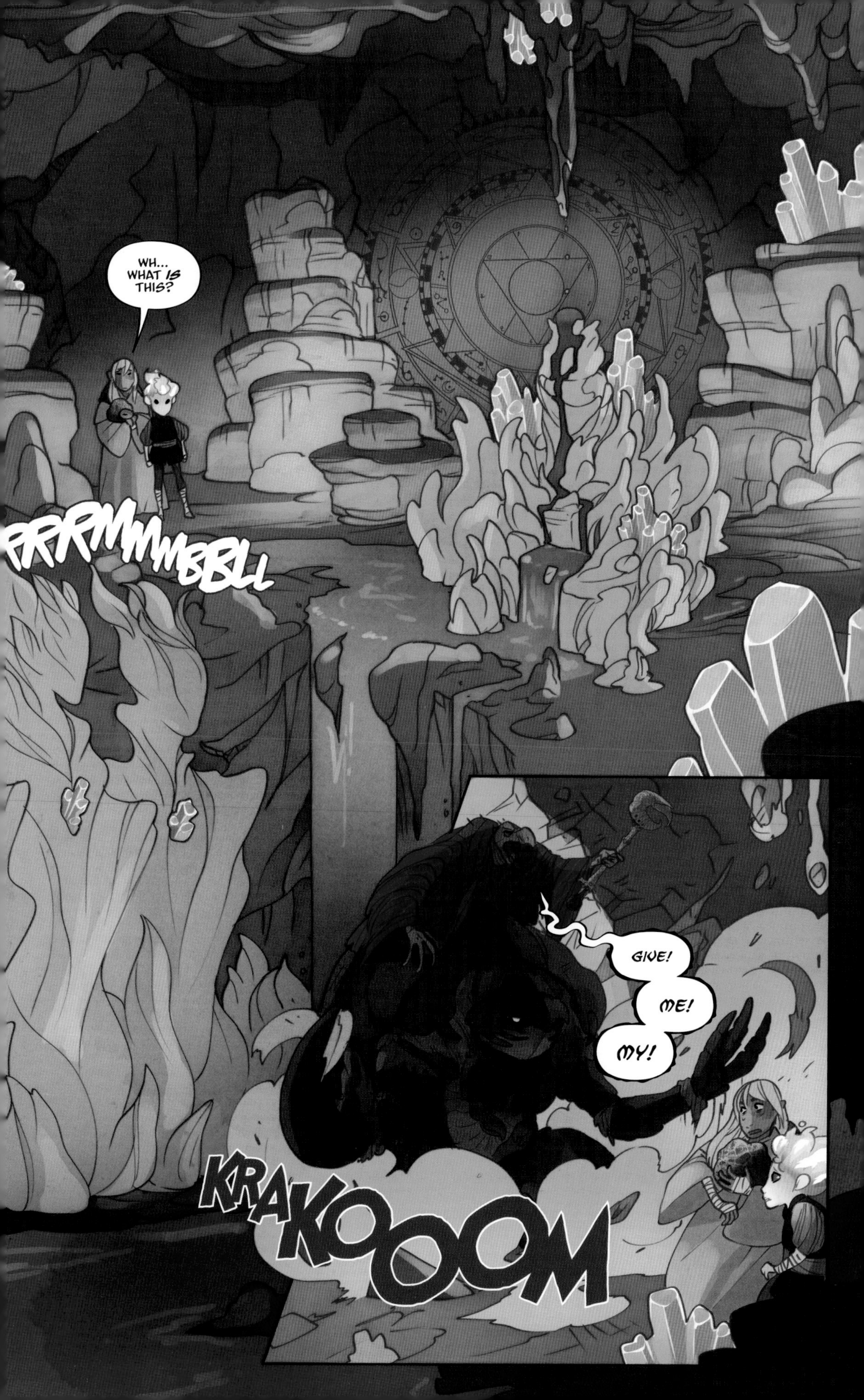
WH... WHAT IS THIS?
PRRMMMBBLL
GIVE!
ME!
MY!
KRAKOOOM

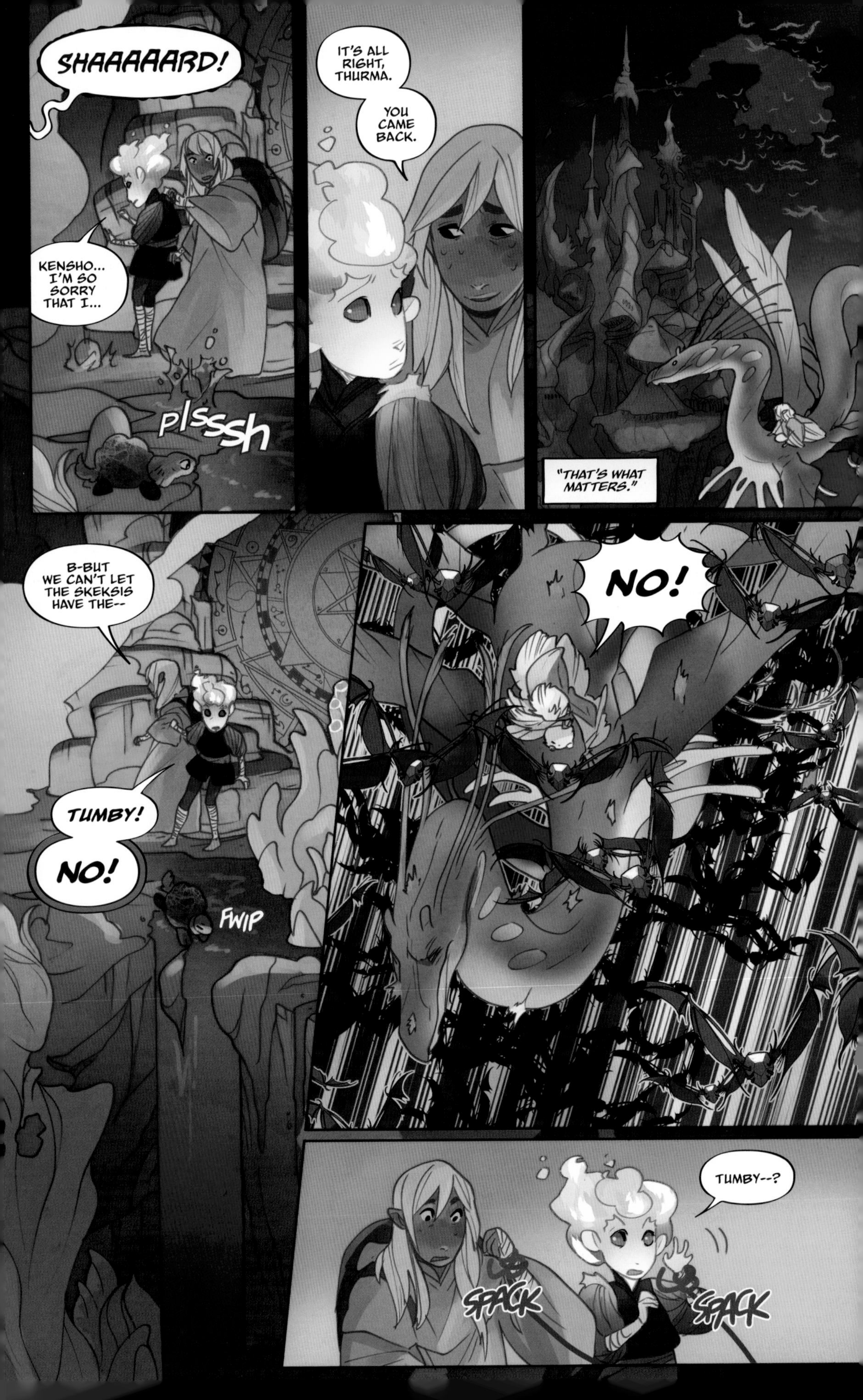
SHAAAAARD!
KENSHO... I'M SO SORRY THAT I...
plsssh
IT'S ALL RIGHT, THURMA.
YOU CAME BACK.
"THAT'S WHAT MATTERS."
B-BUT WE CAN'T LET THE SKEKSIS HAVE THE--
TUMBY!
NO!
FWIP
NO!
TUMBY--?
SPACK
SPACK

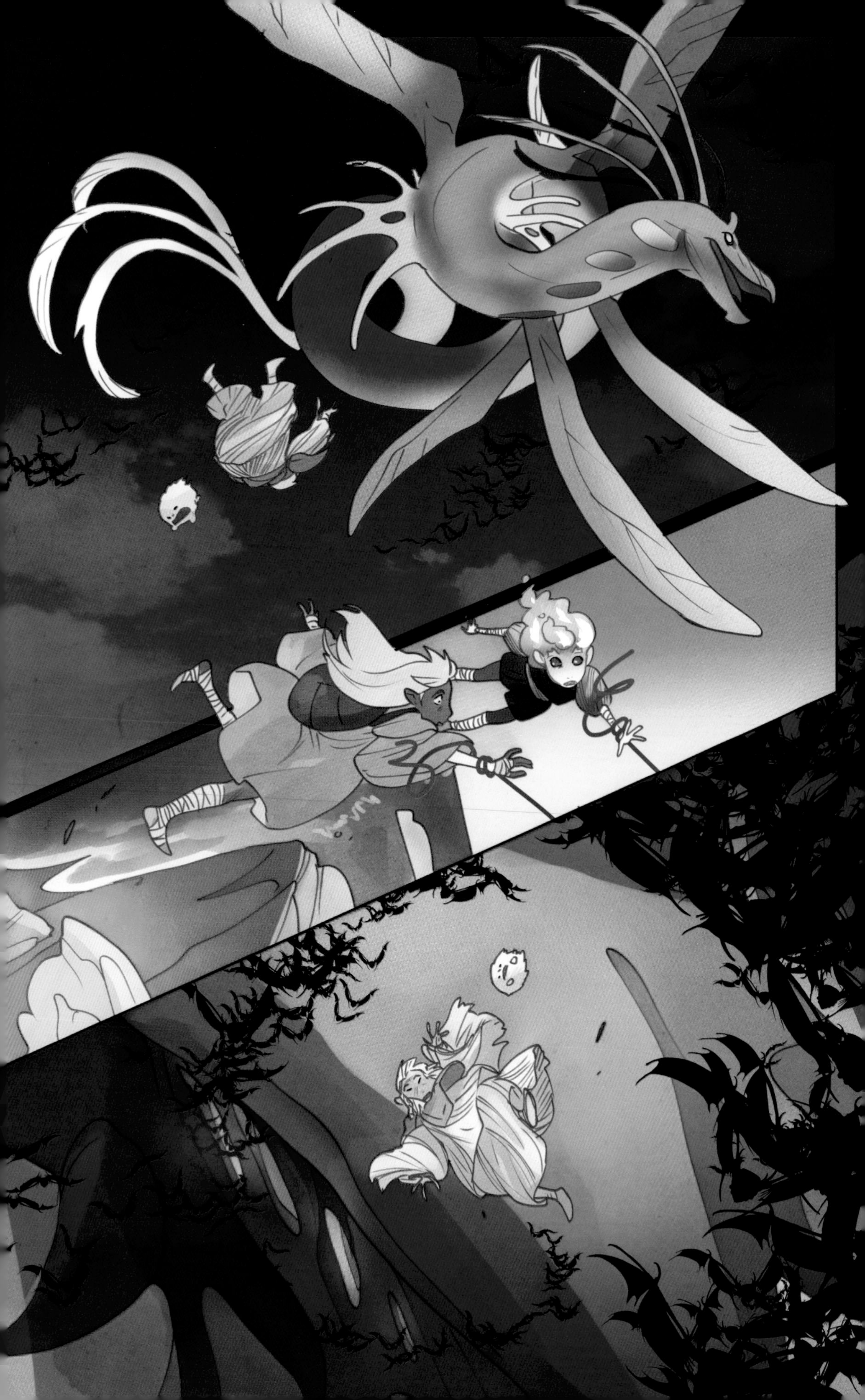

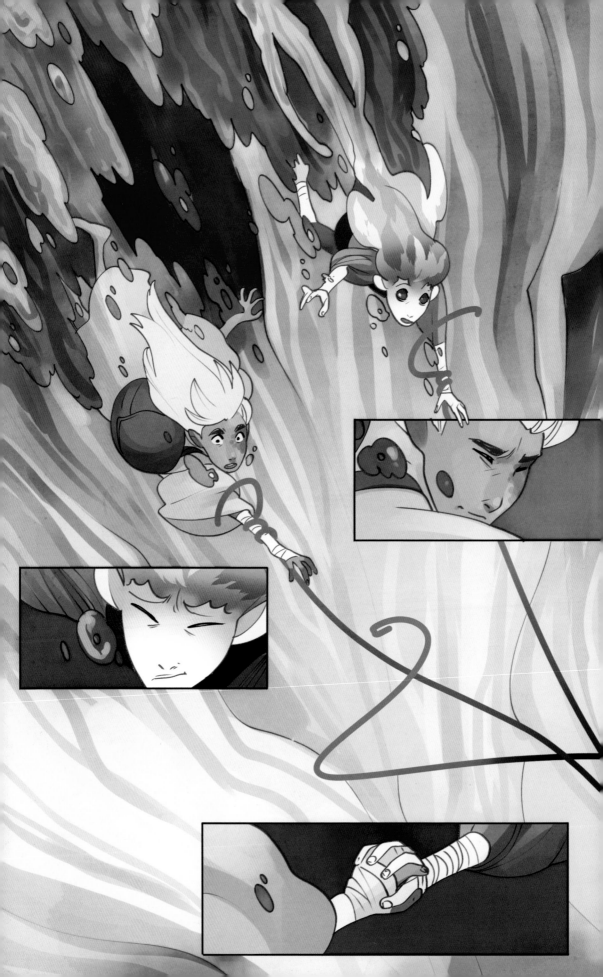

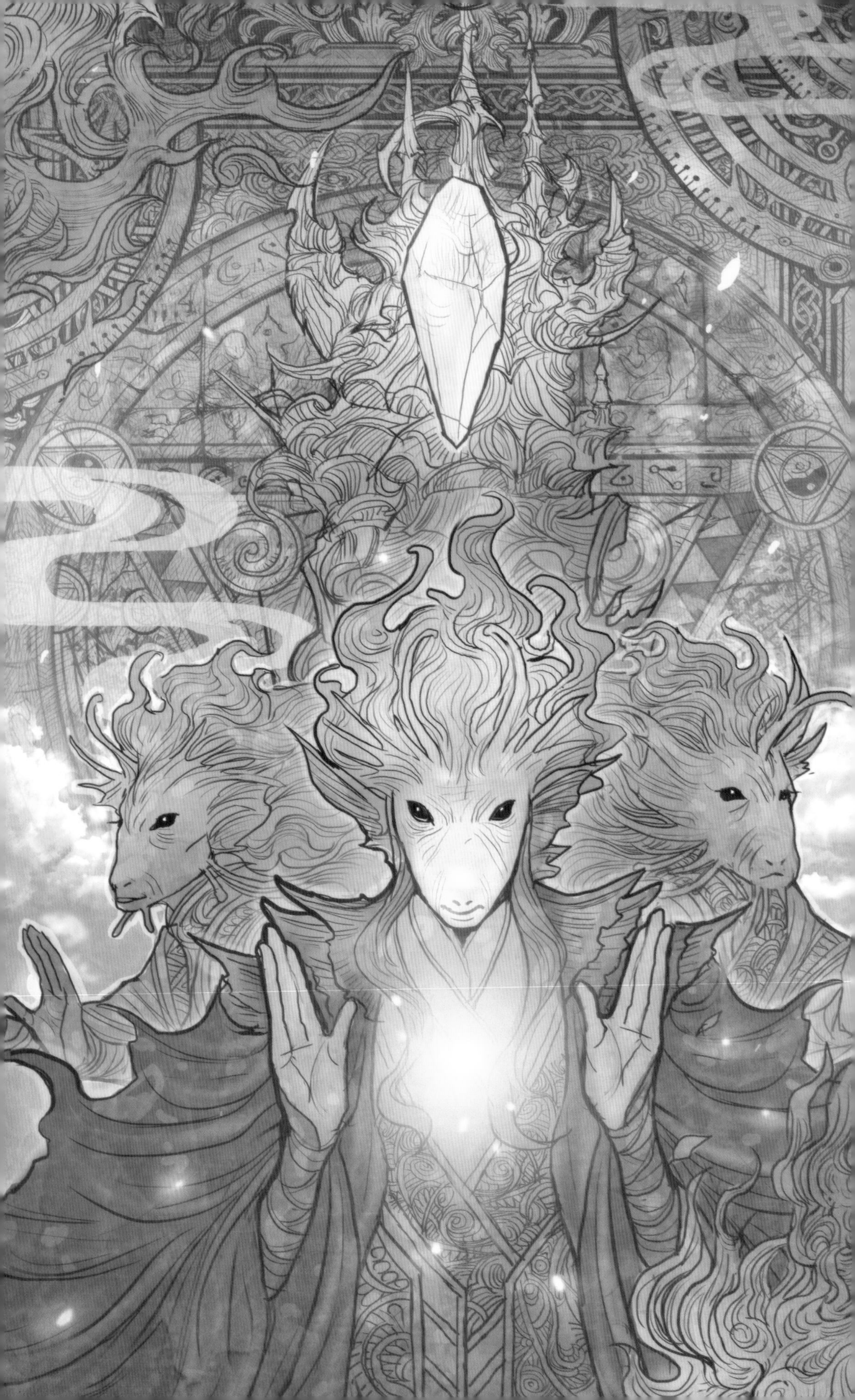

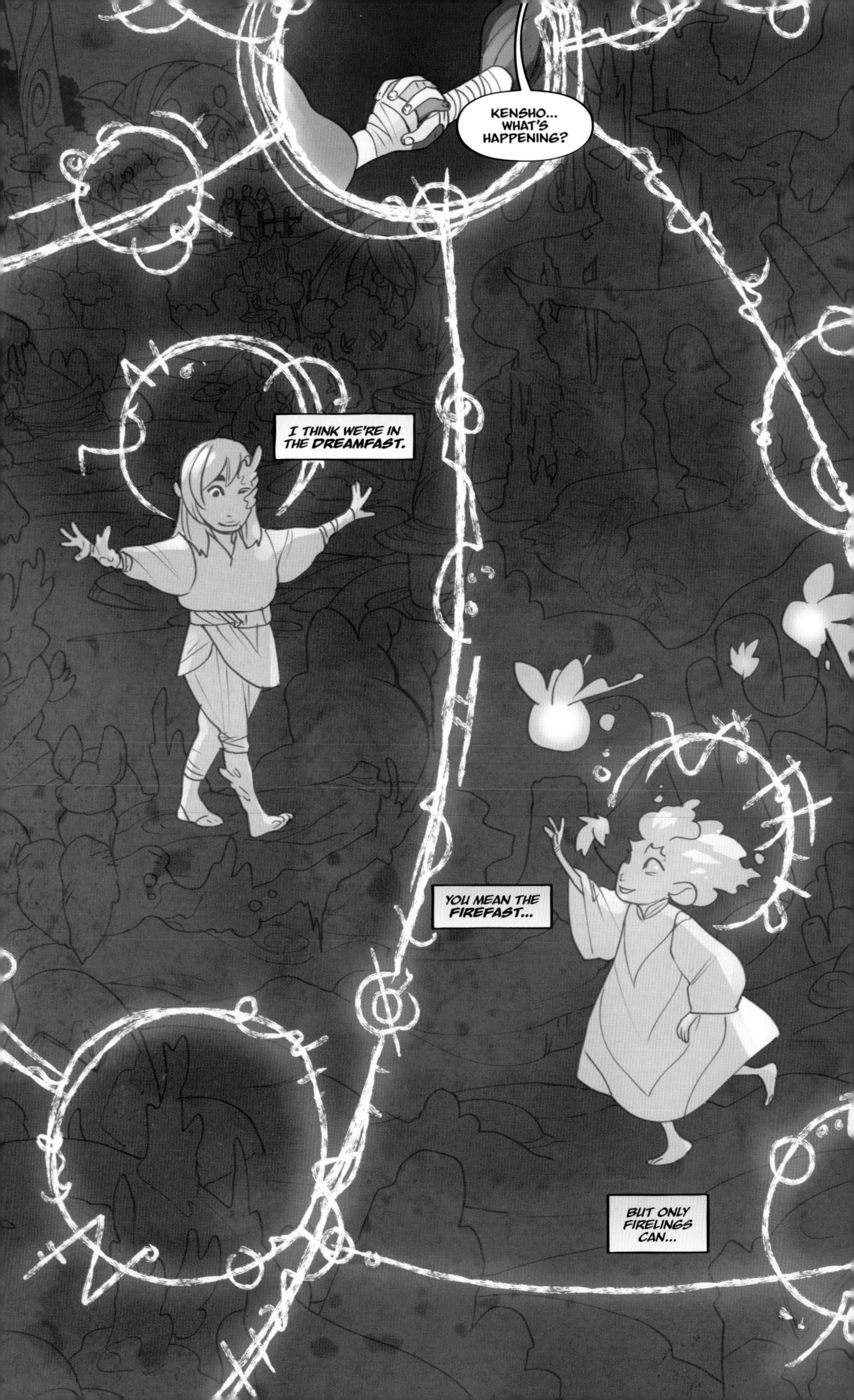
KENSHO... WHAT'S HAPPENING?
I THINK WE'RE IN THE DREAMFAST.
YOU MEAN THE FIREFAST...
BUT ONLY FIRELINGS CAN...

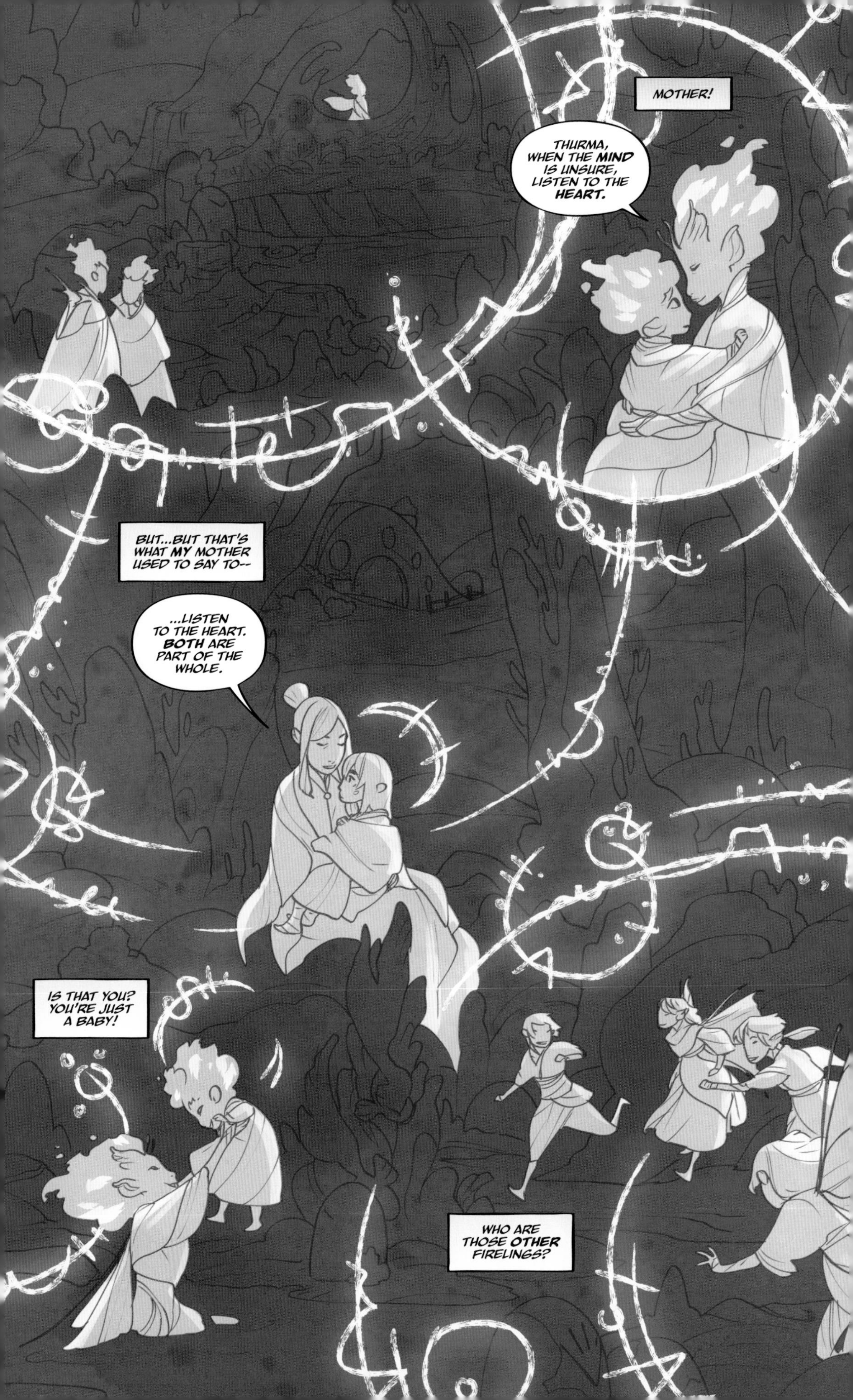
MOTHER!
THURMA, WHEN THE MIND IS UNSURE, LISTEN TO THE HEART.
BUT...BUT THAT'S WHAT MY MOTHER USED TO SAY TO--
...LISTEN TO THE HEART. BOTH ARE PART OF THE WHOLE.
IS THAT YOU? YOU'RE JUST A BABY!
WHO ARE THOSE OTHER FIRELINGS?

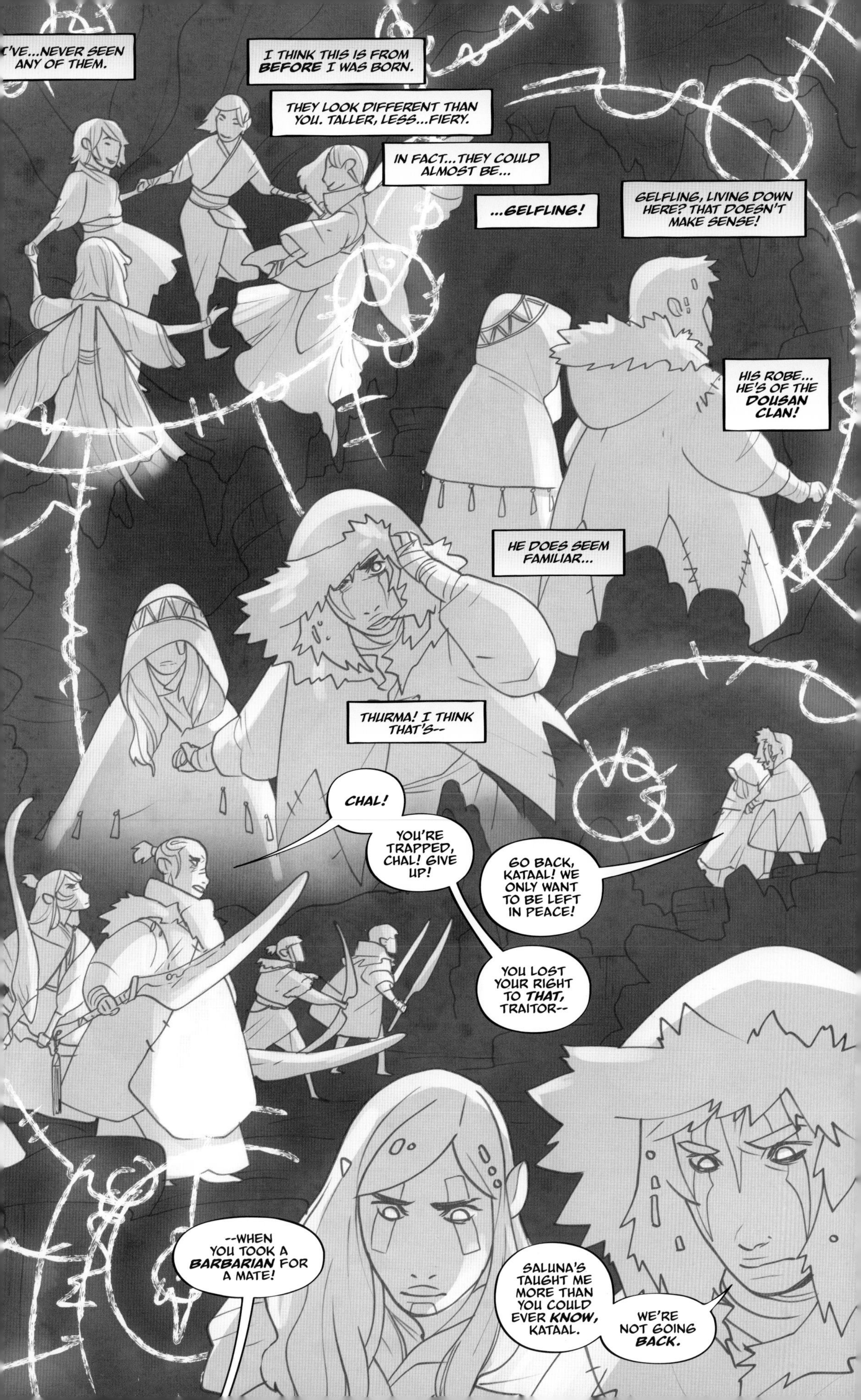
I'VE...NEVER SEEN ANY OF THEM.
I THINK THIS IS FROM BEFORE I WAS BORN.
THEY LOOK DIFFERENT THAN YOU. TALLER, LESS...FIERY.
IN FACT...THEY COULD ALMOST BE...
...GELFLING!
GELFLING, LIVING DOWN HERE? THAT DOESN'T MAKE SENSE!
HIS ROBE... HE'S OF THE DOUSAN CLAN!
HE DOES SEEM FAMILIAR...
THURMA! I THINK THAT'S--
CHAL!
YOU'RE TRAPPED, CHAL! GIVE UP!
GO BACK, KATAAL! WE ONLY WANT TO BE LEFT IN PEACE!
YOU LOST YOUR RIGHT TO THAT, TRAITOR--
--WHEN YOU TOOK A BARBARIAN FOR A MATE!
SALUNA'S TAUGHT ME MORE THAN YOU COULD EVER KNOW, KATAAL.
WE'RE NOT GOING BACK.

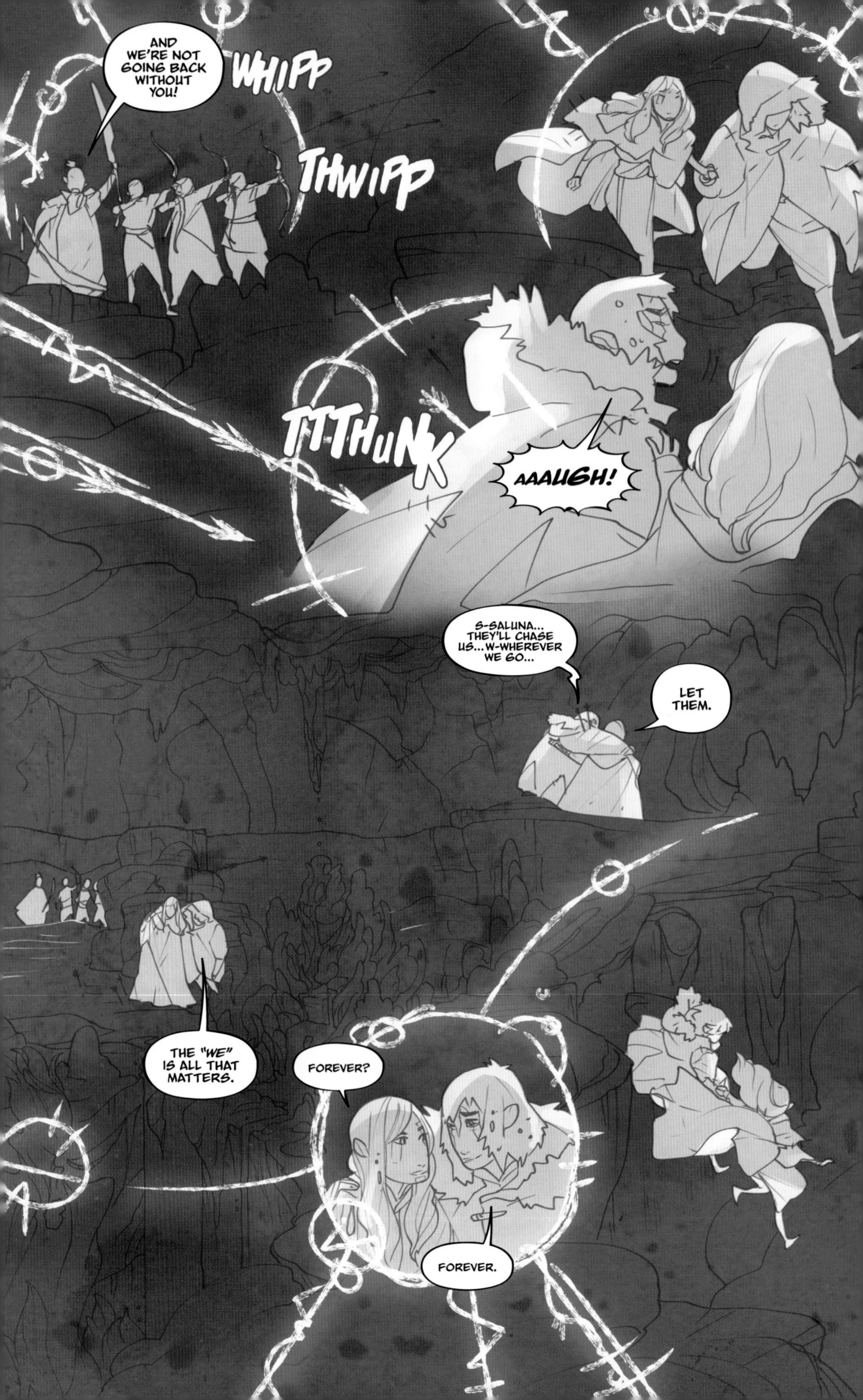
AND WE'RE NOT GOING BACK WITHOUT YOU!
WHIPP
THWIPP
TTTHUNK
AAAUGH!
S-SALUNA... THEY'LL CHASE US...W-WHEREVER WE GO...
LET THEM.
THE "WE" IS ALL THAT MATTERS.
FOREVER?
FOREVER.

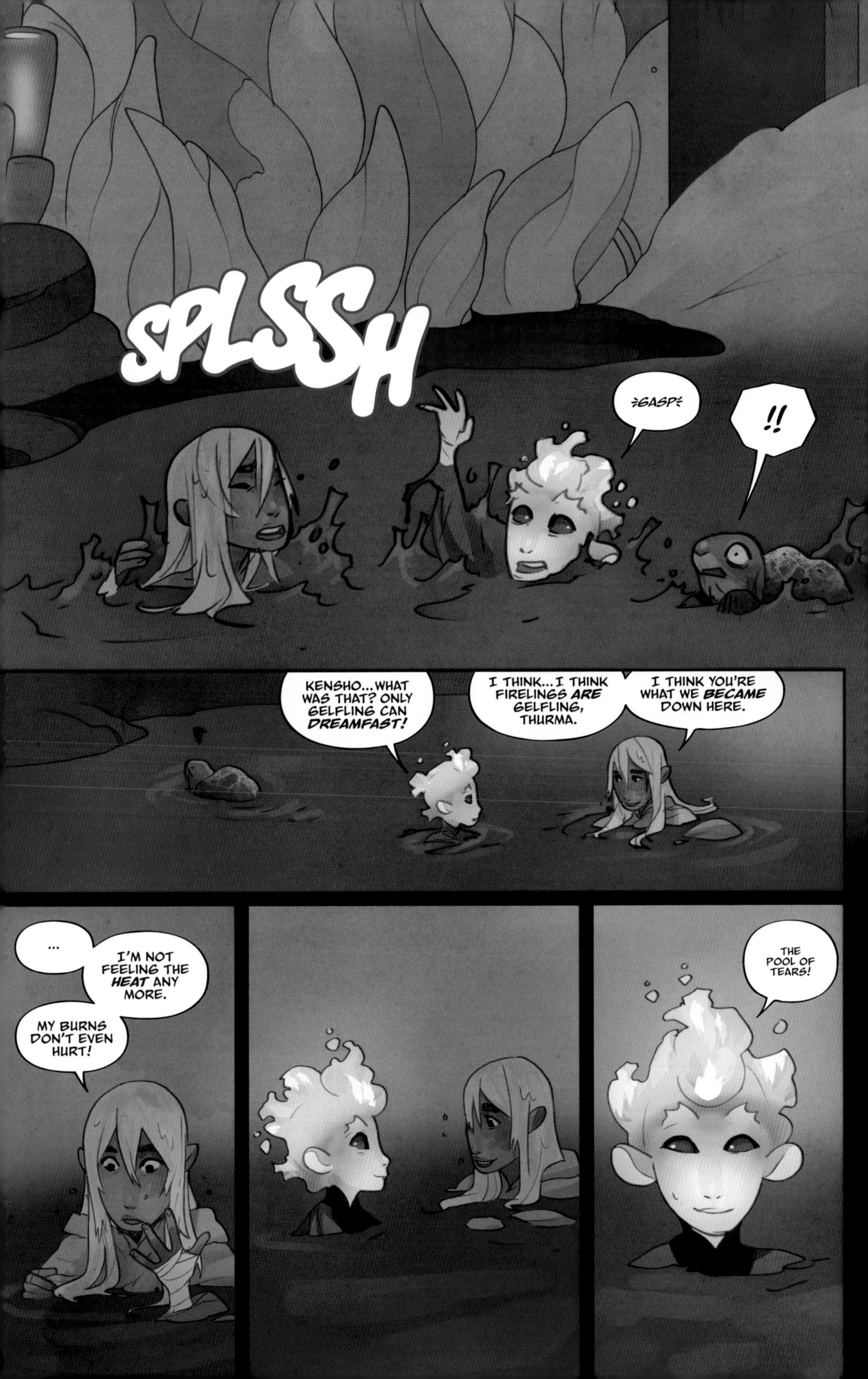
SPLSSH
≠GASP≠
!!
KENSHO...WHAT WAS THAT? ONLY GELFLING CAN *DREAMFAST*!
I THINK...I THINK FIRELINGS *ARE* GELFLING, THURMA.
I THINK YOU'RE WHAT WE *BECAME* DOWN HERE.
...
I'M NOT FEELING THE *HEAT* ANY MORE.
MY BURNS DON'T EVEN HURT!
THE POOL OF TEARS!

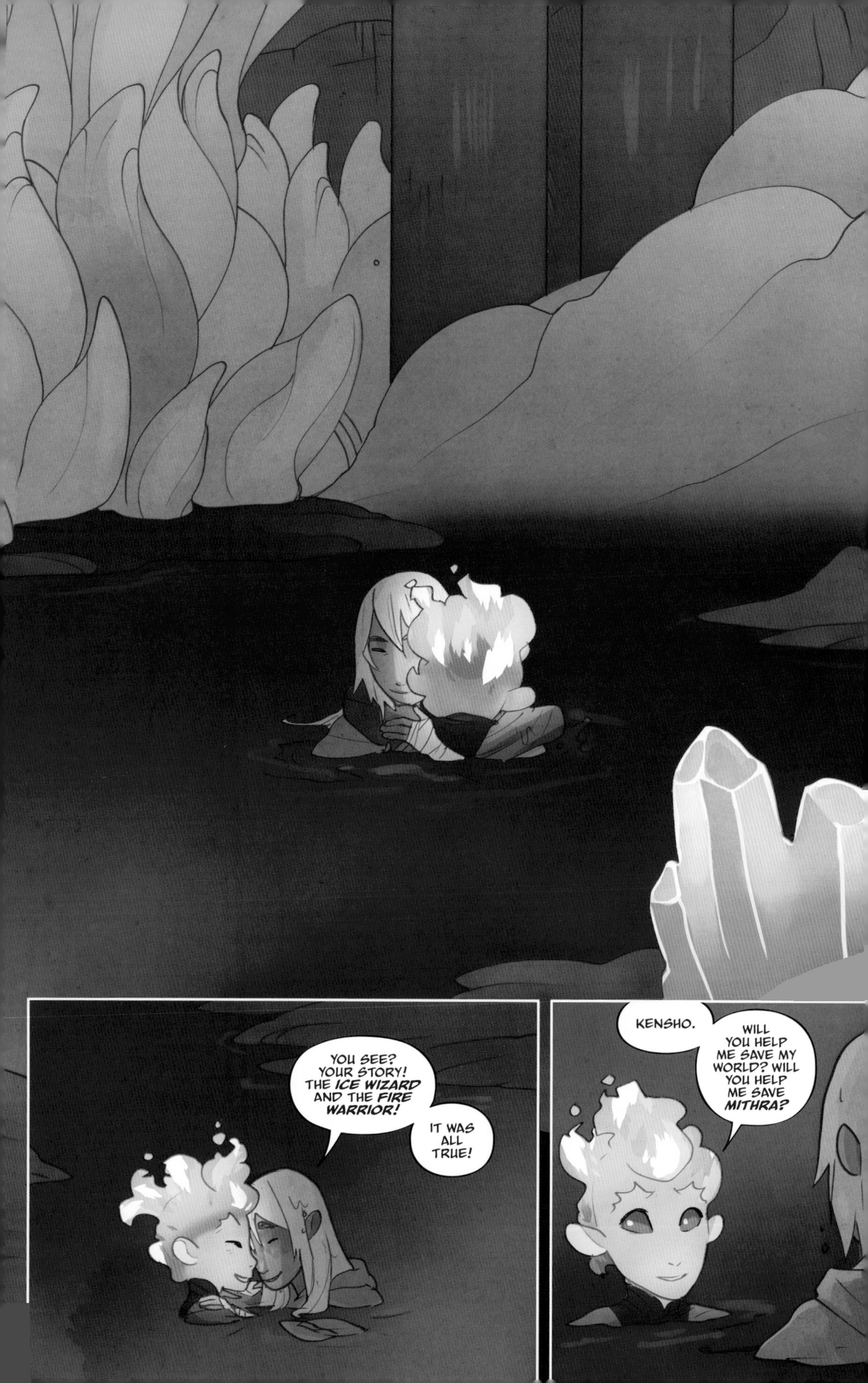
YOU SEE? YOUR STORY! THE ICE WIZARD AND THE FIRE WARRIOR!
IT WAS ALL TRUE!
KENSHO.
WILL YOU HELP ME SAVE MY WORLD? WILL YOU HELP ME SAVE MITHRA?

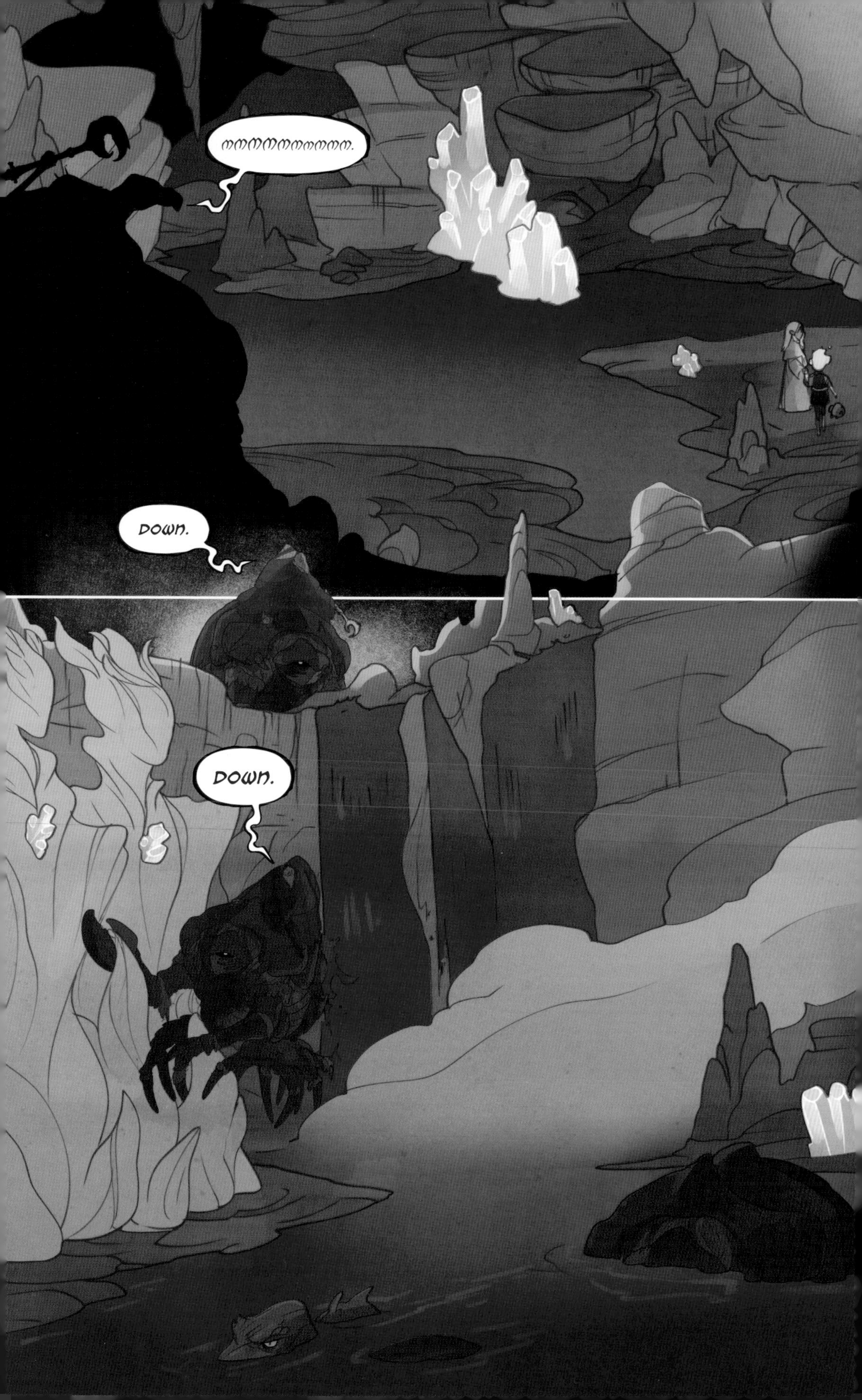

MMMMMMMMMM.
DOWN.
DOWN.

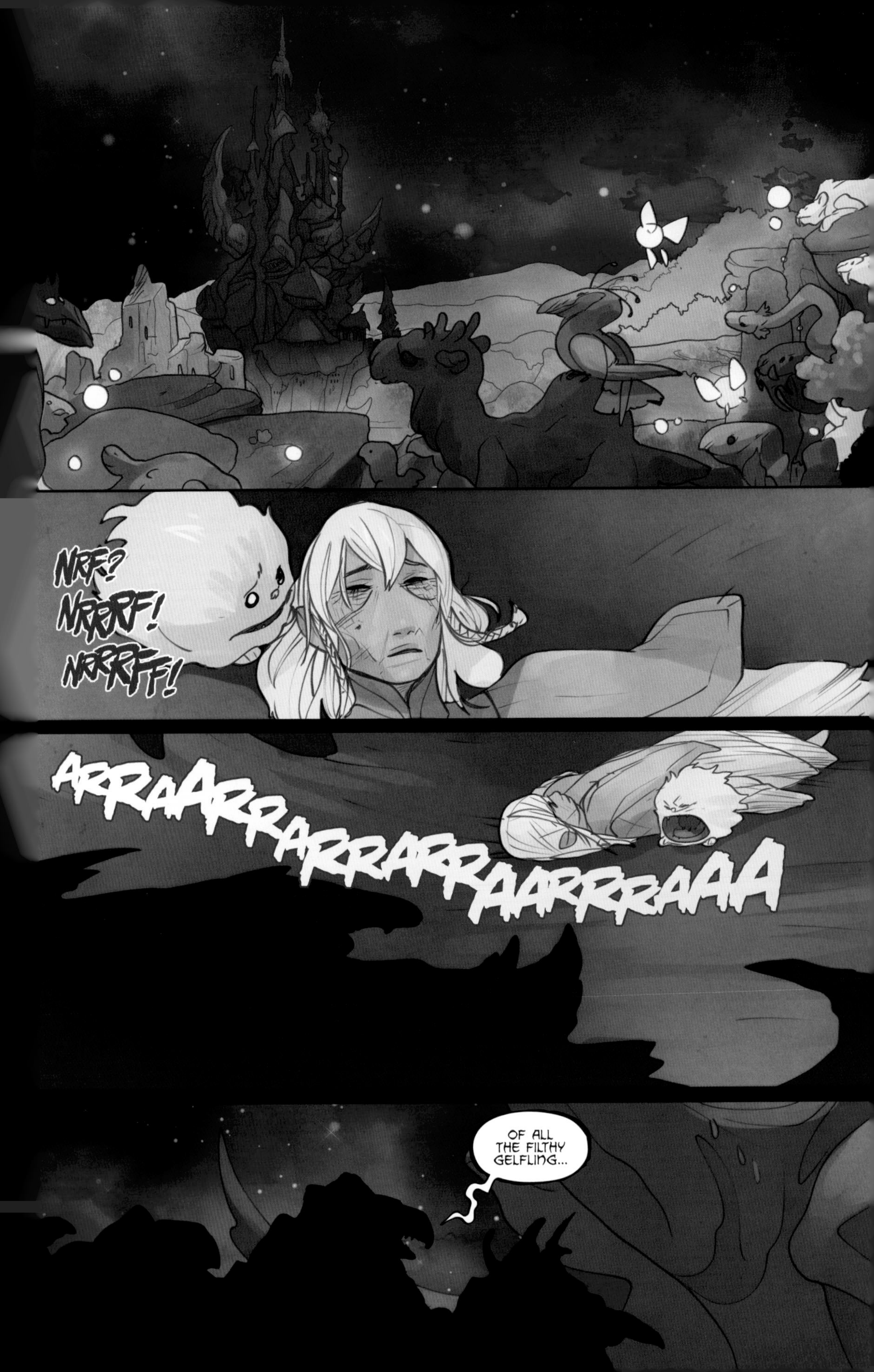

NRF?
NRRRF!
NRRRFF!
ARRAARRARRARRAARRRAAA
OF ALL THE FILTHY GELFLING...

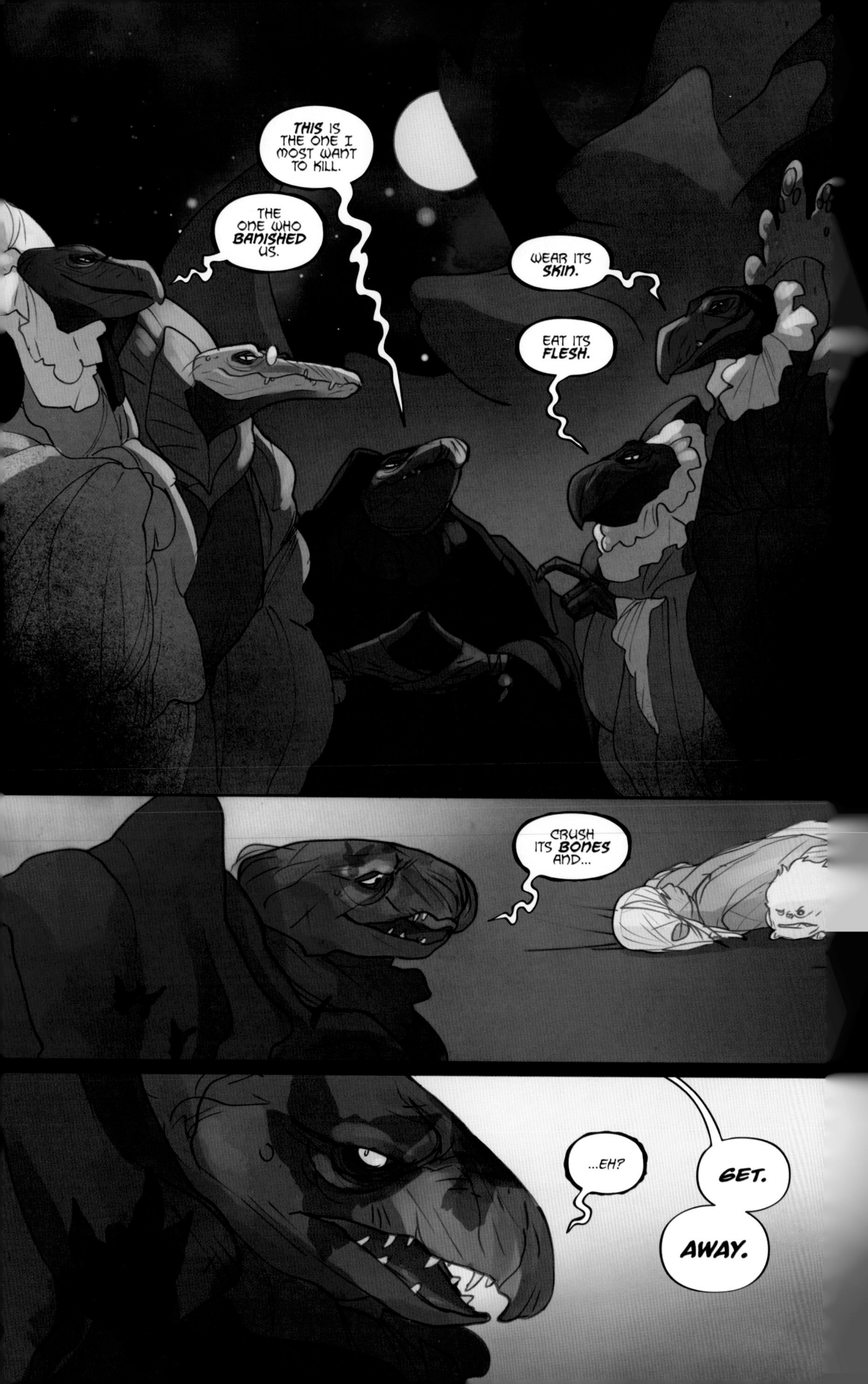
THE ONE WHO BANISHED US.
THIS IS THE ONE I MOST WANT TO KILL.
WEAR ITS SKIN.
EAT ITS FLESH.
CRUSH ITS BONES AND...
...EH?
GET.
AWAY.

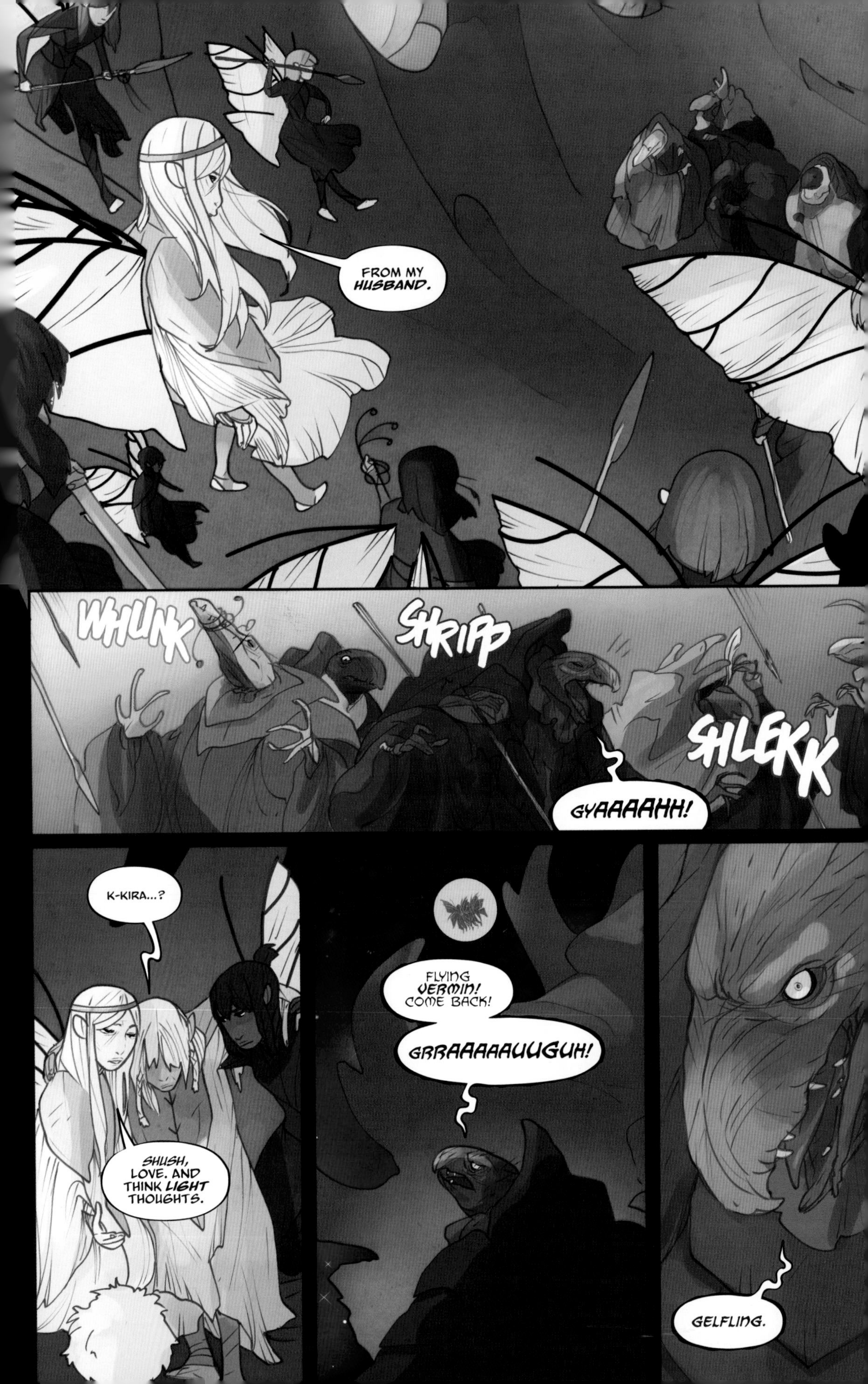
FROM MY HUSBAND.
WHUNK
SHRIPP
SHLEKK
GYAAAAHH!
K-KIRA...?
SHUSH, LOVE. AND THINK LIGHT THOUGHTS.
FLYING VERMIN! COME BACK!
GRRAAAAAUUGUH!
GELFLING.

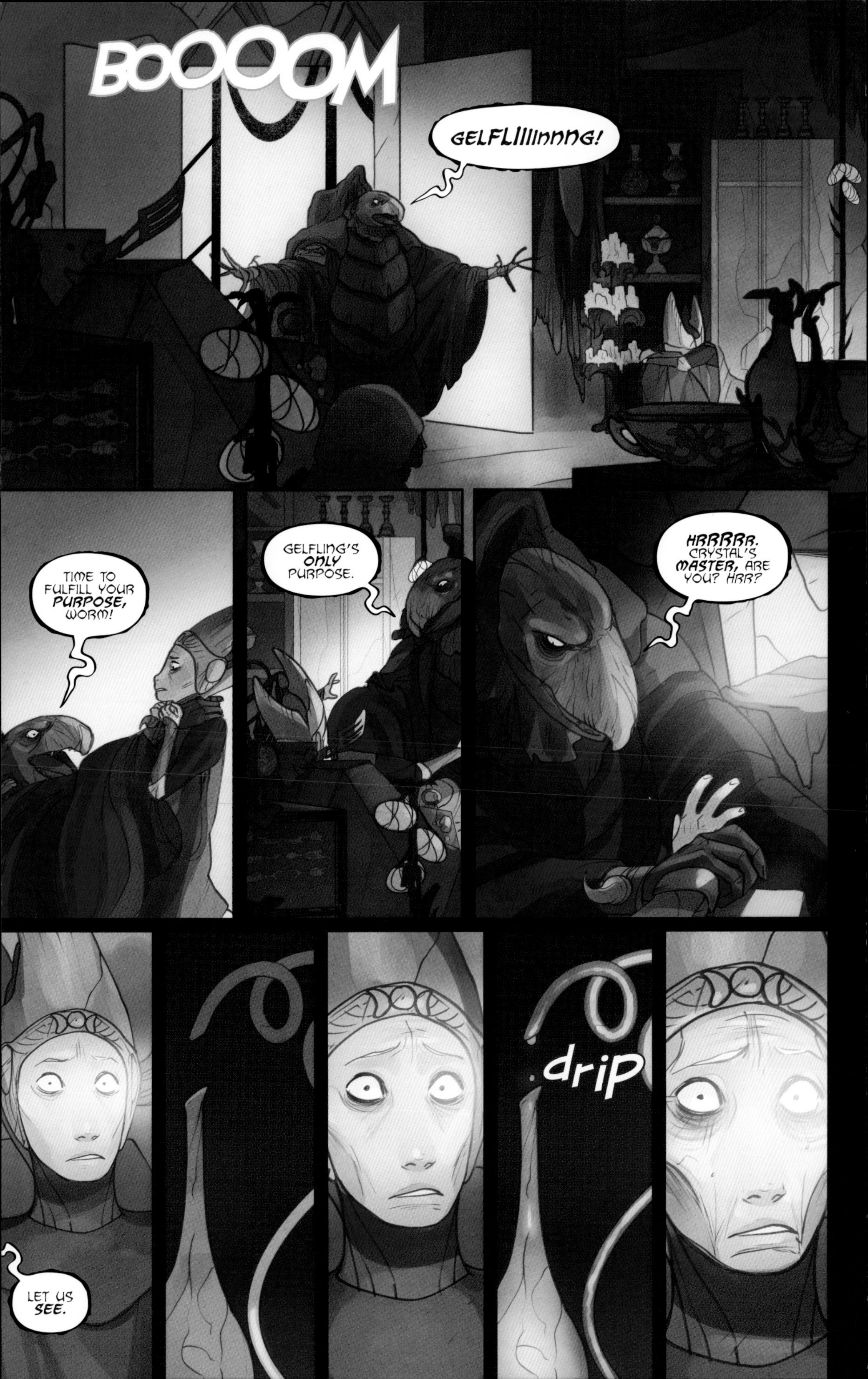
BOOOOM
GELFLIIIIInnng!
TIME TO FULFILL YOUR PURPOSE, WORM!
GELFLING'S ONLY PURPOSE.
HRRRRR. CRYSTAL'S MASTER, ARE YOU? HRR?
LET US SEE.
drip

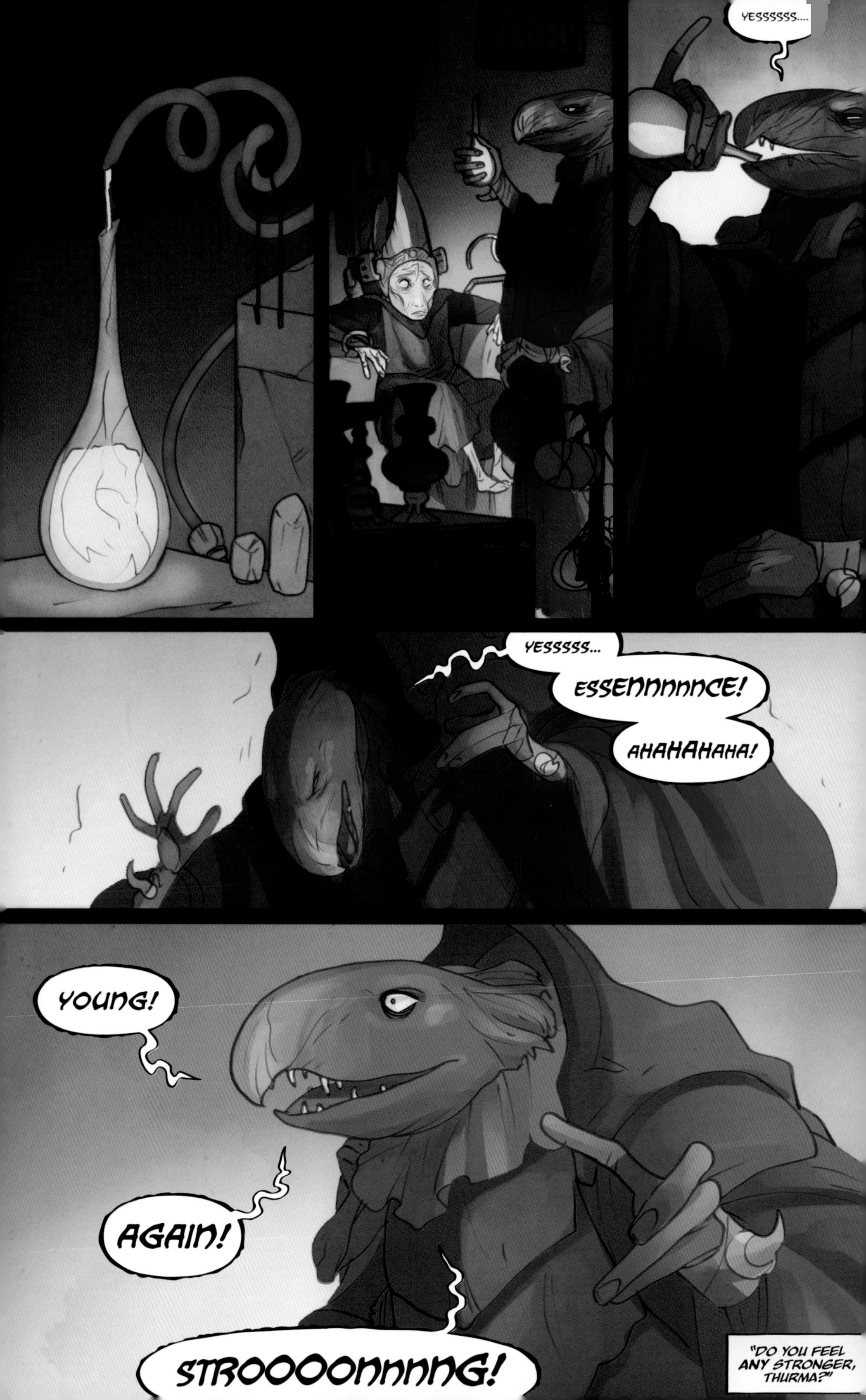
YESSSSSS....
YESSSSS...
ESSENNNNNCE!
AHAHAHAHA!
YOUNG!
AGAIN!
STROOOONNNNG!
"DO YOU FEEL ANY STRONGER, THURMA?"

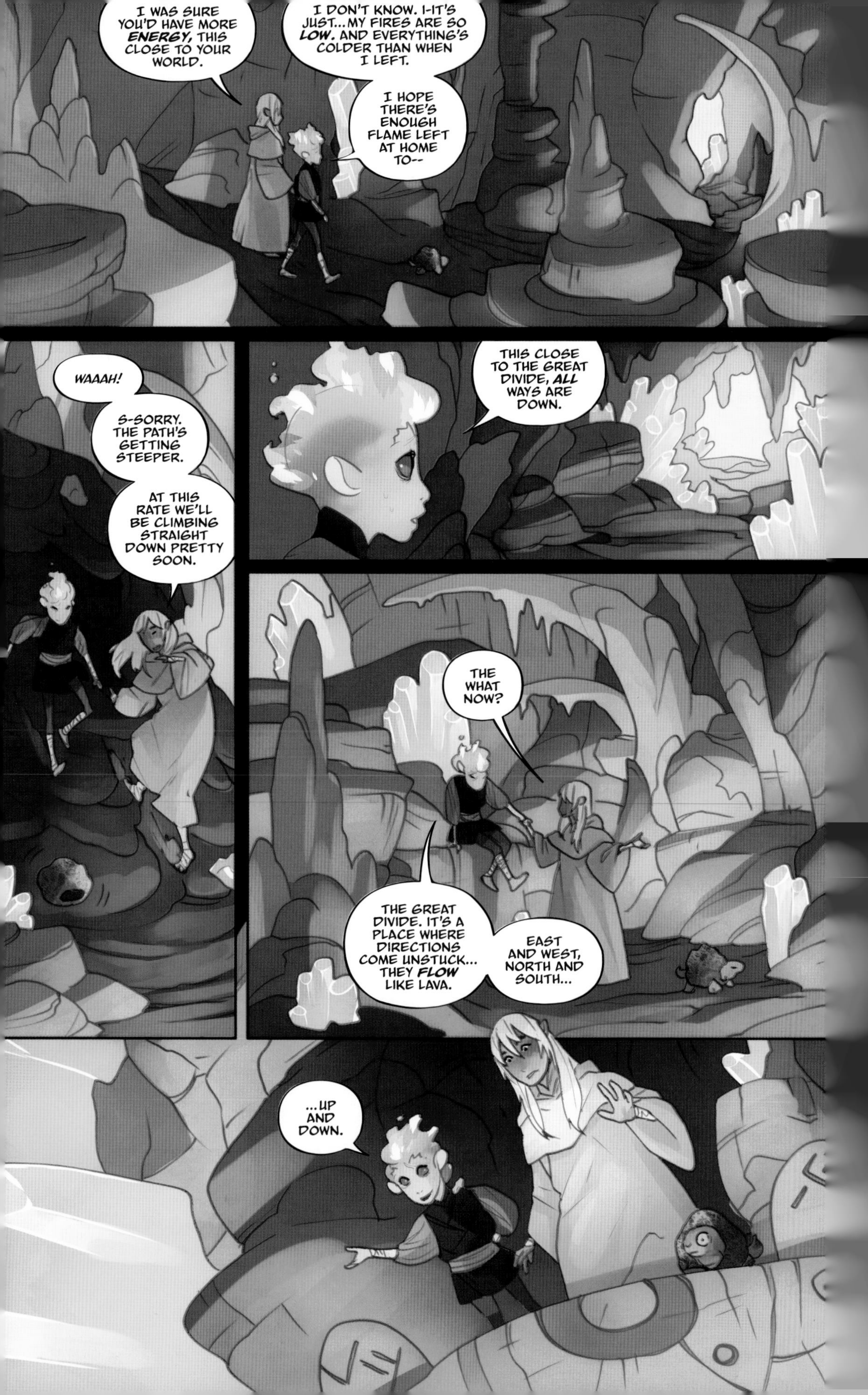
I WAS SURE YOU'D HAVE MORE ENERGY, THIS CLOSE TO YOUR WORLD.
I DON'T KNOW. I-IT'S JUST...MY FIRES ARE SO LOW. AND EVERYTHING'S COLDER THAN WHEN I LEFT.
I HOPE THERE'S ENOUGH FLAME LEFT AT HOME TO--
WAAAH!
S-SORRY. THE PATH'S GETTING STEEPER.
AT THIS RATE WE'LL BE CLIMBING STRAIGHT DOWN PRETTY SOON.
THIS CLOSE TO THE GREAT DIVIDE, ALL WAYS ARE DOWN.
THE WHAT NOW?
THE GREAT DIVIDE. IT'S A PLACE WHERE DIRECTIONS COME UNSTUCK... THEY FLOW LIKE LAVA.
EAST AND WEST, NORTH AND SOUTH...
...UP AND DOWN.

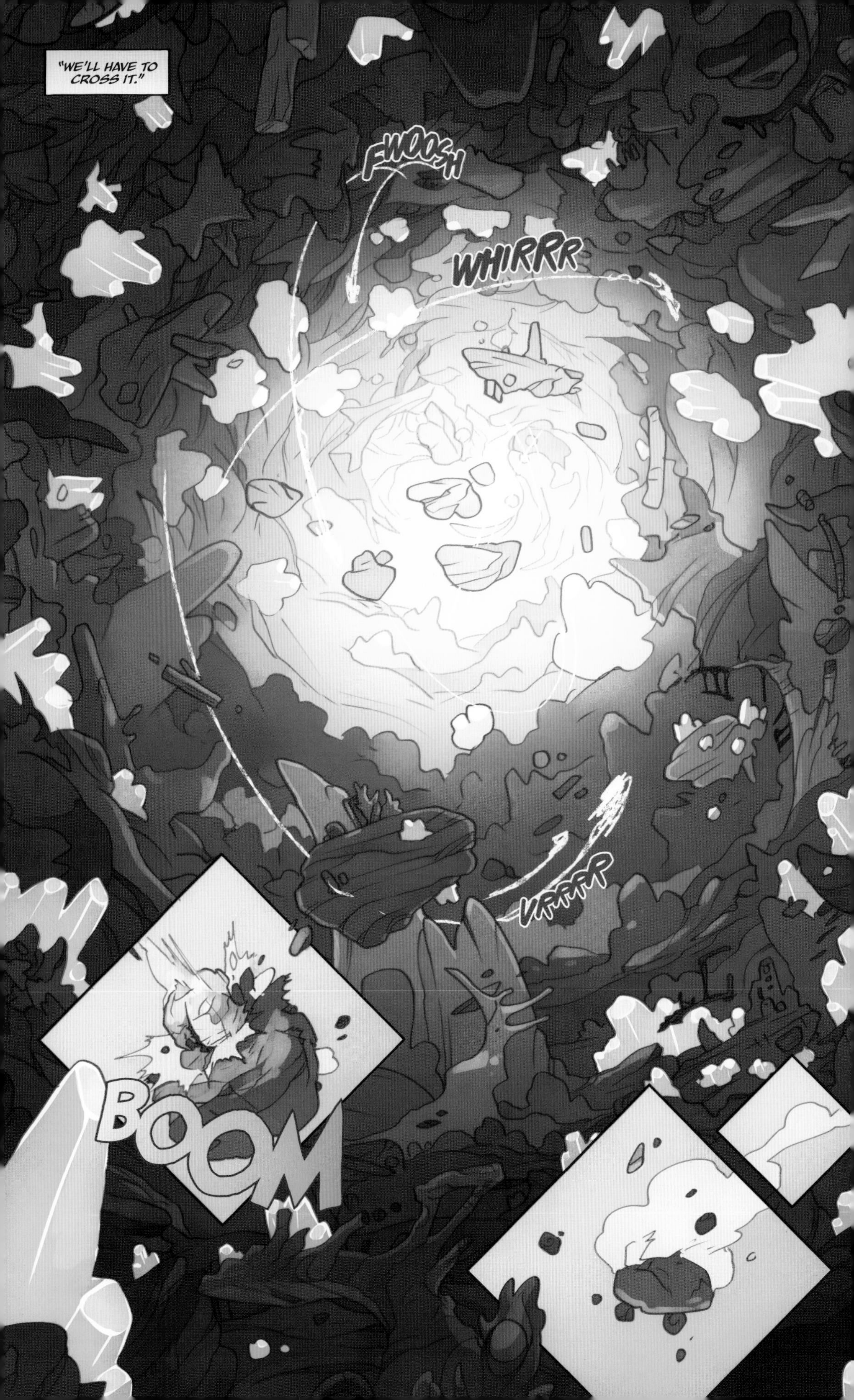
"WE'LL HAVE TO CROSS IT."
FWOOSH
WHIRRR
VRRRR
BOOM

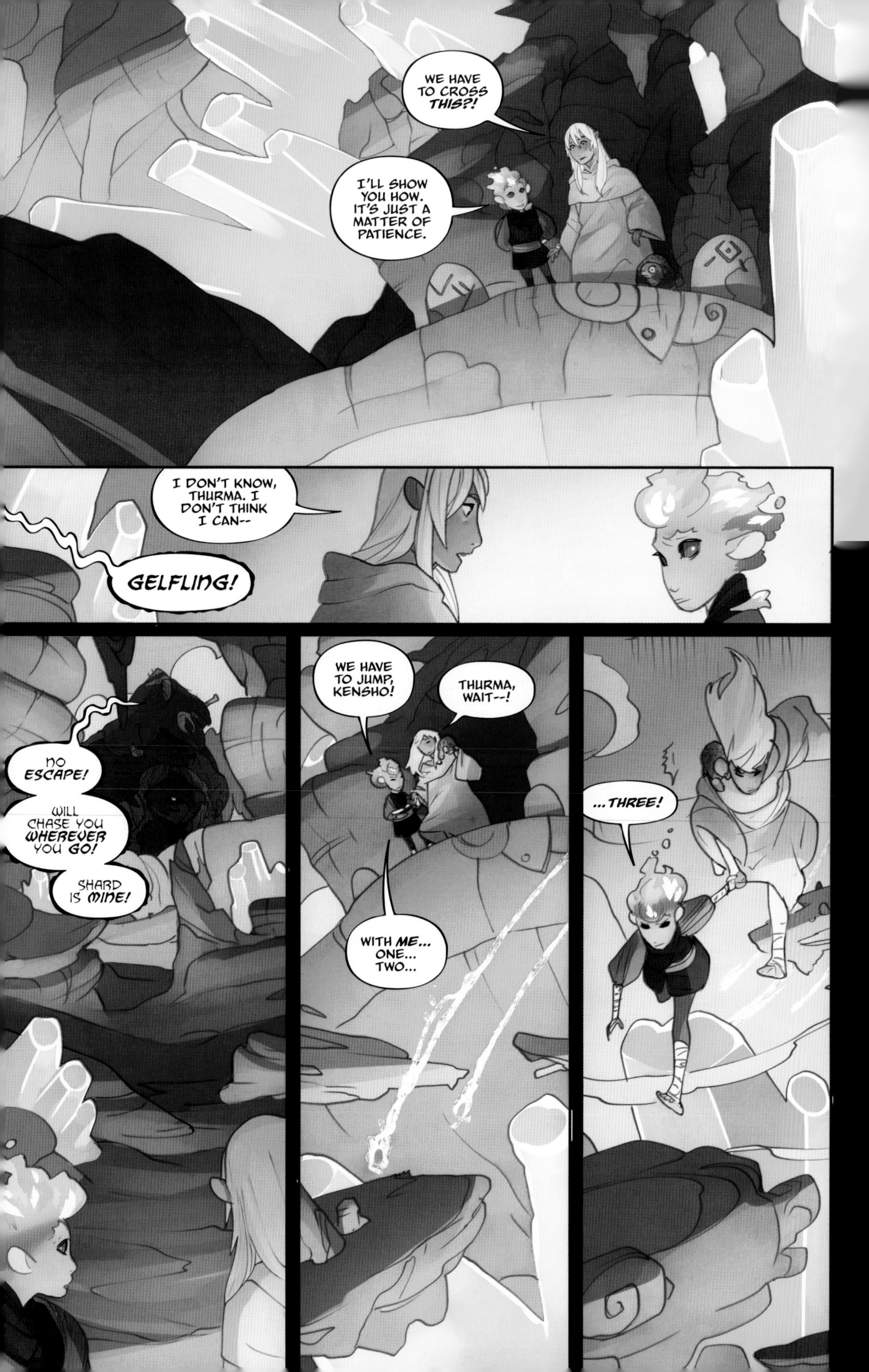
WE HAVE TO CROSS THIS?!
I'LL SHOW YOU HOW. IT'S JUST A MATTER OF PATIENCE.
I DON'T KNOW, THURMA. I DON'T THINK I CAN--
GELFLING!
NO ESCAPE!
WILL CHASE YOU WHEREVER YOU GO!
SHARD IS MINE!
WE HAVE TO JUMP, KENSHO!
THURMA, WAIT--!
WITH ME... ONE... TWO...
...THREE!

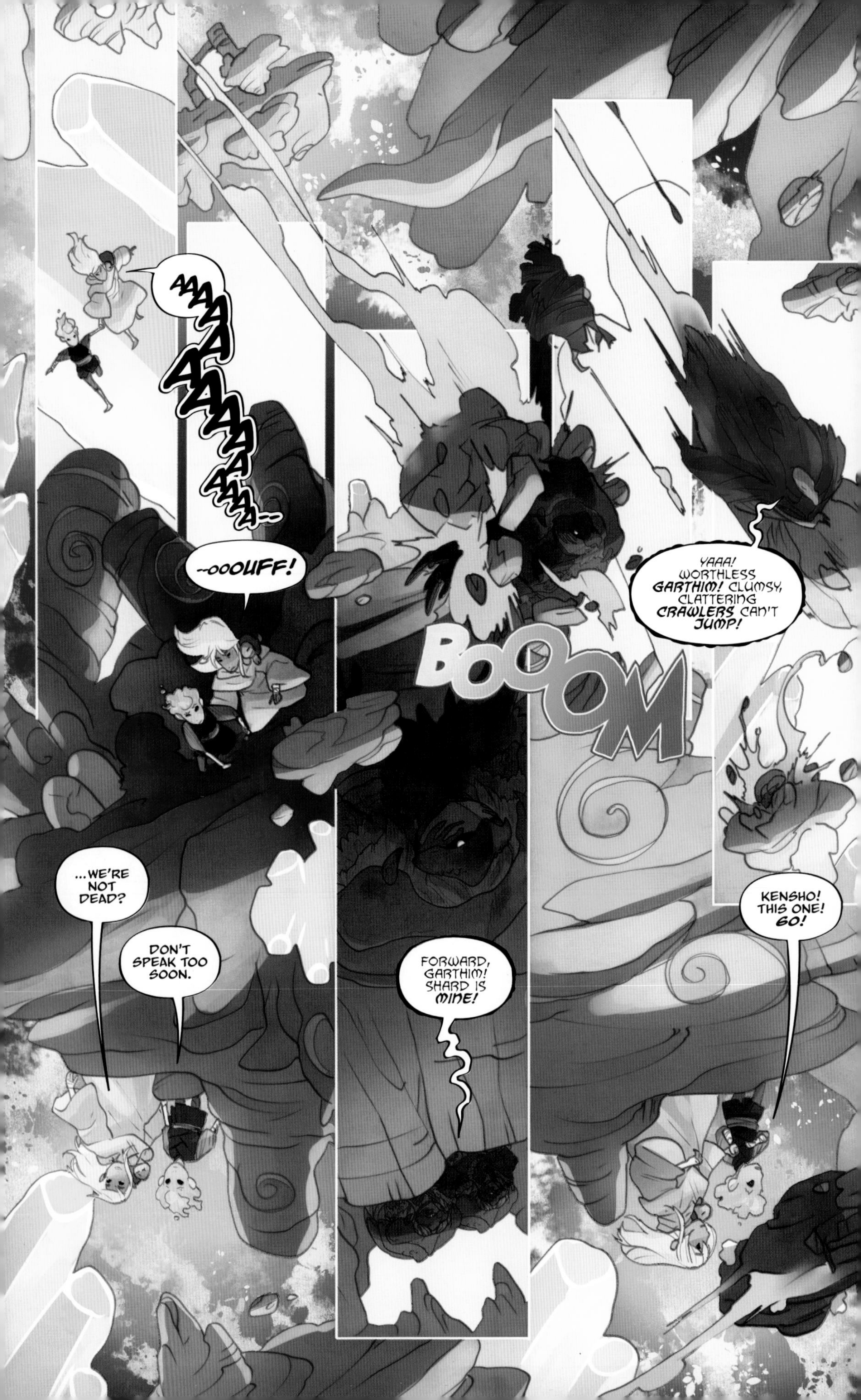
AAAAAAAAAAAAAAA--
--OOOUFF!
BOOOOM
YAAA! WORTHLESS GARTHIM! CLUMSY, CLATTERING CRAWLERS CAN'T JUMP!
...WE'RE NOT DEAD?
DON'T SPEAK TOO SOON.
FORWARD, GARTHIM! SHARD IS MINE!
KENSHO! THIS ONE! GO!

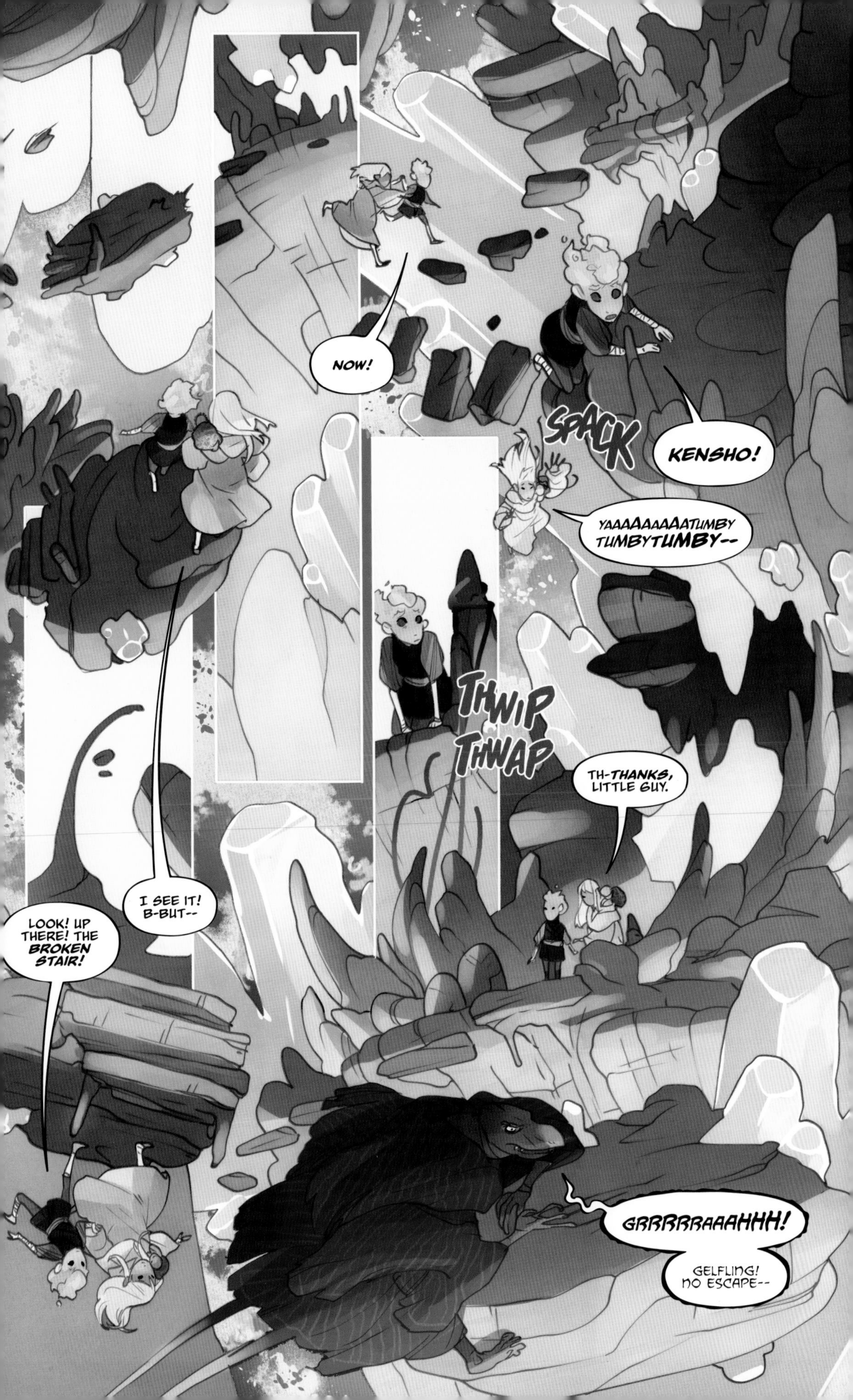
LOOK! UP THERE! THE BROKEN STAIR!
I SEE IT! B-BUT--
NOW!
KENSHO!
SPACK
YAAAAAAAAAATUMBY TUMBYTUMBY--
THWIP THWAP
TH-THANKS, LITTLE GUY.
GRRRRRAAAHHH!
GELFLING! NO ESCAPE--

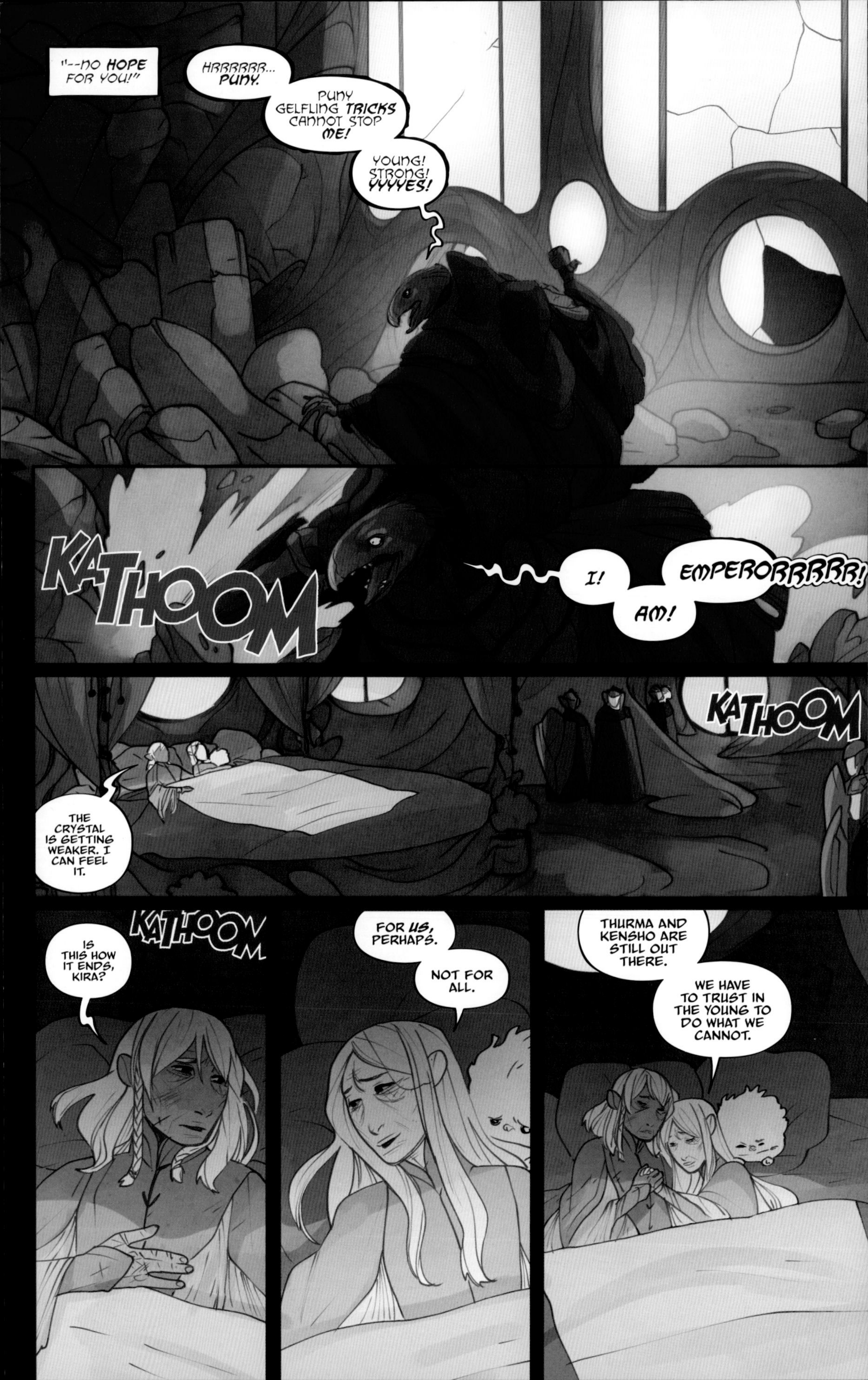

"--NO HOPE FOR YOU!"
HRRRRRR... PUNY.
PUNY GELFLING TRICKS CANNOT STOP ME!
YOUNG! STRONG! YYYYES!
KATHOOM
I!
AM!
EMPERORRRRRR!
KATHOOM
THE CRYSTAL IS GETTING WEAKER. I CAN FEEL IT.
KATHOOM
IS THIS HOW IT ENDS, KIRA?
FOR US, PERHAPS.
NOT FOR ALL.
THURMA AND KENSHO ARE STILL OUT THERE.
WE HAVE TO TRUST IN THE YOUNG TO DO WHAT WE CANNOT.

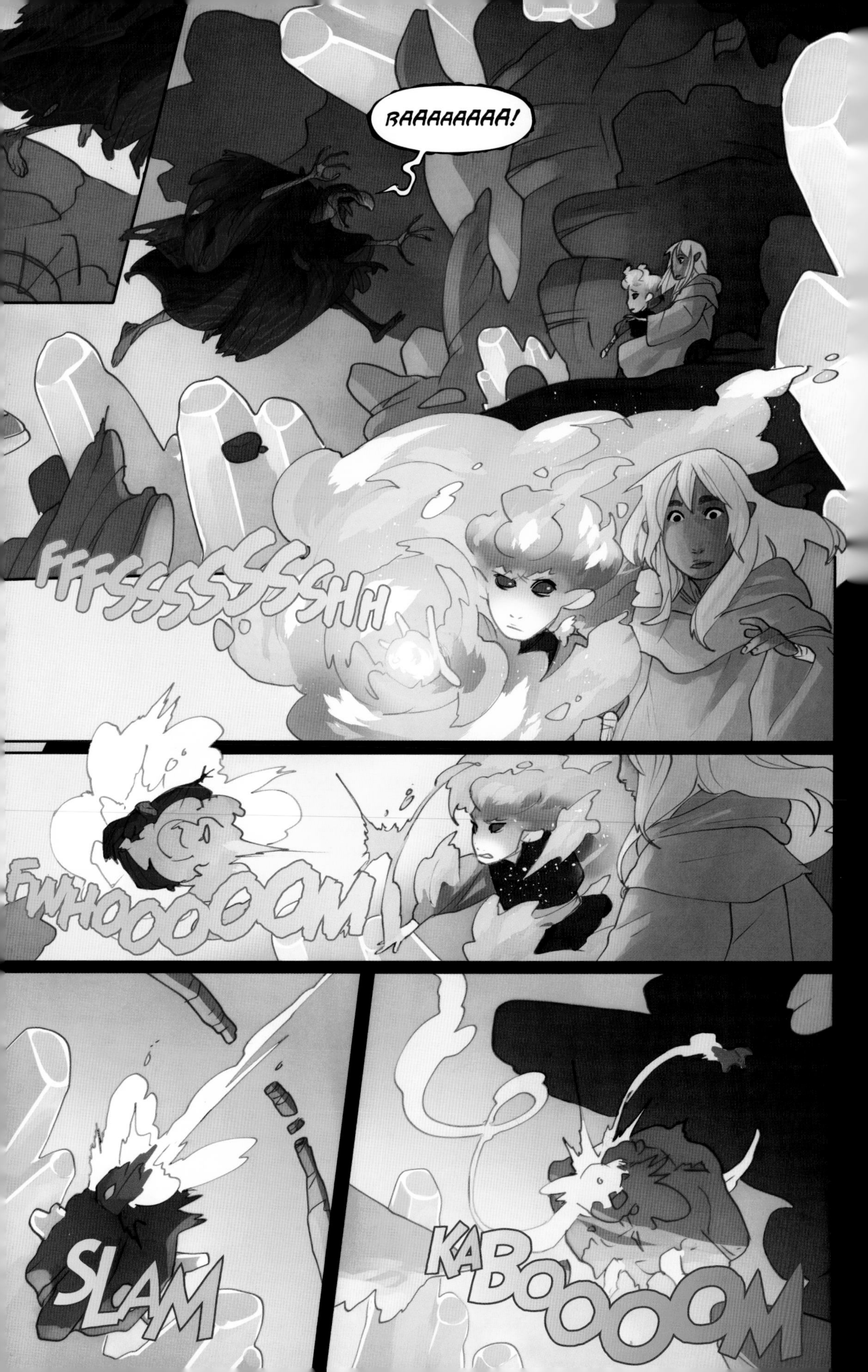

RAAAAAAAA!
FFFSSSSSSSSHH
FWHOOOOOOM
SLAM
KABOOOOOM

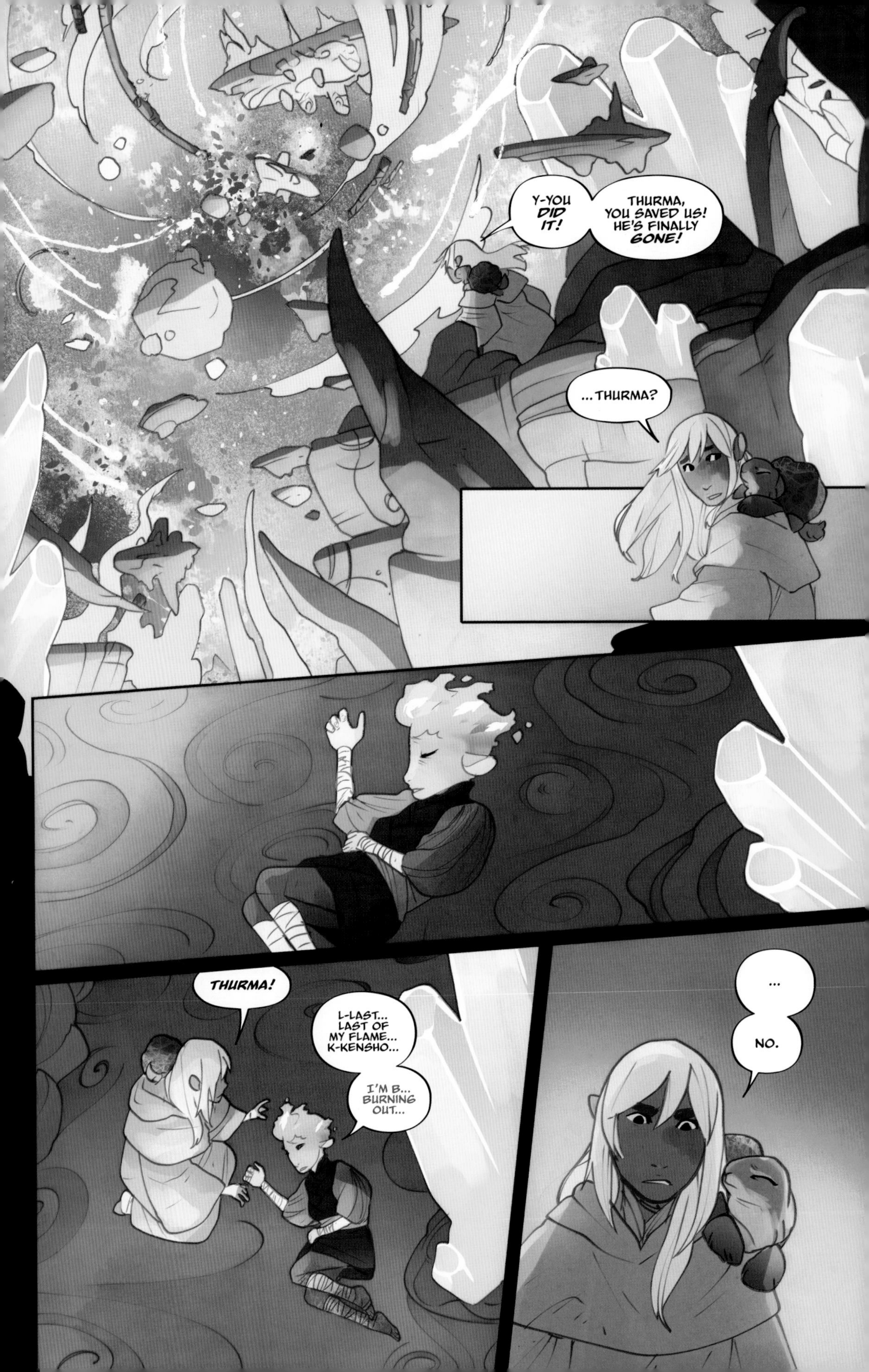
Y-YOU *DID IT!*
THURMA, YOU SAVED US! HE'S FINALLY *GONE!*
...THURMA?
THURMA!
L-LAST... LAST OF MY FLAME... K-KENSHO...
I'M B... BURNING OUT...
...
NO.

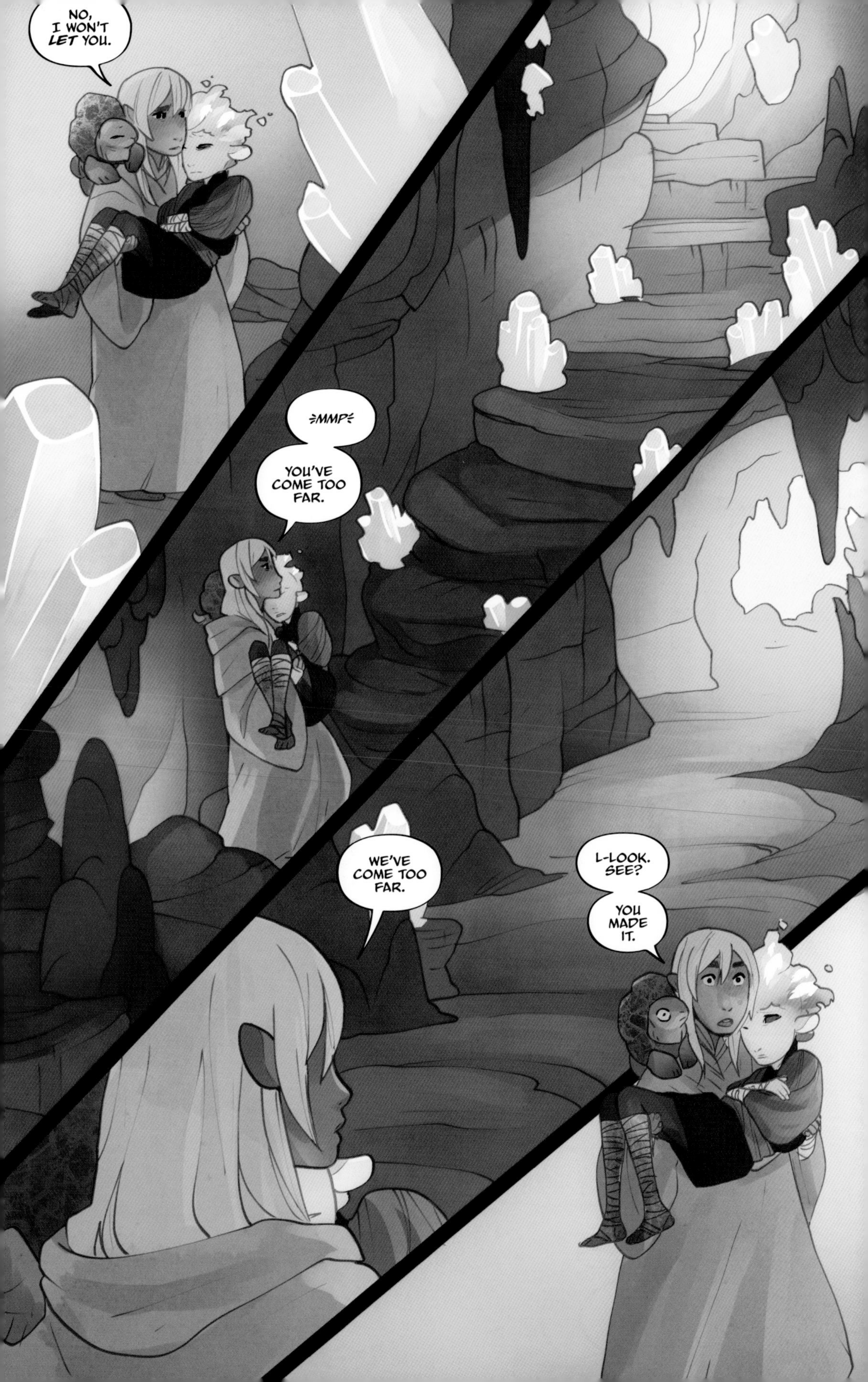
NO, I WON'T *LET* YOU.
⁼MMP⁼
YOU'VE COME TOO FAR.
WE'VE COME TOO FAR.
L-LOOK. SEE?
YOU MADE IT.

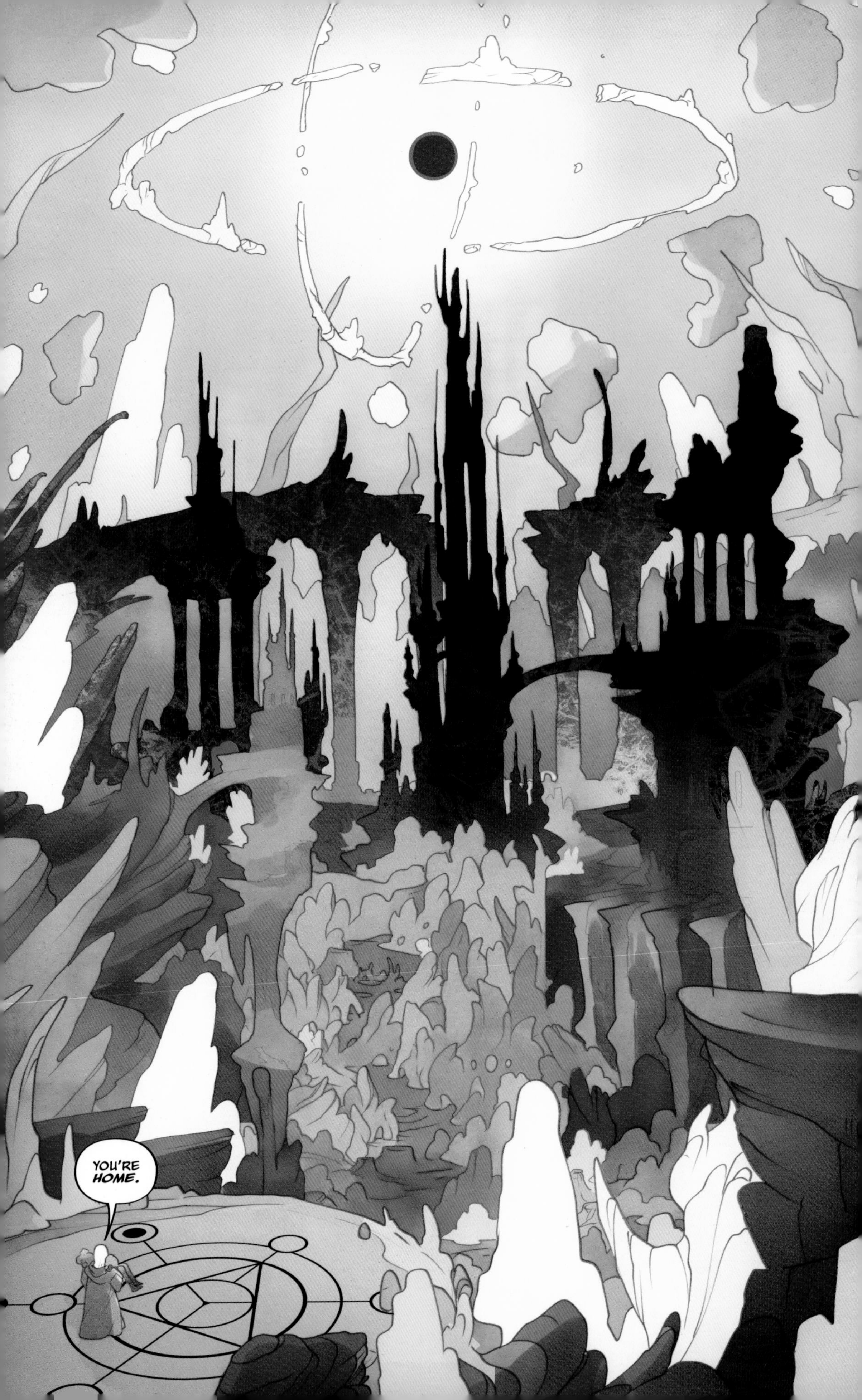
YOU'RE HOME.

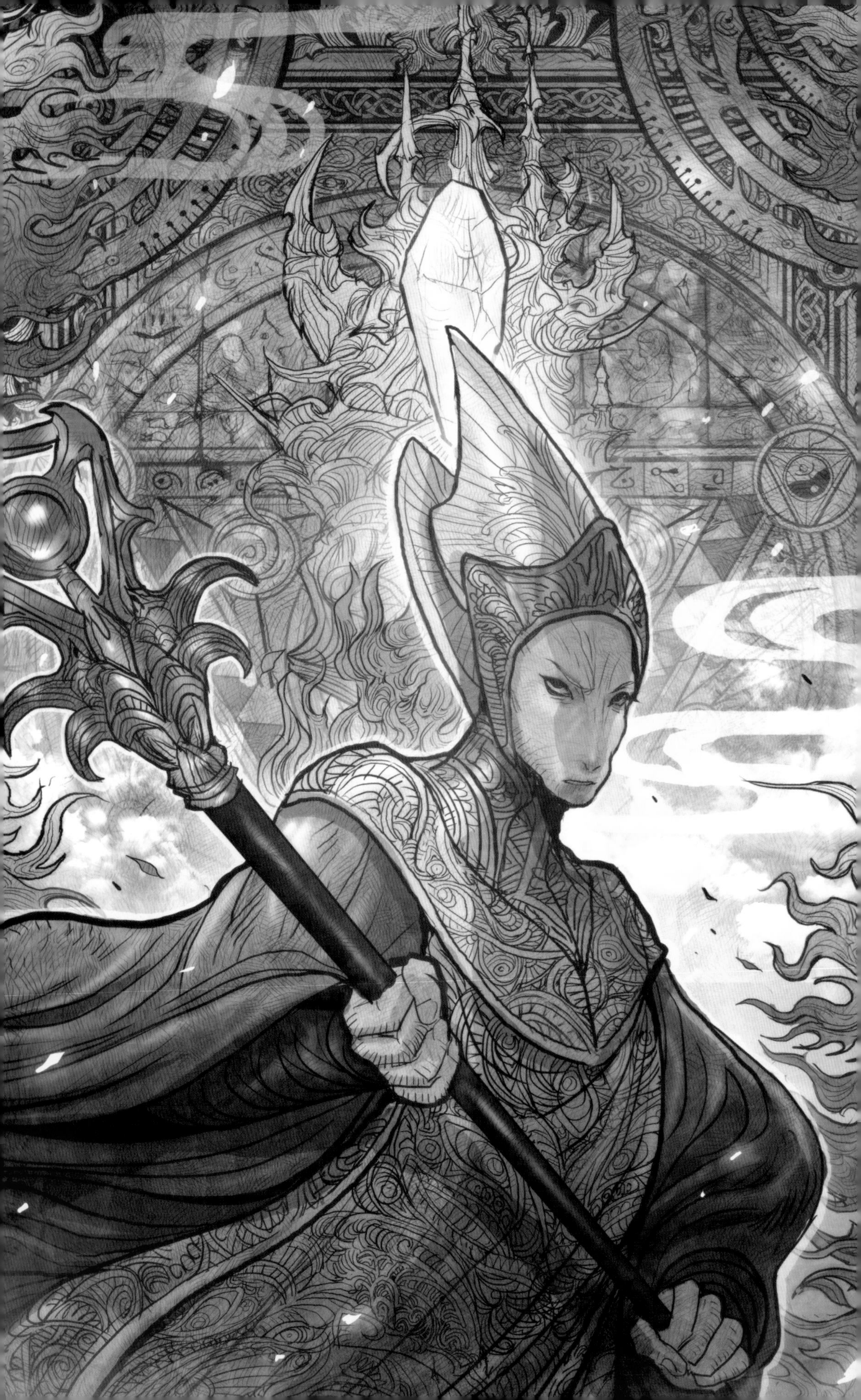

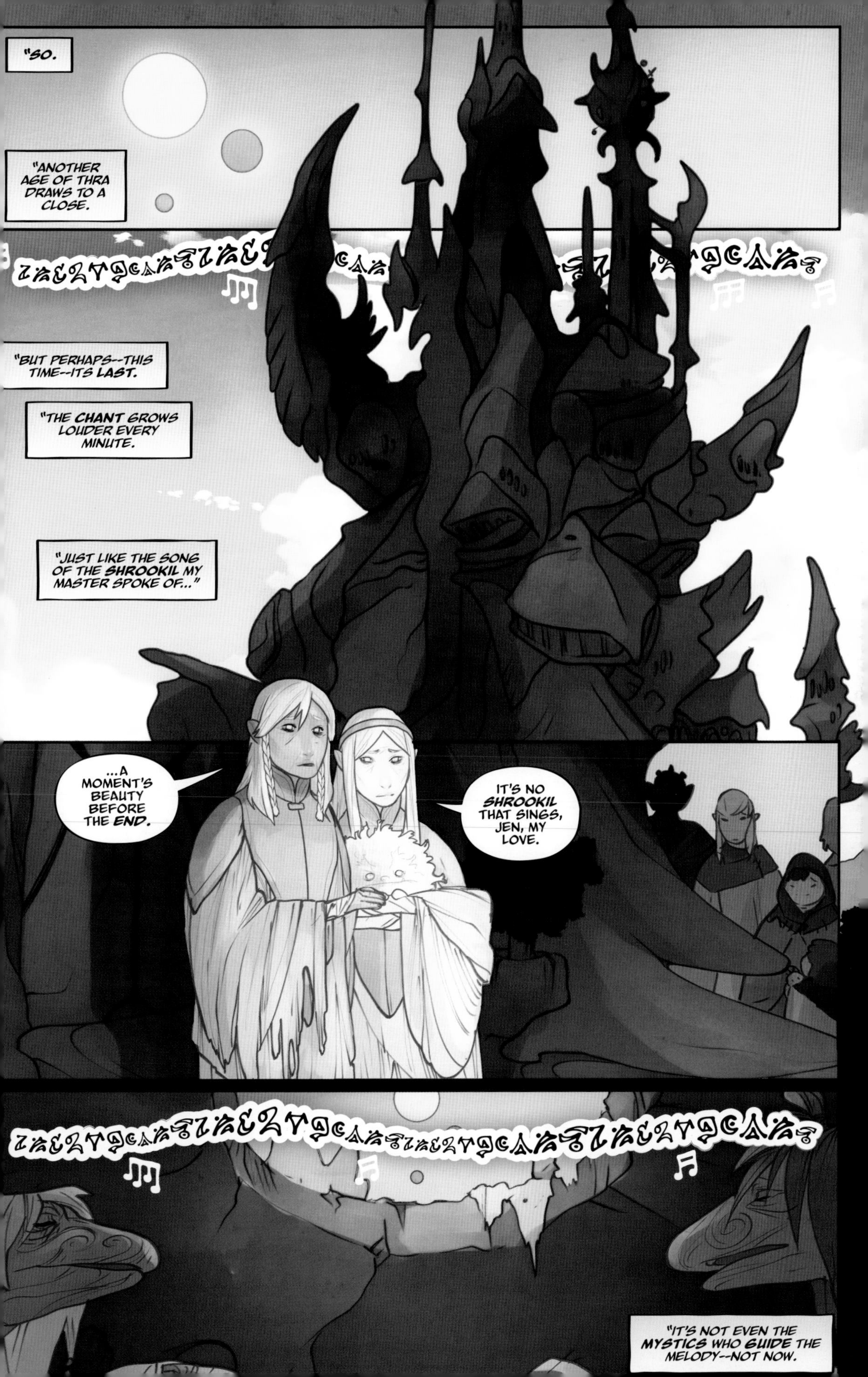

"SO.
"ANOTHER AGE OF THRA DRAWS TO A CLOSE.
"BUT PERHAPS--THIS TIME--ITS **LAST**.
"THE **CHANT** GROWS LOUDER EVERY MINUTE.
"JUST LIKE THE SONG OF THE **SHROOKIL** MY MASTER SPOKE OF..."
...A MOMENT'S BEAUTY BEFORE THE **END**.
IT'S NO **SHROOKIL** THAT SINGS, JEN, MY LOVE.
"IT'S NOT EVEN THE **MYSTICS** WHO **GUIDE** THE MELODY--NOT NOW.

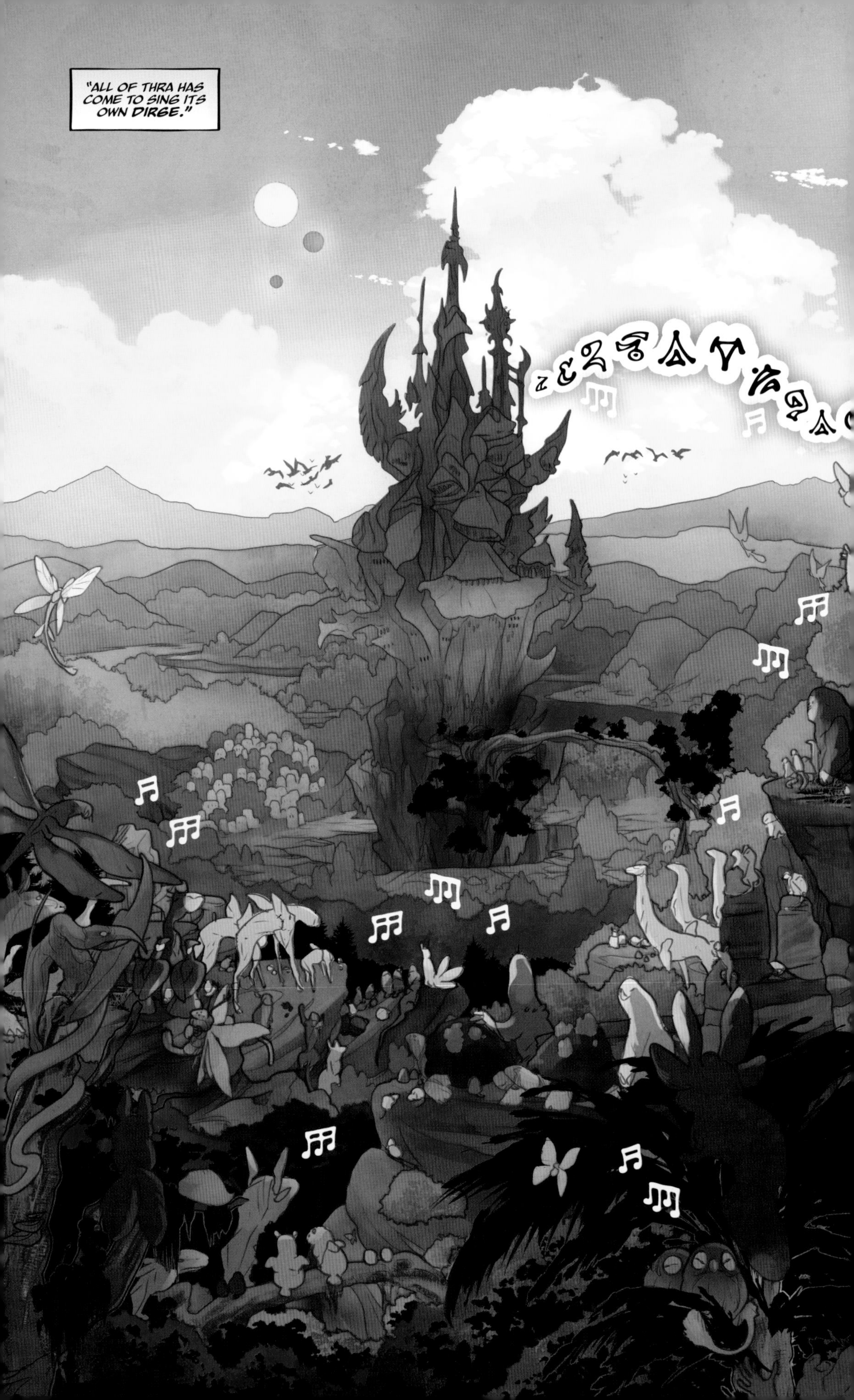
"ALL OF THRA HAS COME TO SING ITS OWN DIRGE."

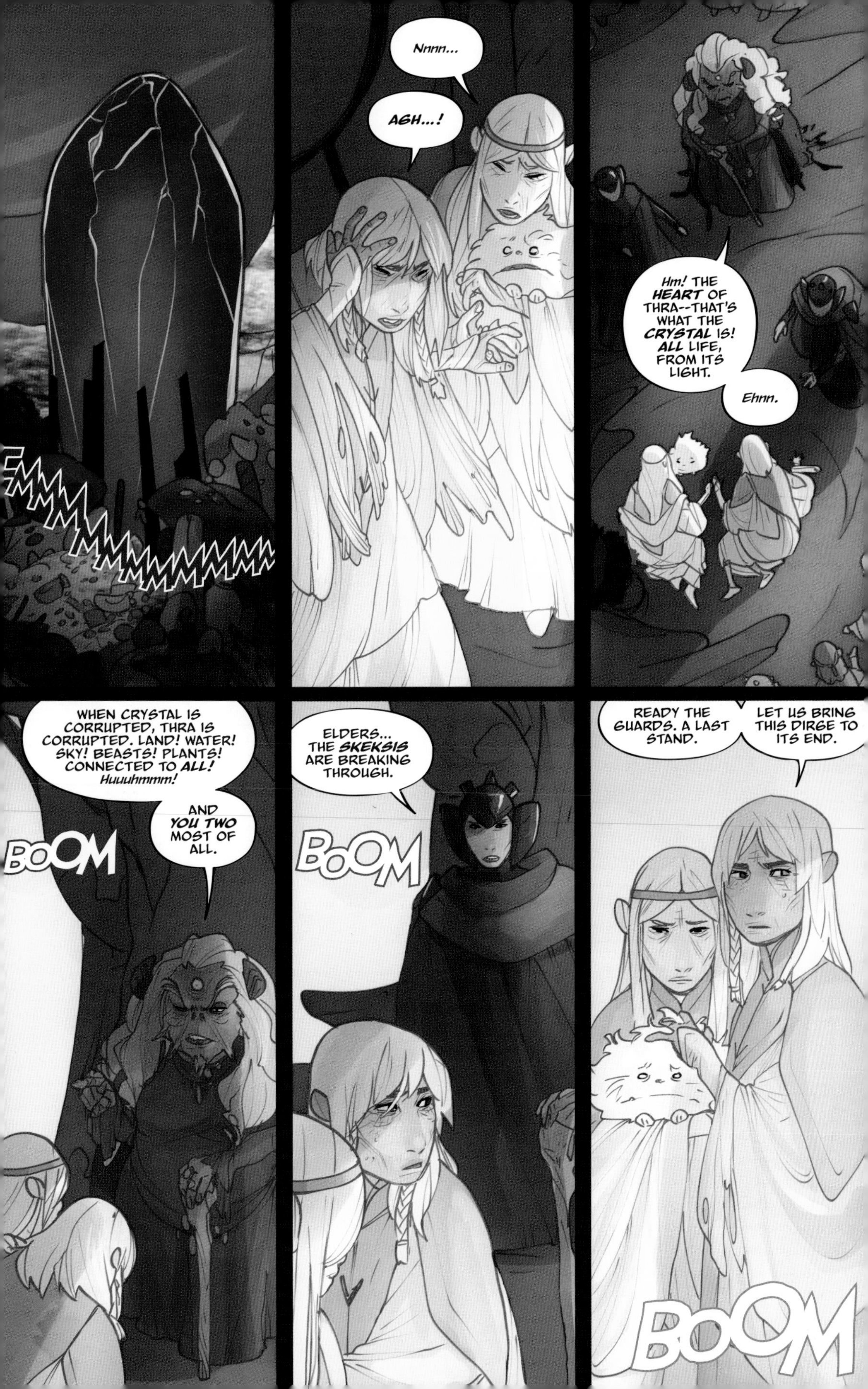
MMMMMMMMMMMMM
Nnnn...
AGH...!
Hm! THE HEART OF THRA--THAT'S WHAT THE CRYSTAL IS! ALL LIFE, FROM ITS LIGHT.
Ehnn.
WHEN CRYSTAL IS CORRUPTED, THRA IS CORRUPTED. LAND! WATER! SKY! BEASTS! PLANTS! CONNECTED TO ALL! Huuuhmmm!
BOOM
AND YOU TWO MOST OF ALL.
ELDERS... THE SKEKSIS ARE BREAKING THROUGH.
BOOM
READY THE GUARDS. A LAST STAND.
LET US BRING THIS DIRGE TO ITS END.
BOOM

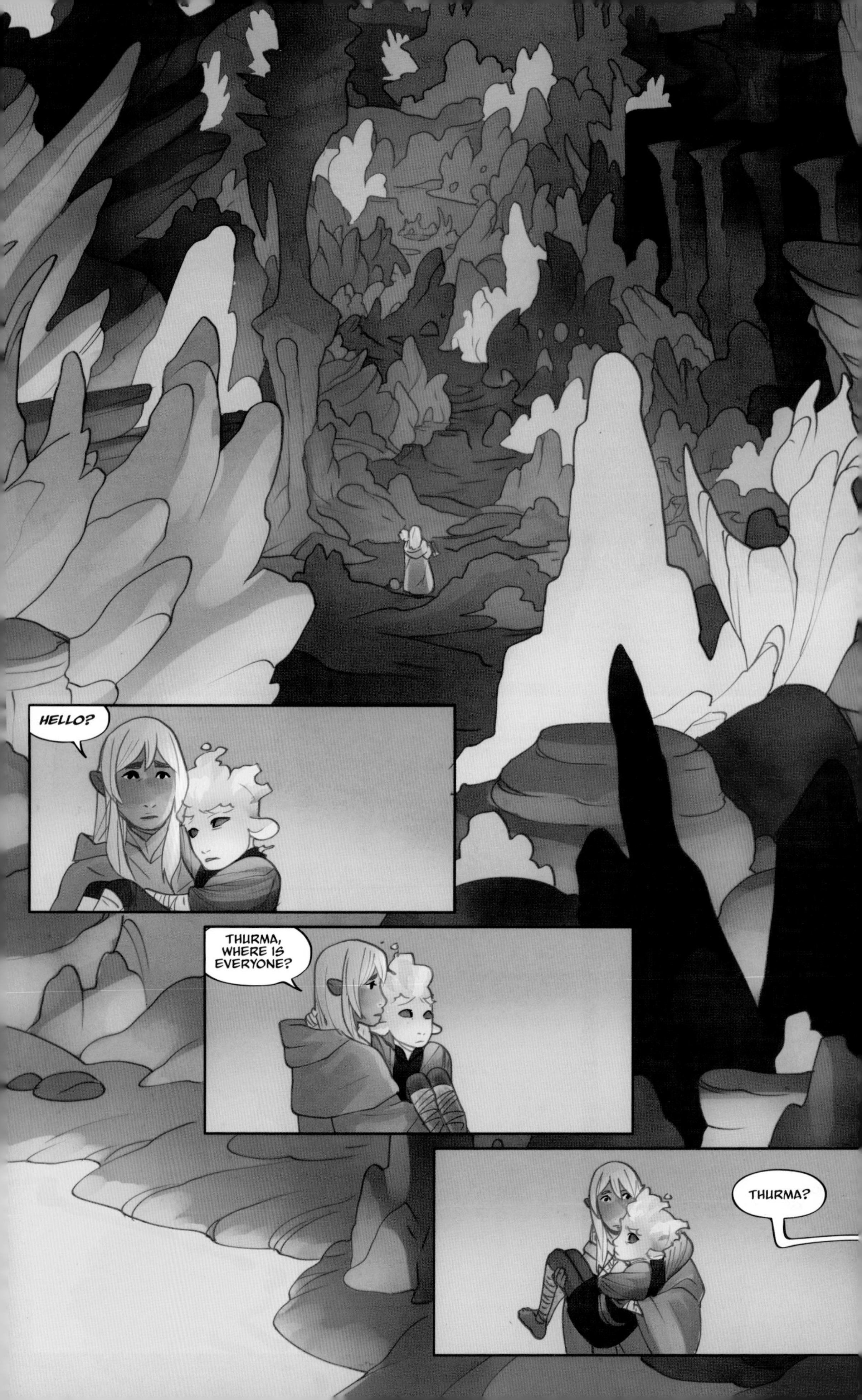
HELLO?
THURMA, WHERE IS EVERYONE?
THURMA?

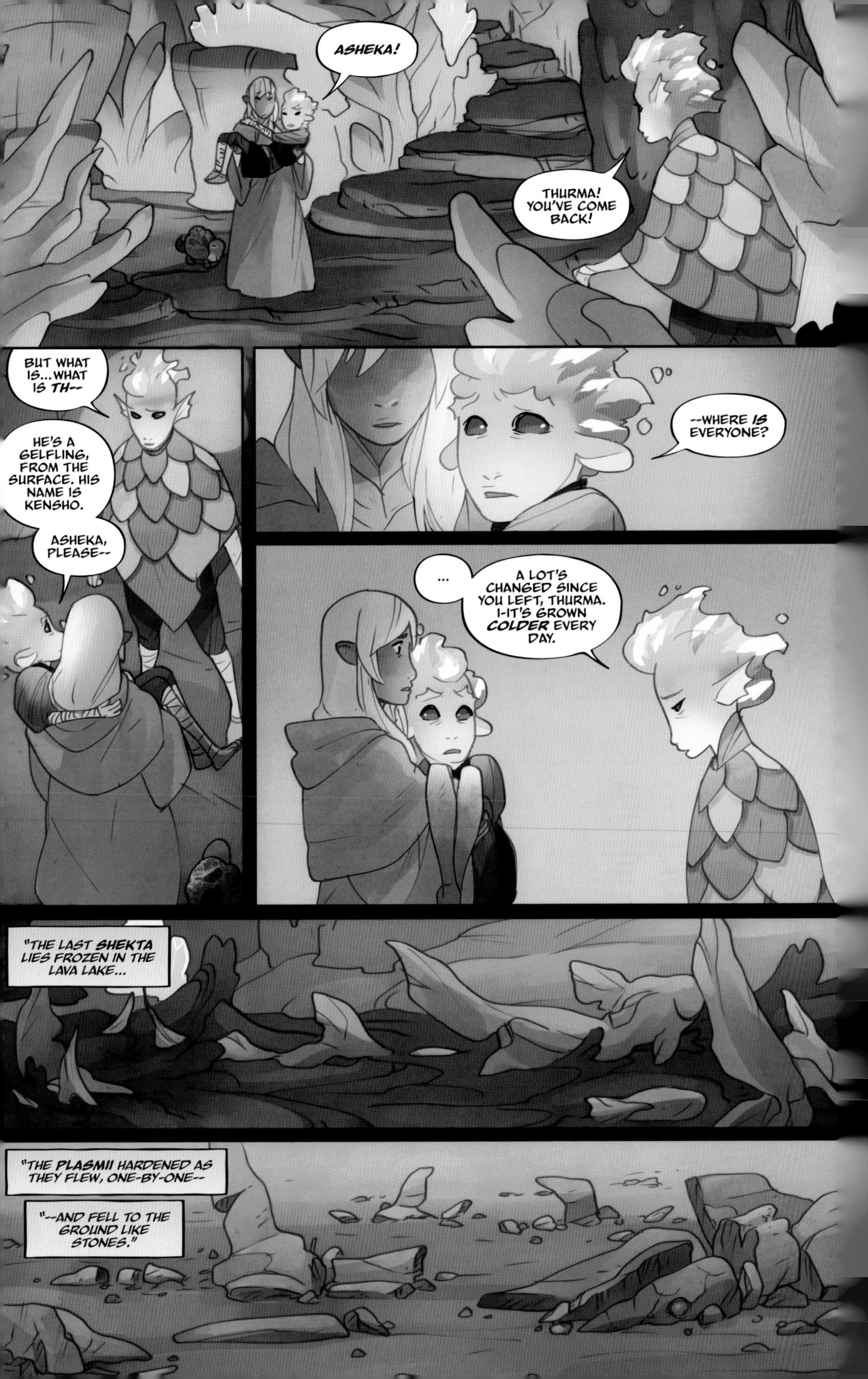
ASHEKA!
THURMA! YOU'VE COME BACK!
BUT WHAT IS...WHAT IS TH--
HE'S A GELFLING, FROM THE SURFACE. HIS NAME IS KENSHO.
ASHEKA, PLEASE--
--WHERE IS EVERYONE?
...
A LOT'S CHANGED SINCE YOU LEFT, THURMA. I-IT'S GROWN COLDER EVERY DAY.
"THE LAST SHEKTA LIES FROZEN IN THE LAVA LAKE...
"THE PLASMII HARDENED AS THEY FLEW, ONE-BY-ONE--
"--AND FELL TO THE GROUND LIKE STONES."

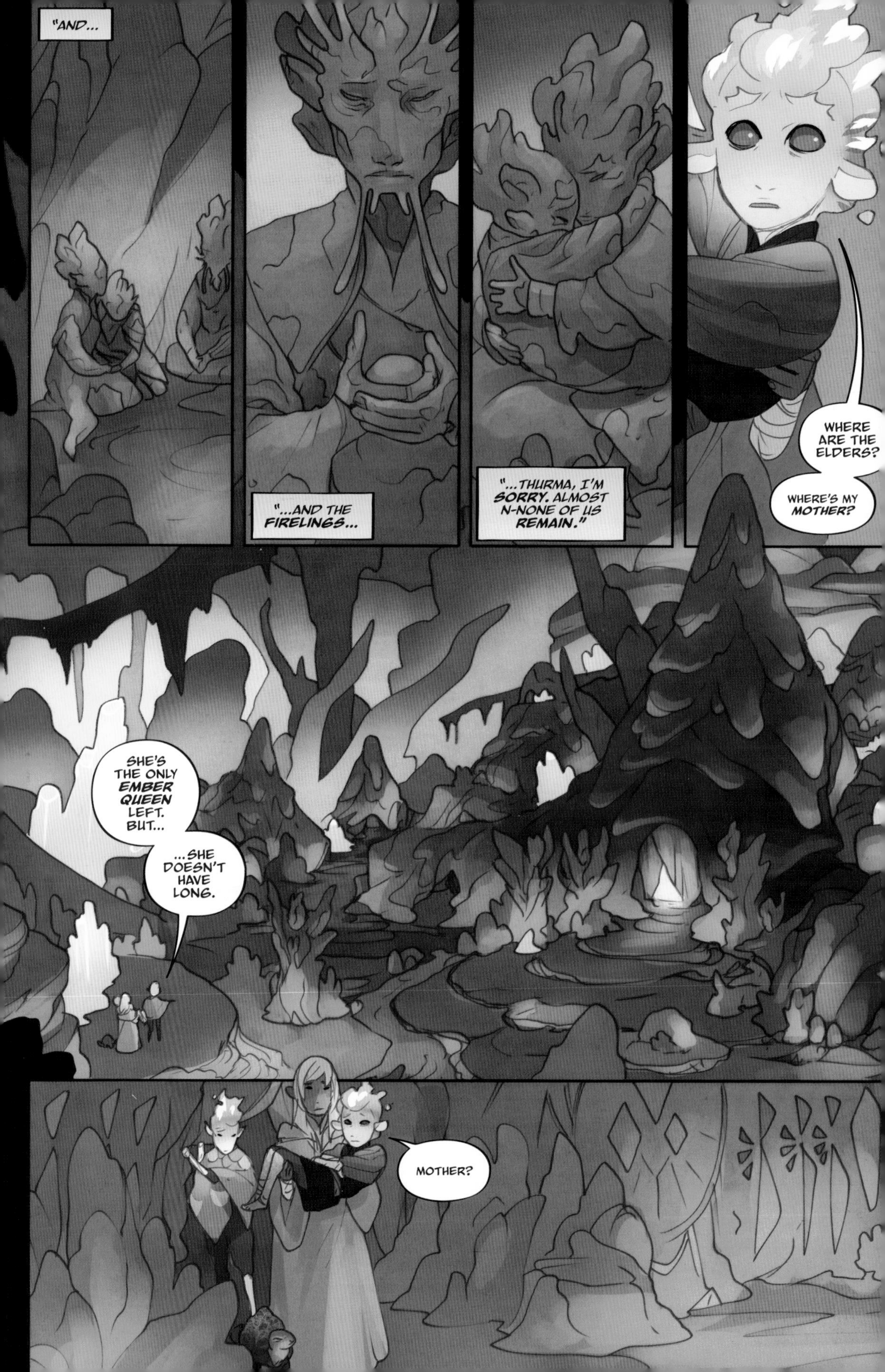
"AND...
"...AND THE FIRELINGS...
"...THURMA, I'M SORRY. ALMOST N-NONE OF US REMAIN."
WHERE ARE THE ELDERS?
WHERE'S MY MOTHER?
SHE'S THE ONLY EMBER QUEEN LEFT. BUT...
...SHE DOESN'T HAVE LONG.
MOTHER?

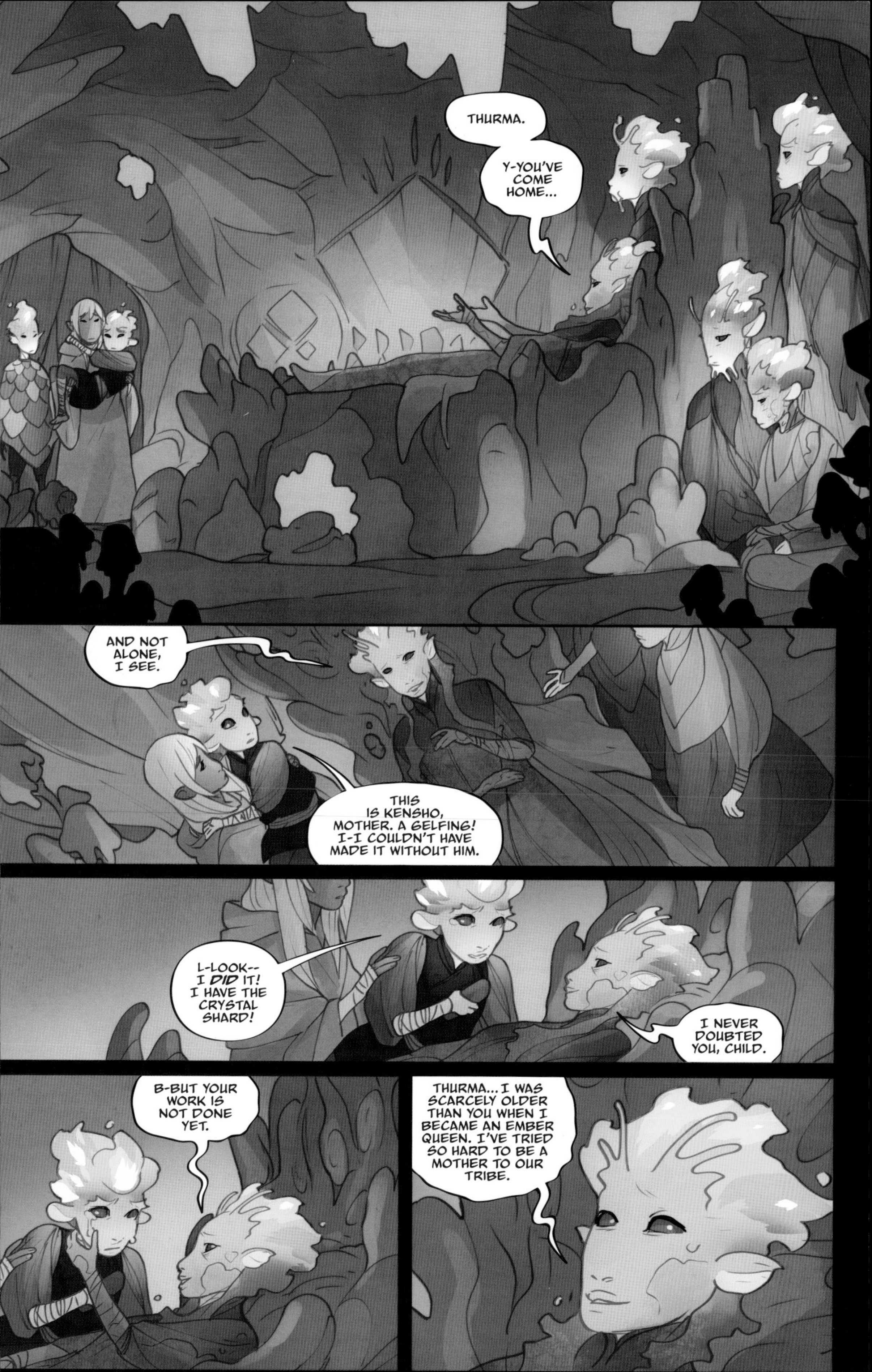
THURMA.
Y-YOU'VE COME HOME...
AND NOT ALONE, I SEE.
THIS IS KENSHO, MOTHER. A GELFING! I-I COULDN'T HAVE MADE IT WITHOUT HIM.
L-LOOK-- I *DID* IT! I HAVE THE CRYSTAL SHARD!
I NEVER DOUBTED YOU, CHILD.
B-BUT YOUR WORK IS NOT DONE YET.
THURMA... I WAS SCARCELY OLDER THAN YOU WHEN I BECAME AN EMBER QUEEN. I'VE TRIED SO HARD TO BE A MOTHER TO OUR TRIBE.

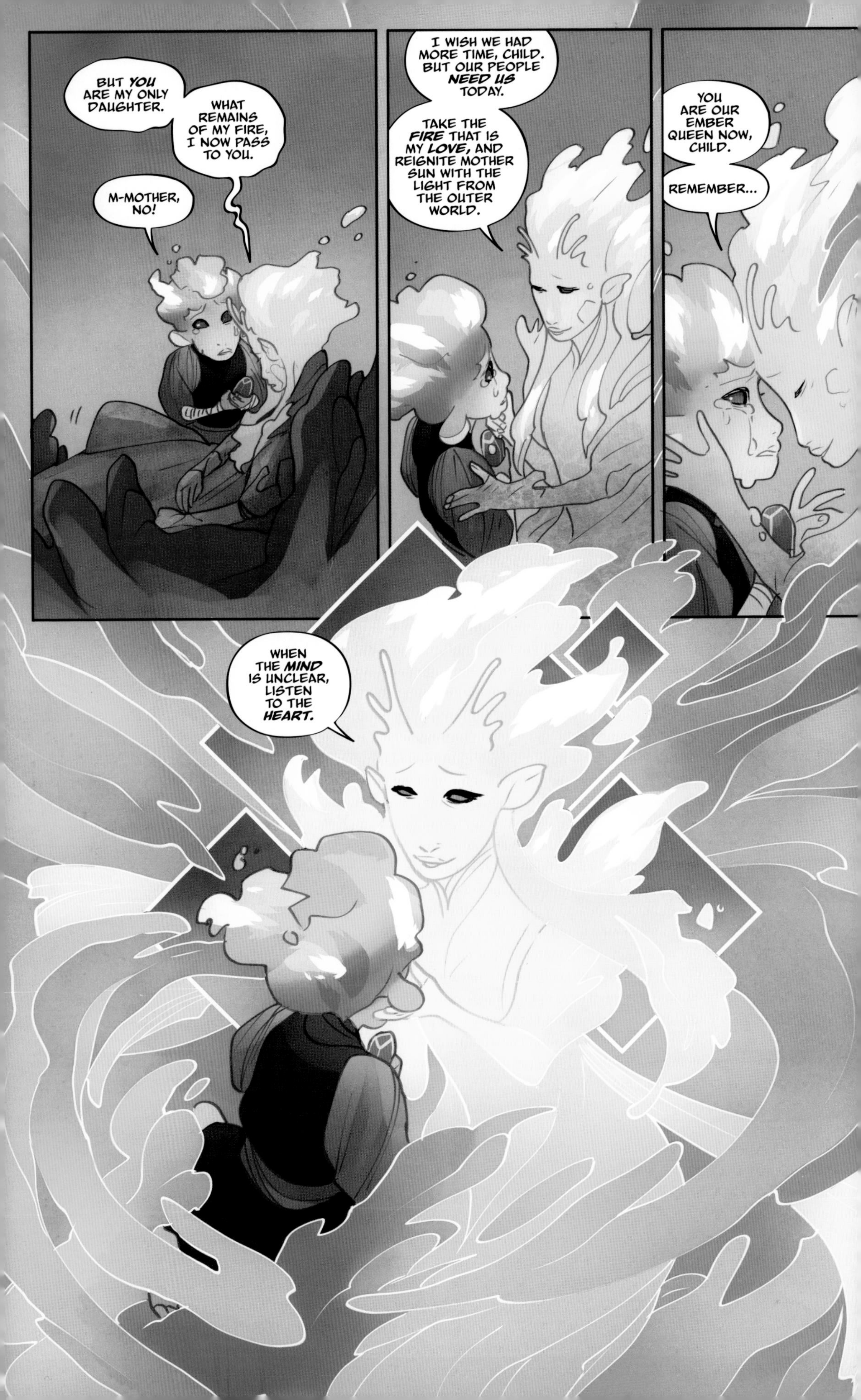
BUT YOU ARE MY ONLY DAUGHTER.
WHAT REMAINS OF MY FIRE, I NOW PASS TO YOU.
M-MOTHER, NO!
I WISH WE HAD MORE TIME, CHILD. BUT OUR PEOPLE NEED US TODAY.
TAKE THE FIRE THAT IS MY LOVE, AND REIGNITE MOTHER SUN WITH THE LIGHT FROM THE OUTER WORLD.
YOU ARE OUR EMBER QUEEN NOW, CHILD.
REMEMBER...
WHEN THE MIND IS UNCLEAR, LISTEN TO THE HEART.

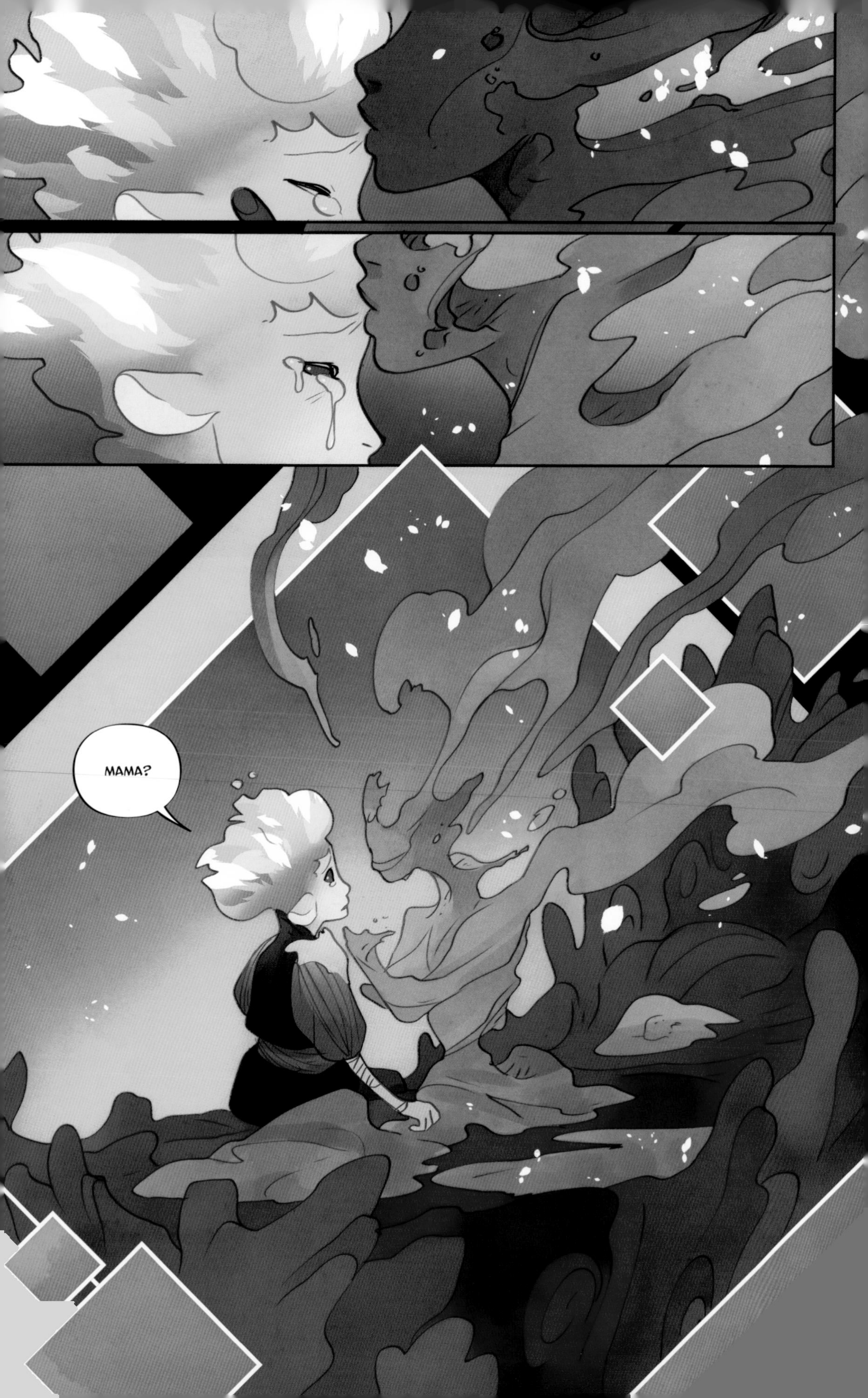
MAMA?

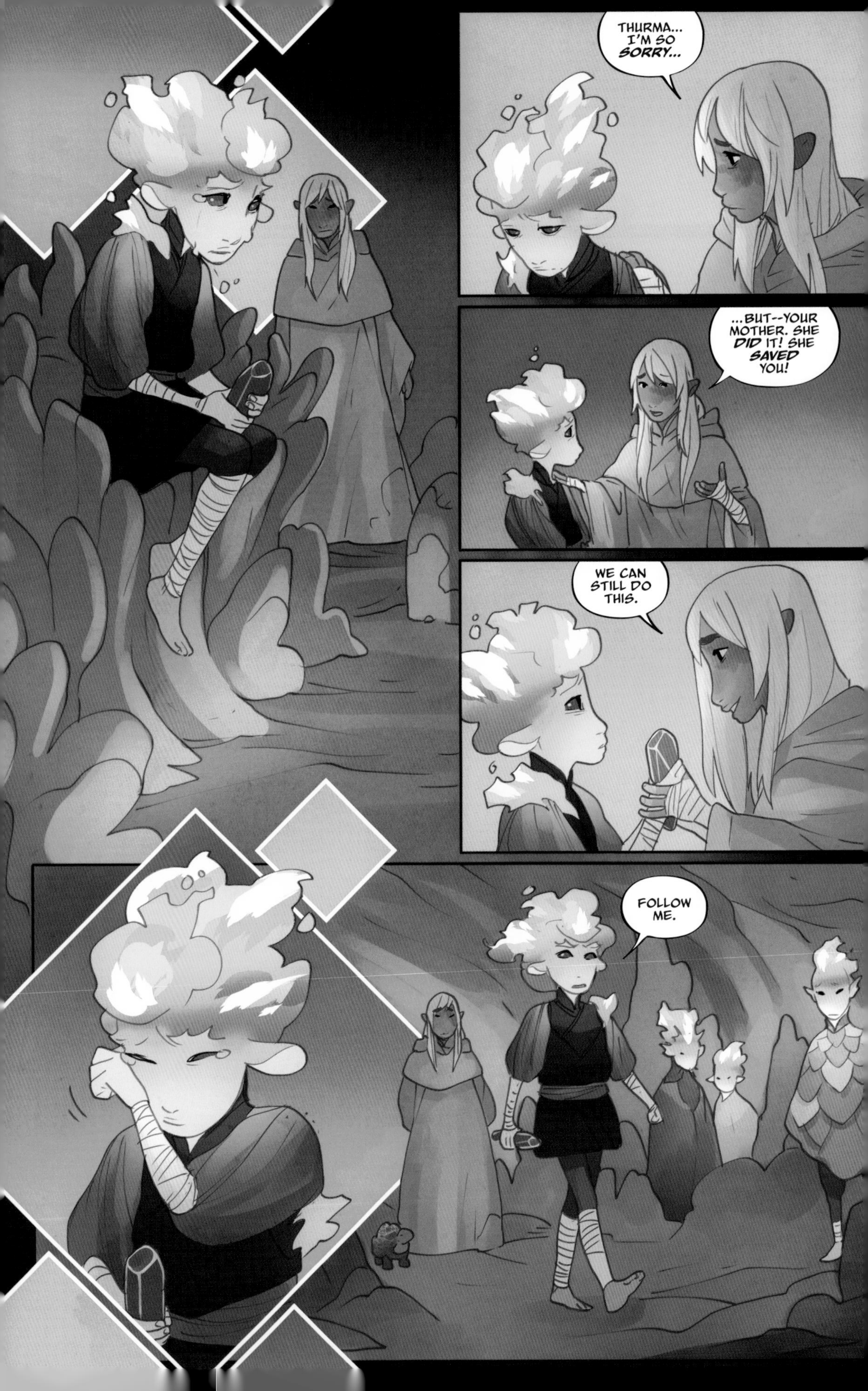
THURMA... I'M SO SORRY...
...BUT--YOUR MOTHER. SHE DID IT! SHE SAVED YOU!
WE CAN STILL DO THIS.
FOLLOW ME.

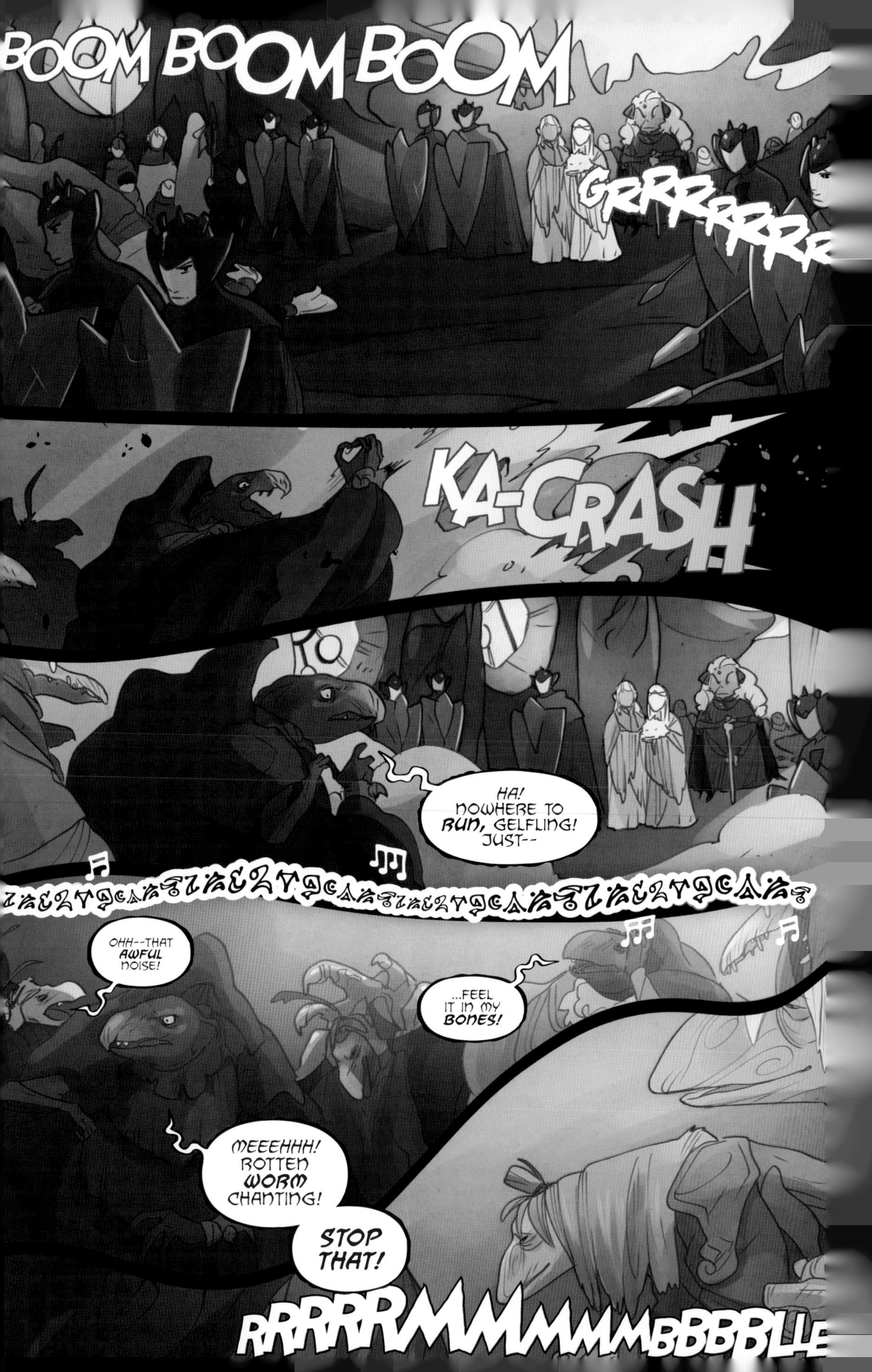
BOOM BOOM BOOM
GRRRRRRRR
KA-CRASH
HA! NOWHERE TO RUN, GELFLING! JUST--
OHH--THAT AWFUL NOISE!
...FEEL IT IN MY BONES!
MEEEHHH! ROTTEN WORM CHANTING!
STOP THAT!
RRRRRMMMMMMBBBBLLE

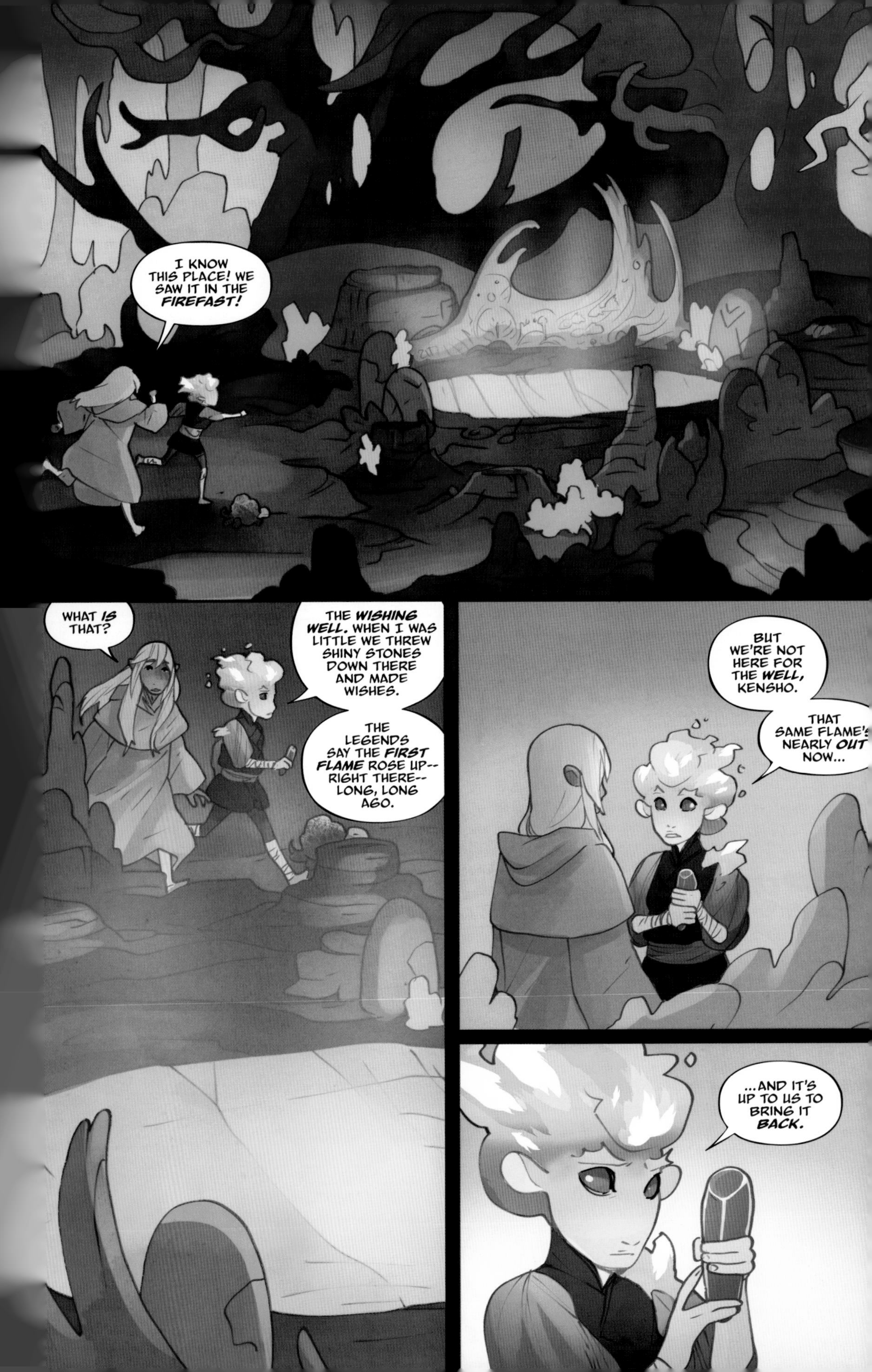
I KNOW THIS PLACE! WE SAW IT IN THE FIREFAST!
WHAT IS THAT?
THE WISHING WELL. WHEN I WAS LITTLE WE THREW SHINY STONES DOWN THERE AND MADE WISHES.
THE LEGENDS SAY THE FIRST FLAME ROSE UP-- RIGHT THERE-- LONG, LONG AGO.
BUT WE'RE NOT HERE FOR THE WELL, KENSHO.
THAT SAME FLAME'S NEARLY OUT NOW...
...AND IT'S UP TO US TO BRING IT BACK.

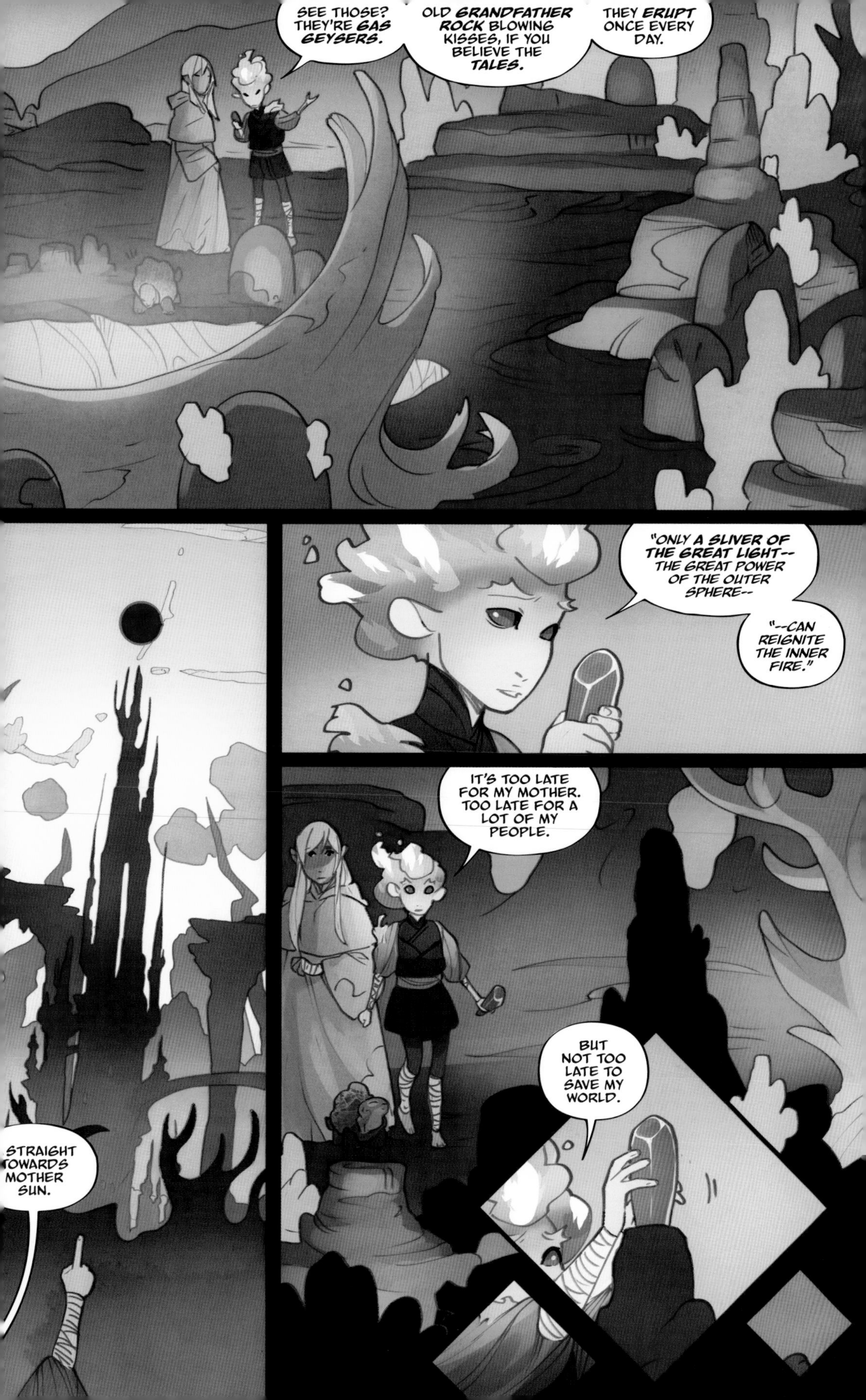
SEE THOSE? THEY'RE GAS GEYSERS.
OLD GRANDFATHER ROCK BLOWING KISSES, IF YOU BELIEVE THE TALES.
THEY ERUPT ONCE EVERY DAY.
STRAIGHT TOWARDS MOTHER SUN.
"ONLY A SLIVER OF THE GREAT LIGHT-- THE GREAT POWER OF THE OUTER SPHERE--
"--CAN REIGNITE THE INNER FIRE."
IT'S TOO LATE FOR MY MOTHER. TOO LATE FOR A LOT OF MY PEOPLE.
BUT NOT TOO LATE TO SAVE MY WORLD.

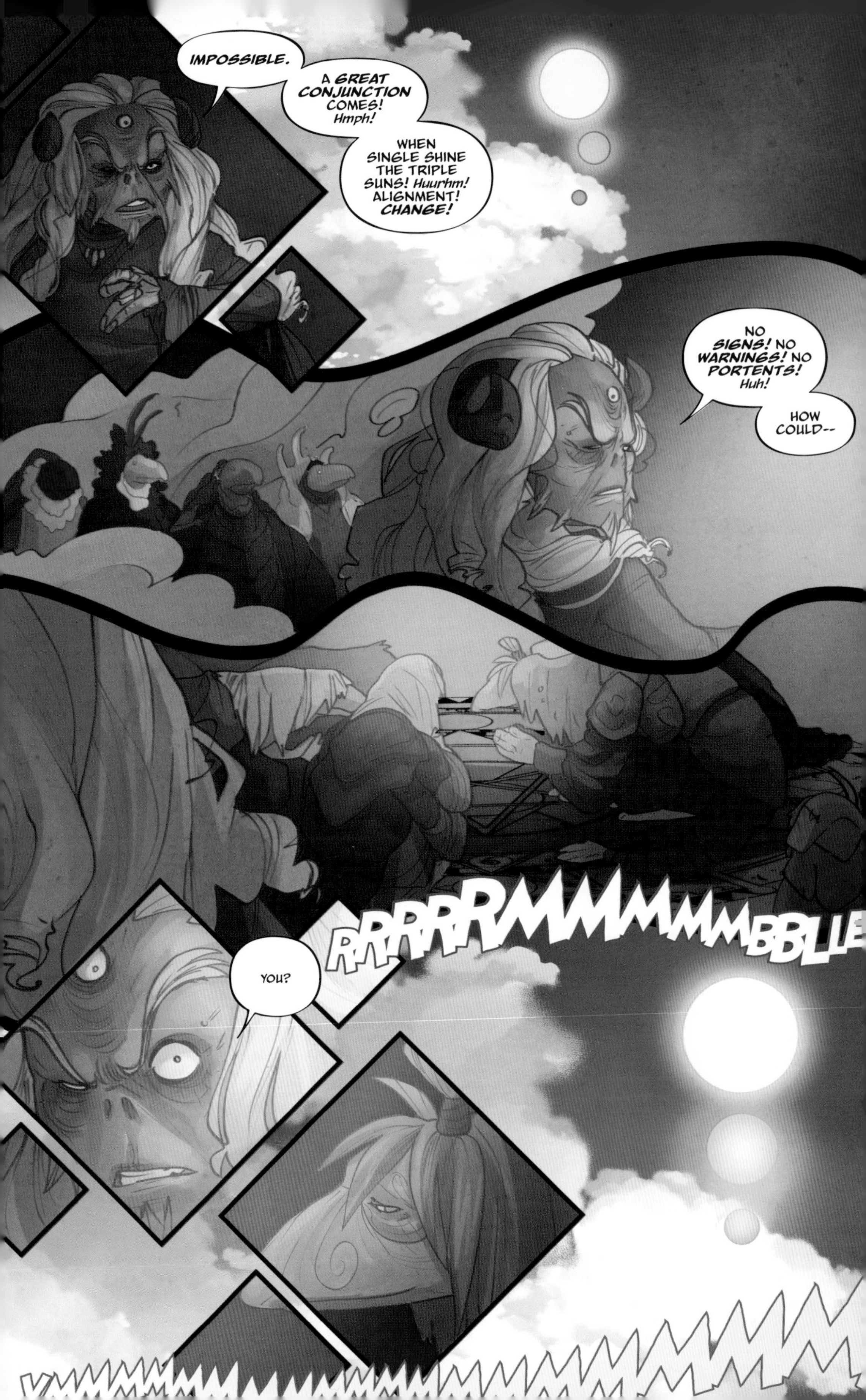

IMPOSSIBLE.
A GREAT CONJUNCTION COMES! Hmph!
WHEN SINGLE SHINE THE TRIPLE SUNS! Huurhm! ALIGNMENT! CHANGE!
NO SIGNS! NO WARNINGS! NO PORTENTS! Huh!
HOW COULD--
RRRRRMMMMMMMBBLLE
YOU?

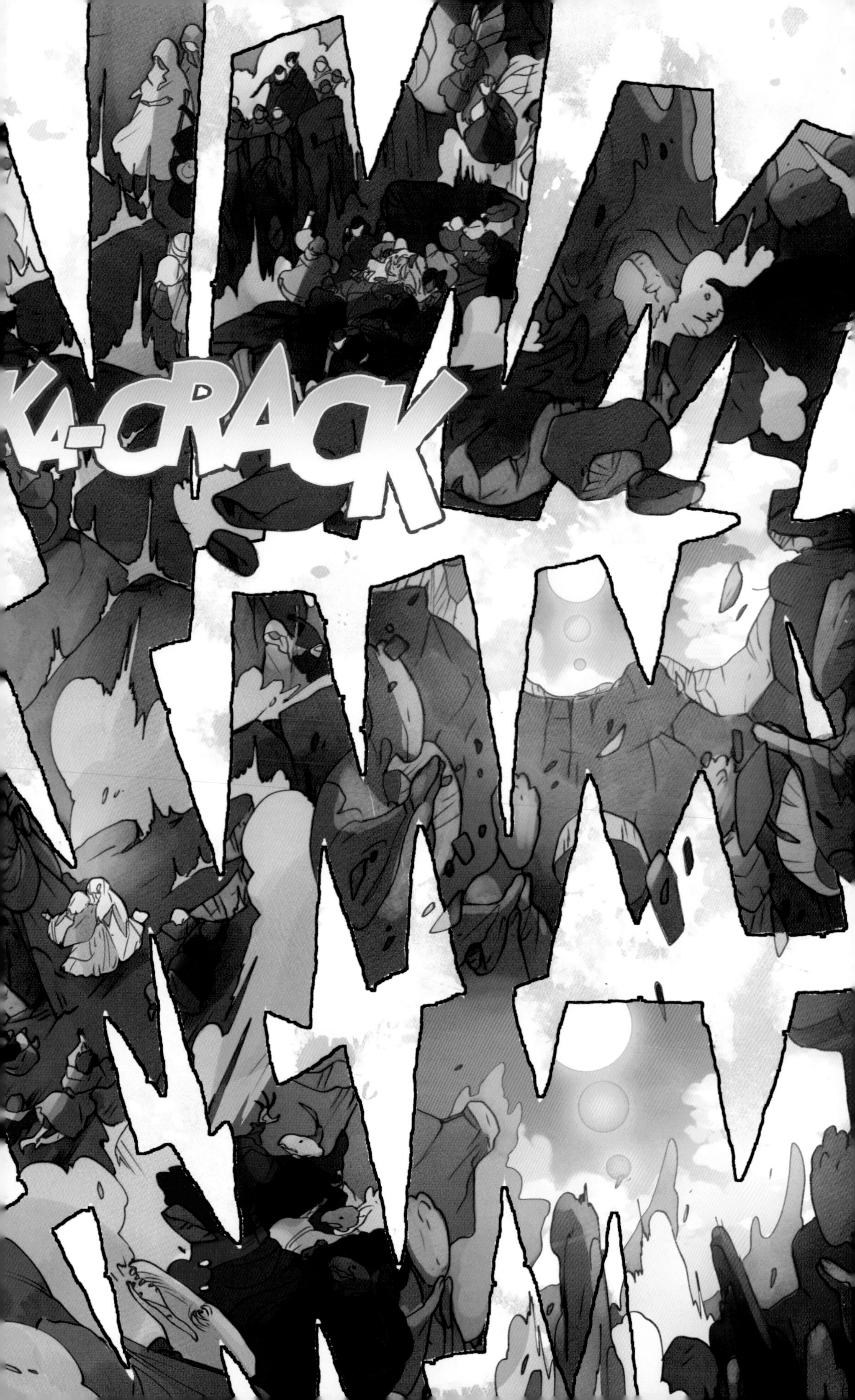
KA-CRACK

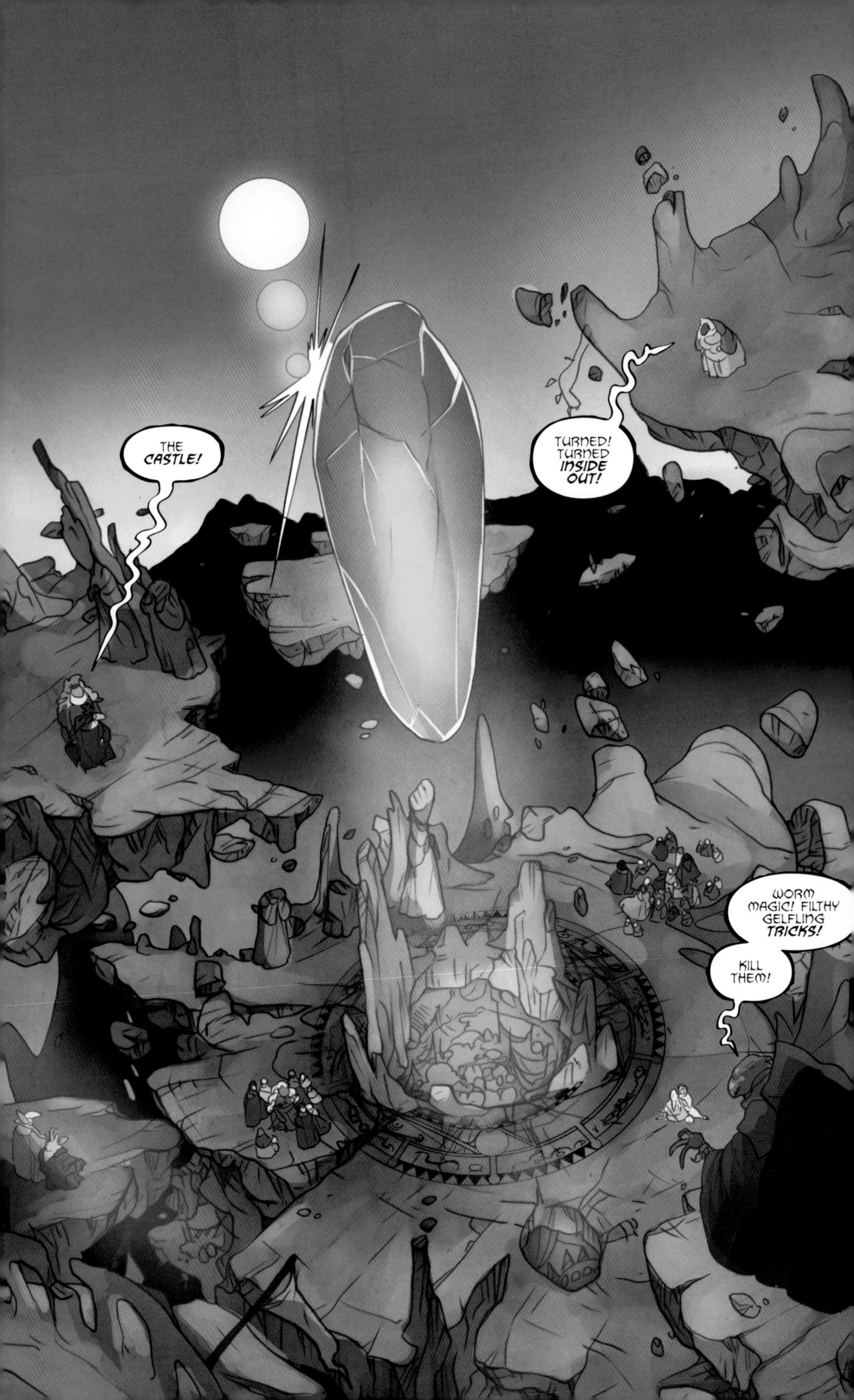
THE CASTLE!
TURNED! TURNED INSIDE OUT!
WORM MAGIC! FILTHY GELFLING TRICKS!
KILL THEM!

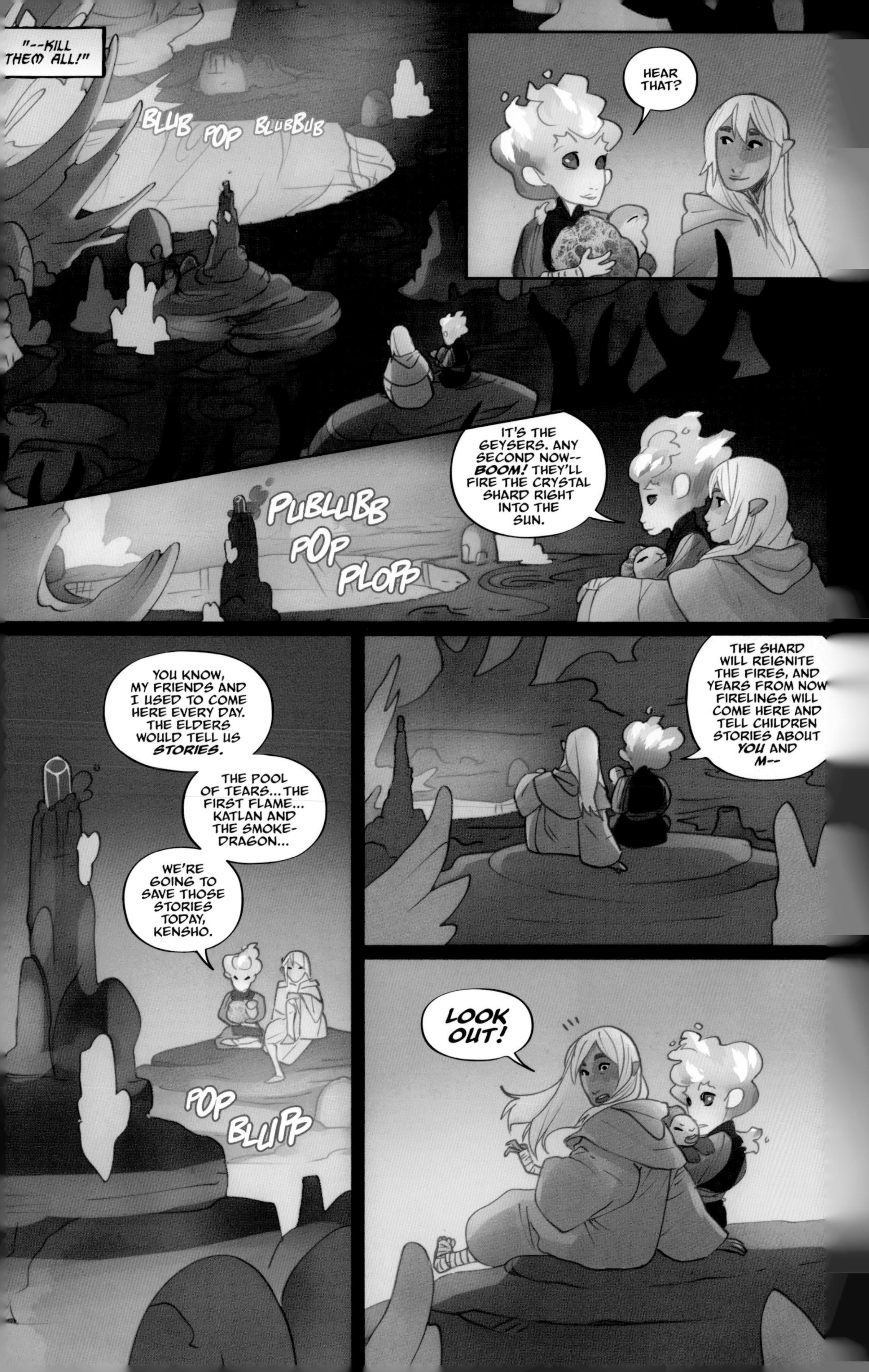
"--KILL THEM ALL!"
BLUB POP BLUBBUB
HEAR THAT?
IT'S THE GEYSERS. ANY SECOND NOW-- BOOM! THEY'LL FIRE THE CRYSTAL SHARD RIGHT INTO THE SUN.
PUBLUBB POP PLOPP
YOU KNOW, MY FRIENDS AND I USED TO COME HERE EVERY DAY. THE ELDERS WOULD TELL US STORIES.
THE POOL OF TEARS... THE FIRST FLAME... KATLAN AND THE SMOKE-DRAGON...
WE'RE GOING TO SAVE THOSE STORIES TODAY, KENSHO.
POP BLUPP
THE SHARD WILL REIGNITE THE FIRES, AND YEARS FROM NOW FIRELINGS WILL COME HERE AND TELL CHILDREN STORIES ABOUT YOU AND M--
LOOK OUT!

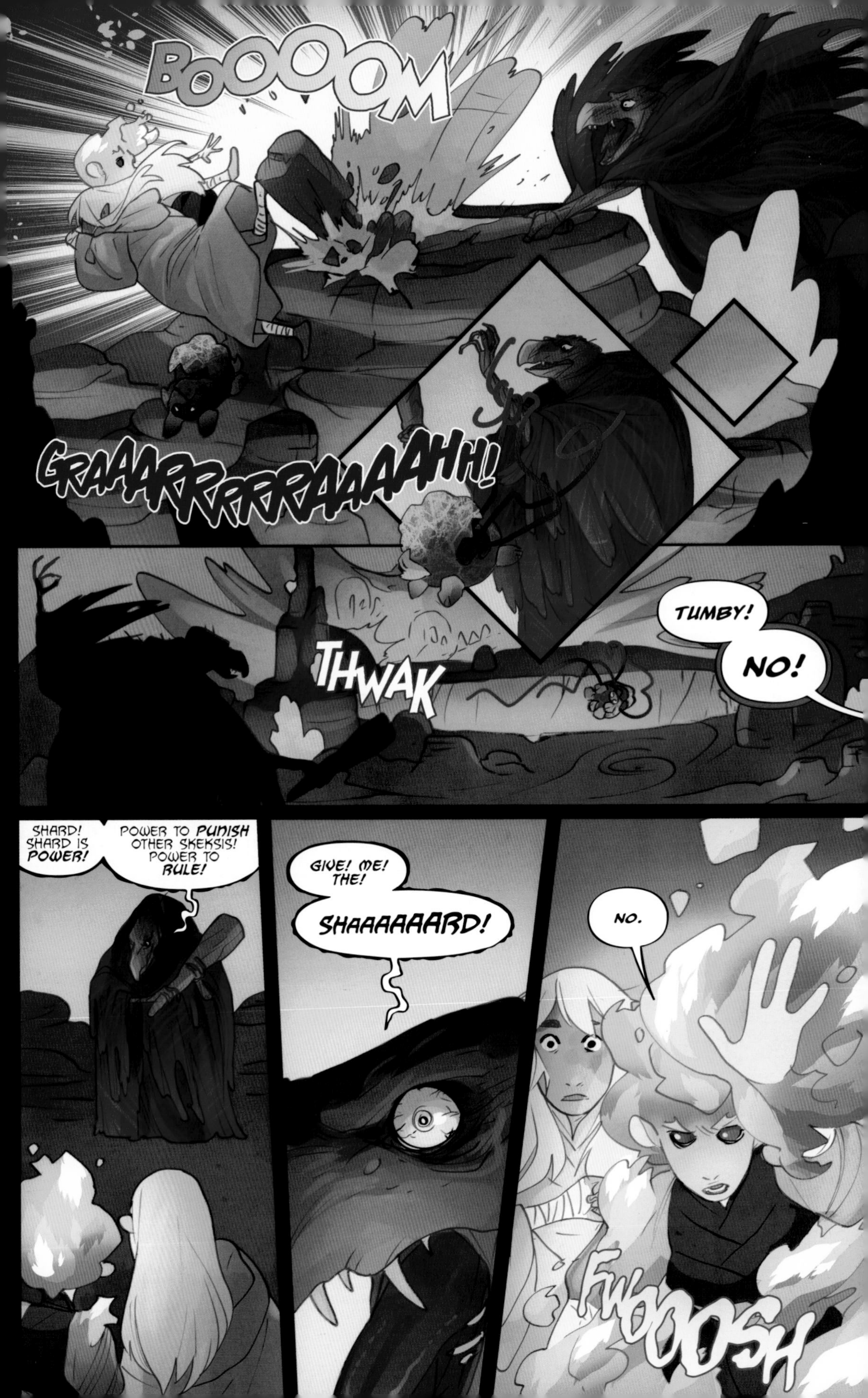
BOOOOOM
GRAAARRRRRRAAAAAHHH!
THWAK
TUMBY!
NO!
SHARD! SHARD IS POWER!
POWER TO PUNISH OTHER SKEKSIS! POWER TO RULE!
GIVE! ME! THE!
SHAAAAAARD!
NO.
FWOOOSH

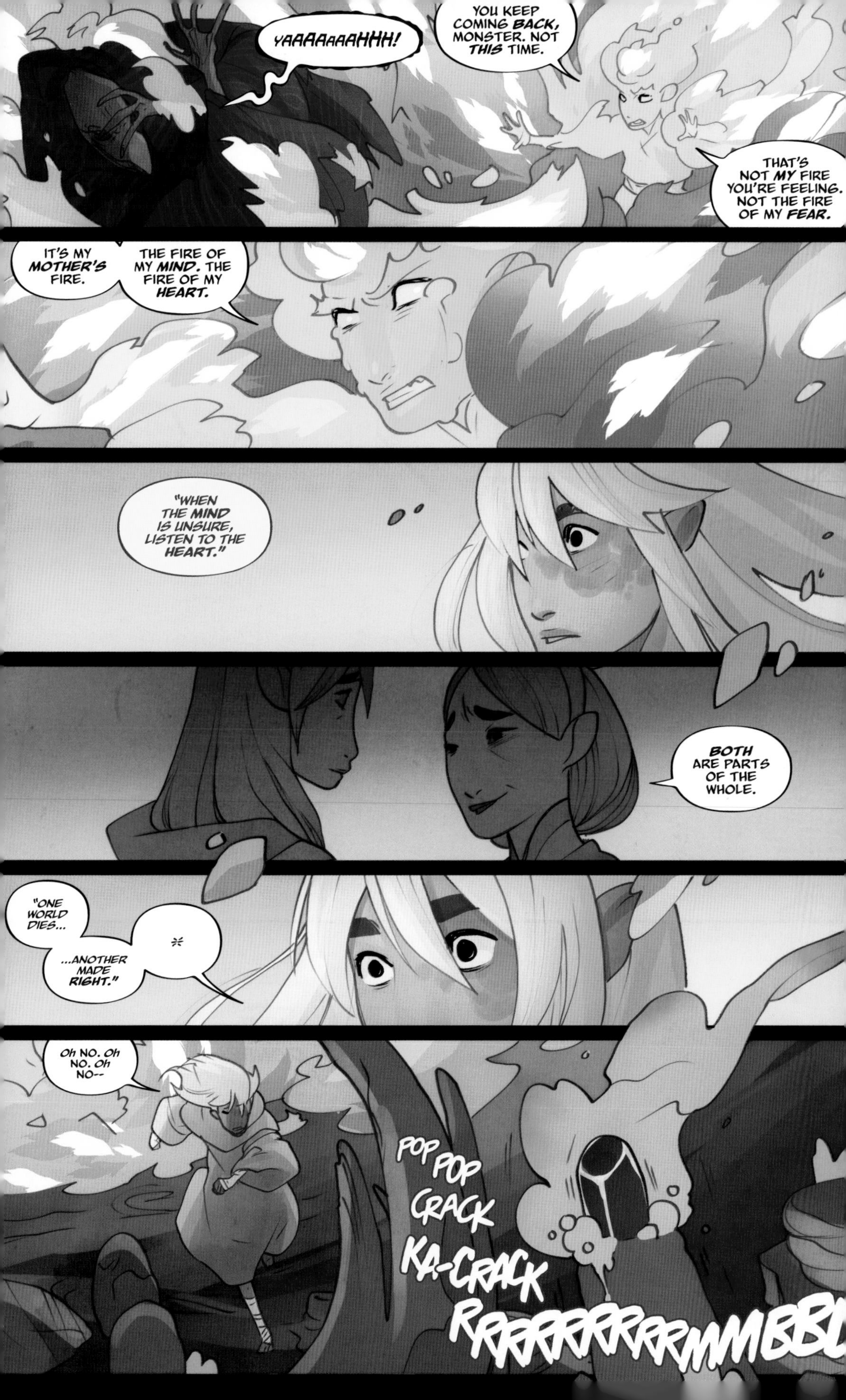
YAAAAAAAHHH!
YOU KEEP COMING BACK, MONSTER. NOT THIS TIME.
THAT'S NOT MY FIRE YOU'RE FEELING. NOT THE FIRE OF MY FEAR.
IT'S MY MOTHER'S FIRE.
THE FIRE OF MY MIND. THE FIRE OF MY HEART.
"WHEN THE MIND IS UNSURE, LISTEN TO THE HEART."
BOTH ARE PARTS OF THE WHOLE.
"ONE WORLD DIES...
...ANOTHER MADE RIGHT."
Oh NO. Oh NO. Oh NO--
POP POP
CRACK
KA-CRACK
RRRRRRRRRRMMBBL

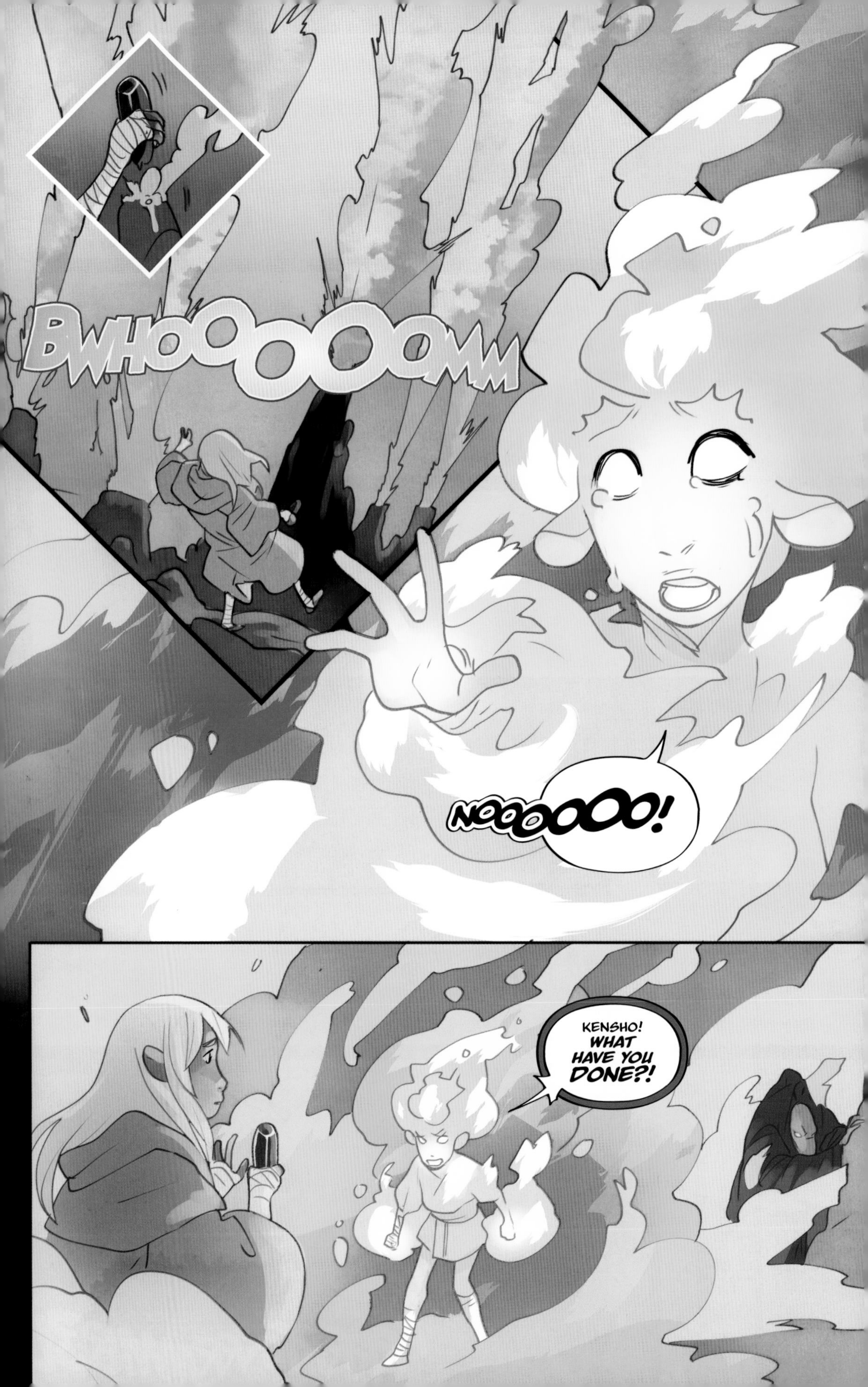
BWHOOOOOOMM
NOOOOOOO!
KENSHO! WHAT HAVE YOU DONE?!

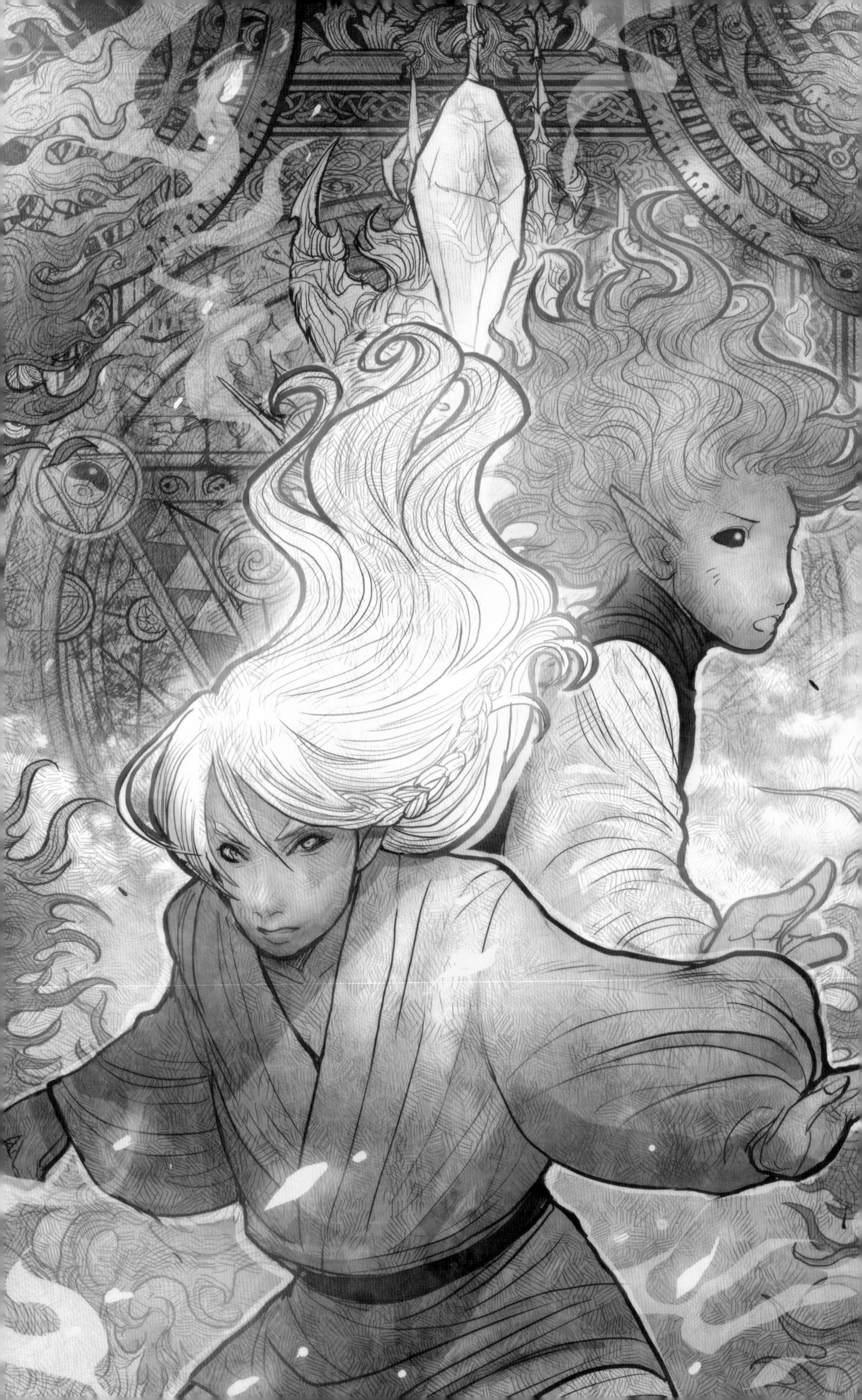

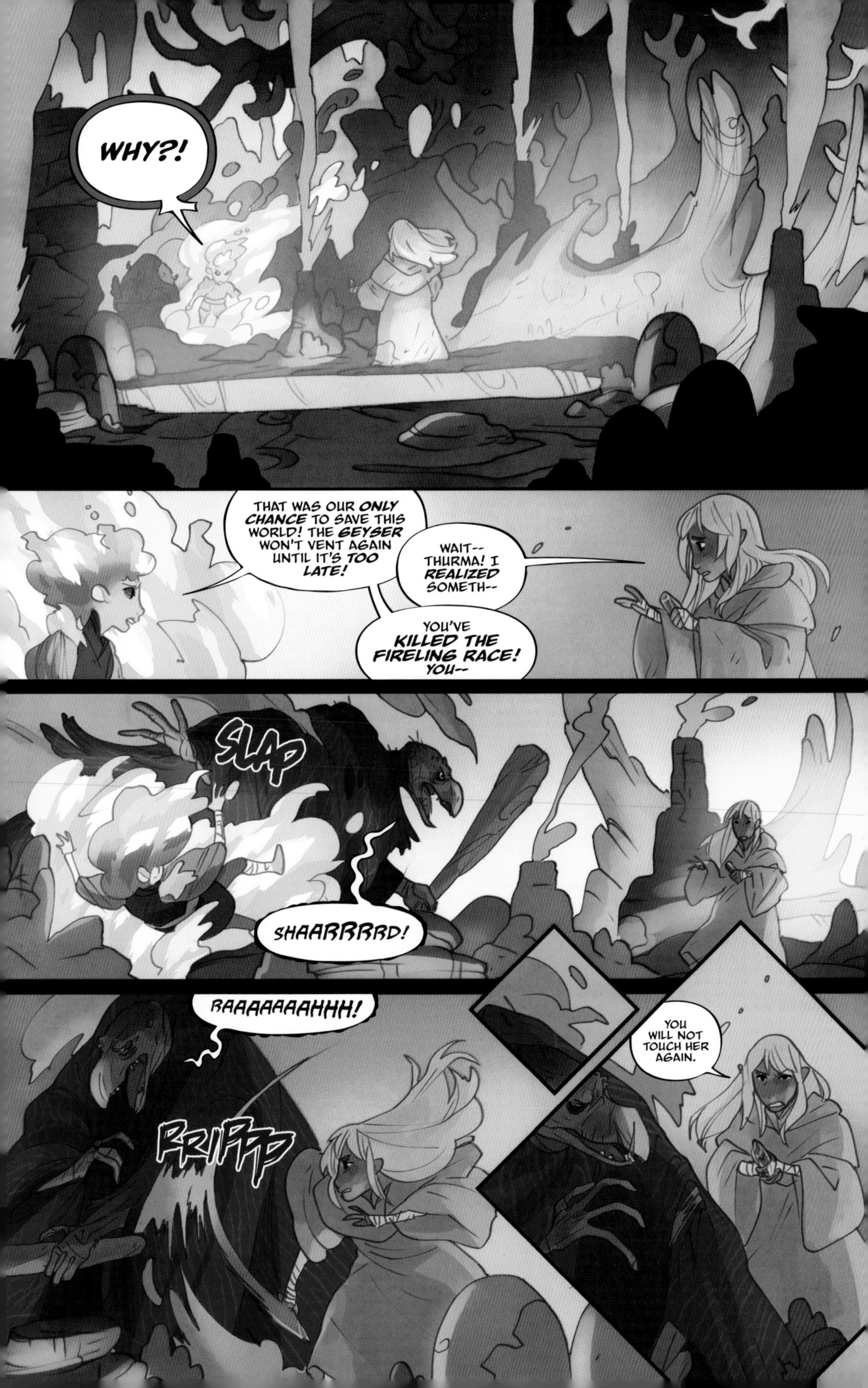
WHY?!
THAT WAS OUR ONLY CHANCE TO SAVE THIS WORLD! THE GEYSER WON'T VENT AGAIN UNTIL IT'S TOO LATE!
WAIT-- THURMA! I REALIZED SOMETH--
YOU'VE KILLED THE FIRELING RACE! YOU--
SLAP
SHAARRRRD!
RAAAAAAAHHH!
RRIPPP
YOU WILL NOT TOUCH HER AGAIN.

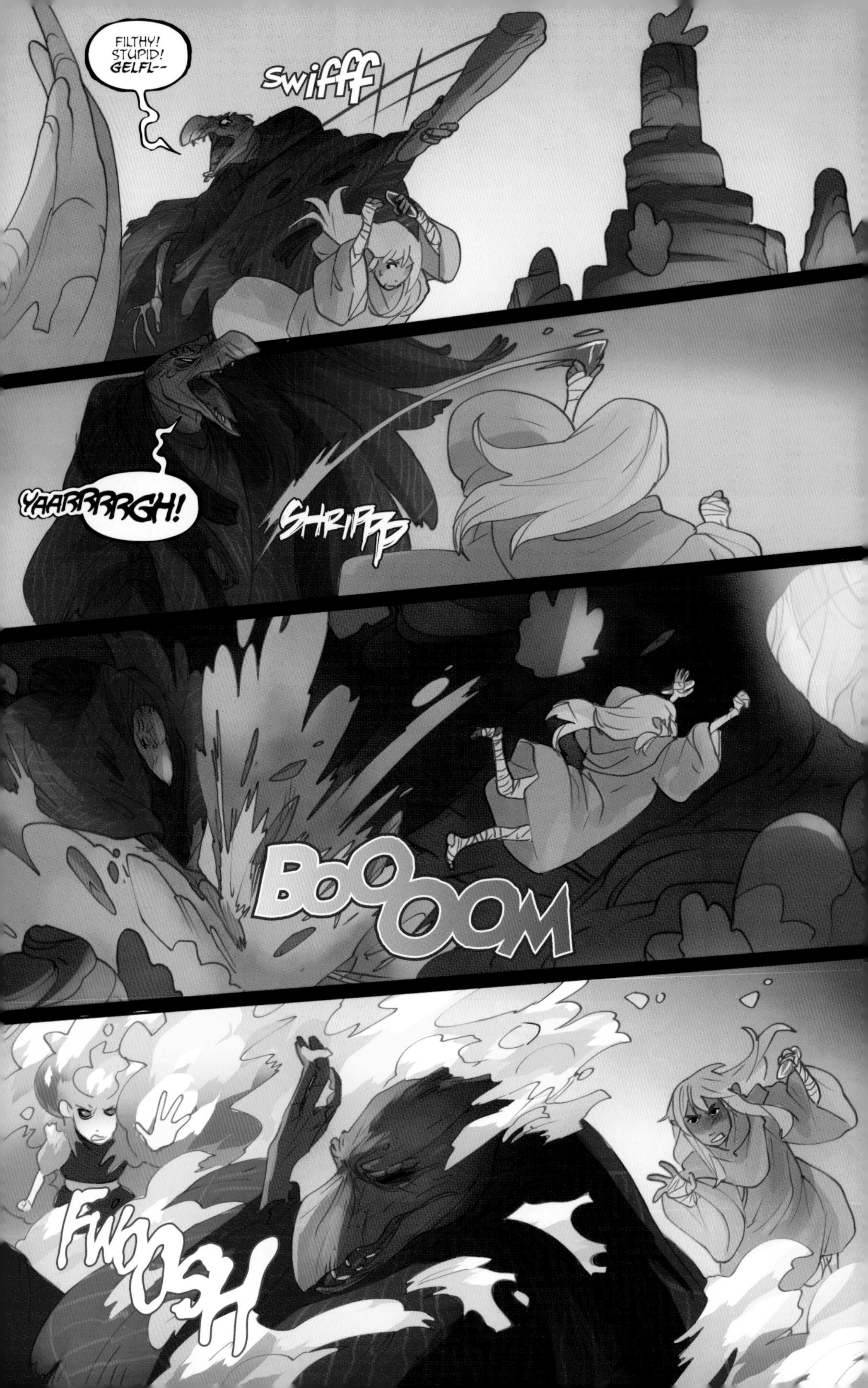
FILTHY! STUPID! GELFL--
SWIFFF
YAARRRRRGH!
SHRIPPP
BOOOOOM
!
FWOOSH

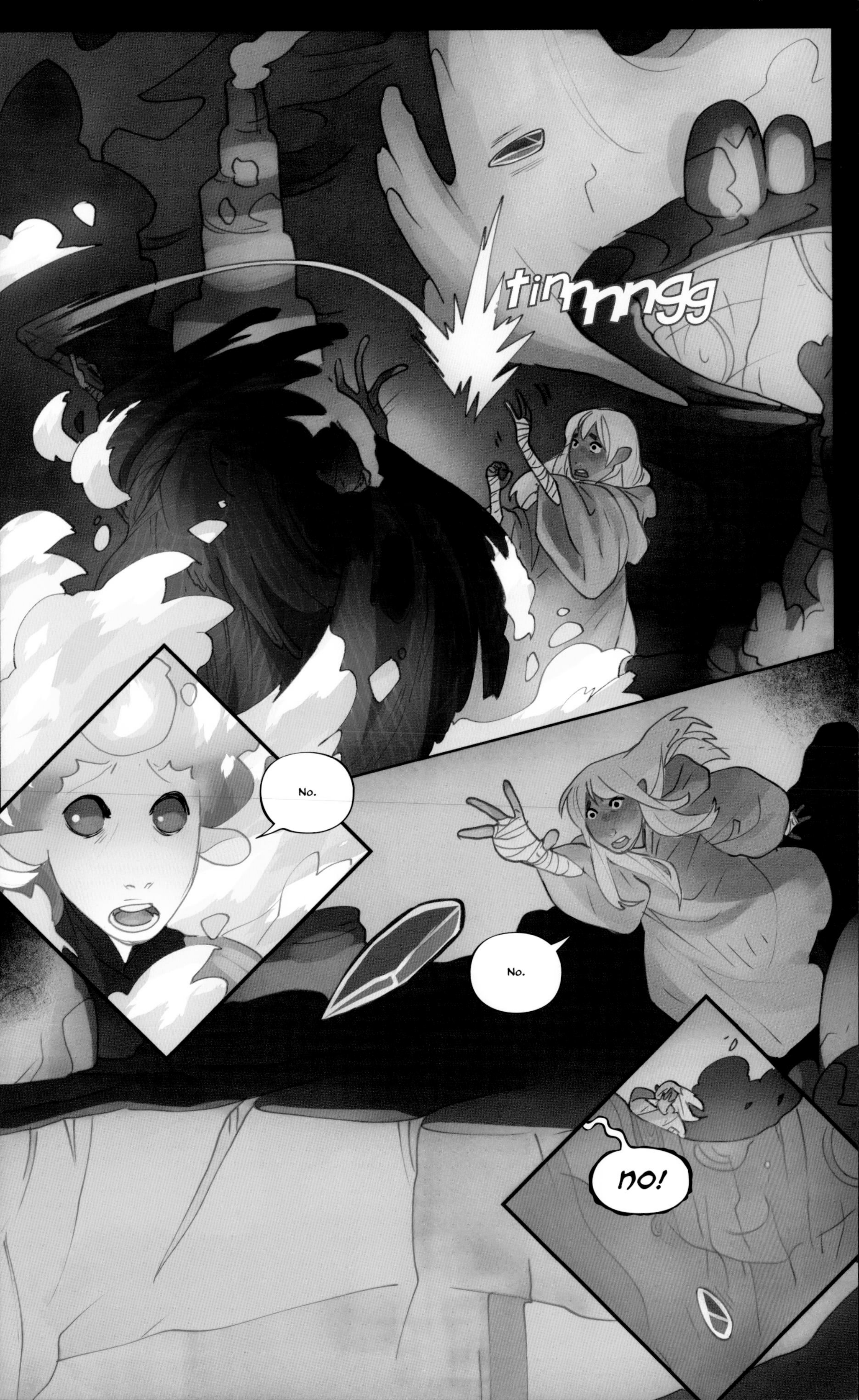
tinnnngg
No.
No.
no!

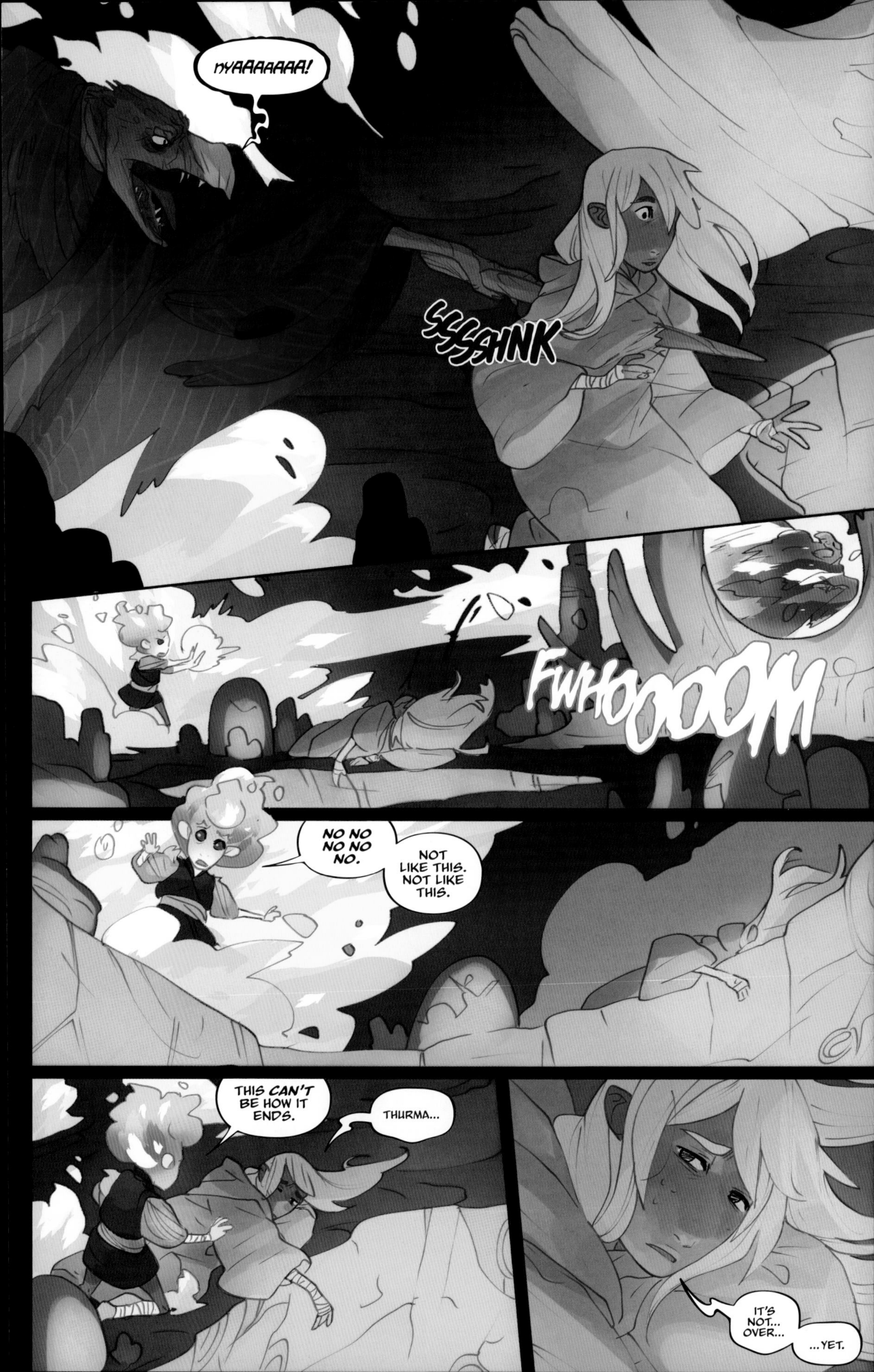

NYAAAAAAA!
SSSSHNK
FWHOOOOM
NO NO NO NO NO.
NOT LIKE THIS. NOT LIKE THIS.
THIS CAN'T BE HOW IT ENDS.
THURMA...
IT'S NOT... OVER...
...YET.

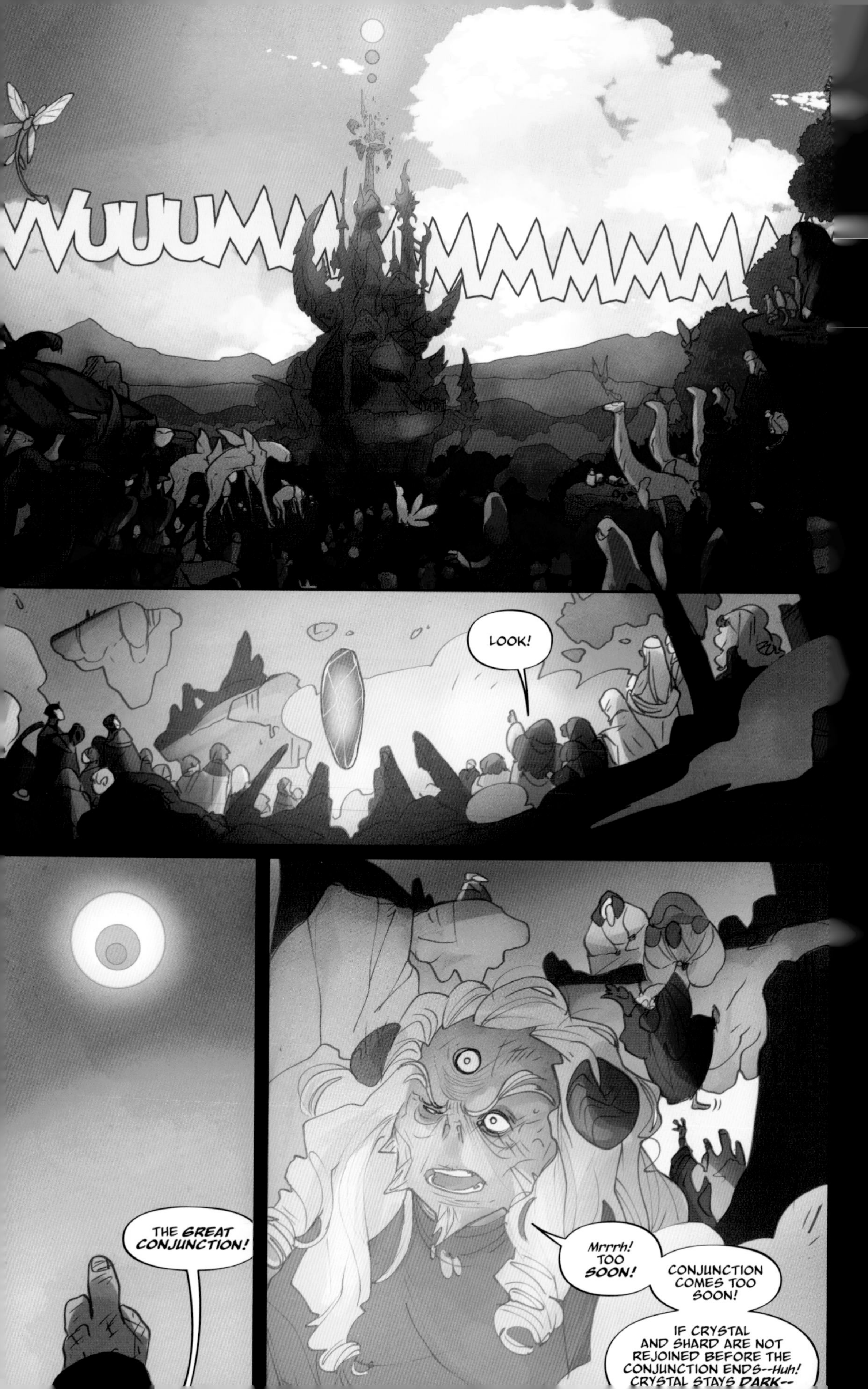

VVUUUMMMMMMMMMMM
LOOK!
THE GREAT CONJUNCTION!
Mrrrh! TOO SOON!
CONJUNCTION COMES TOO SOON!
IF CRYSTAL AND SHARD ARE NOT REJOINED BEFORE THE CONJUNCTION ENDS--Huh! CRYSTAL STAYS DARK--

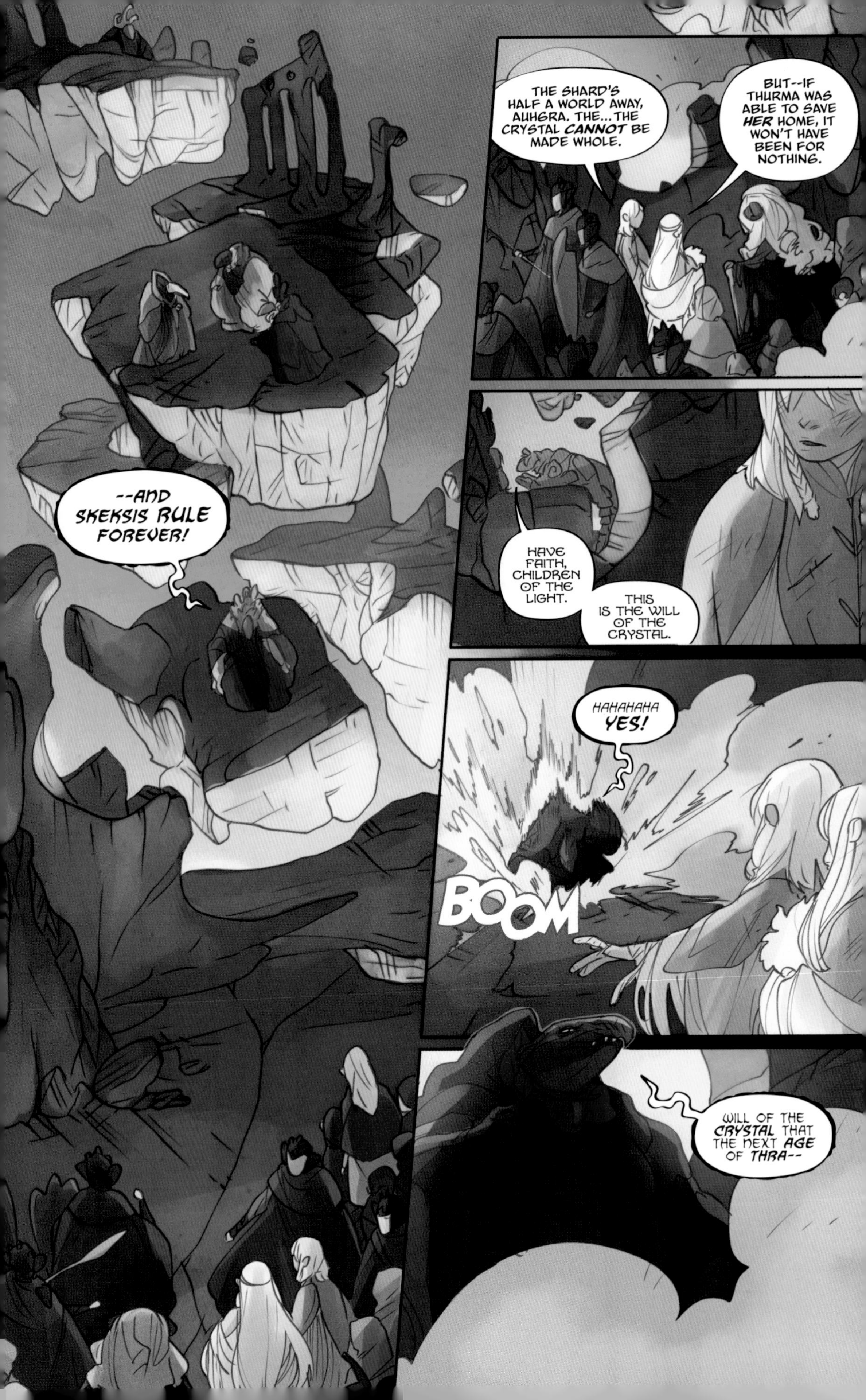
--AND SKEKSIS RULE FOREVER!
THE SHARD'S HALF A WORLD AWAY, AUGHRA. THE...THE CRYSTAL CANNOT BE MADE WHOLE.
BUT--IF THURMA WAS ABLE TO SAVE HER HOME, IT WON'T HAVE BEEN FOR NOTHING.
HAVE FAITH, CHILDREN OF THE LIGHT.
THIS IS THE WILL OF THE CRYSTAL.
HAHAHAHA YES!
BOOM
WILL OF THE CRYSTAL THAT THE NEXT AGE OF THRA--

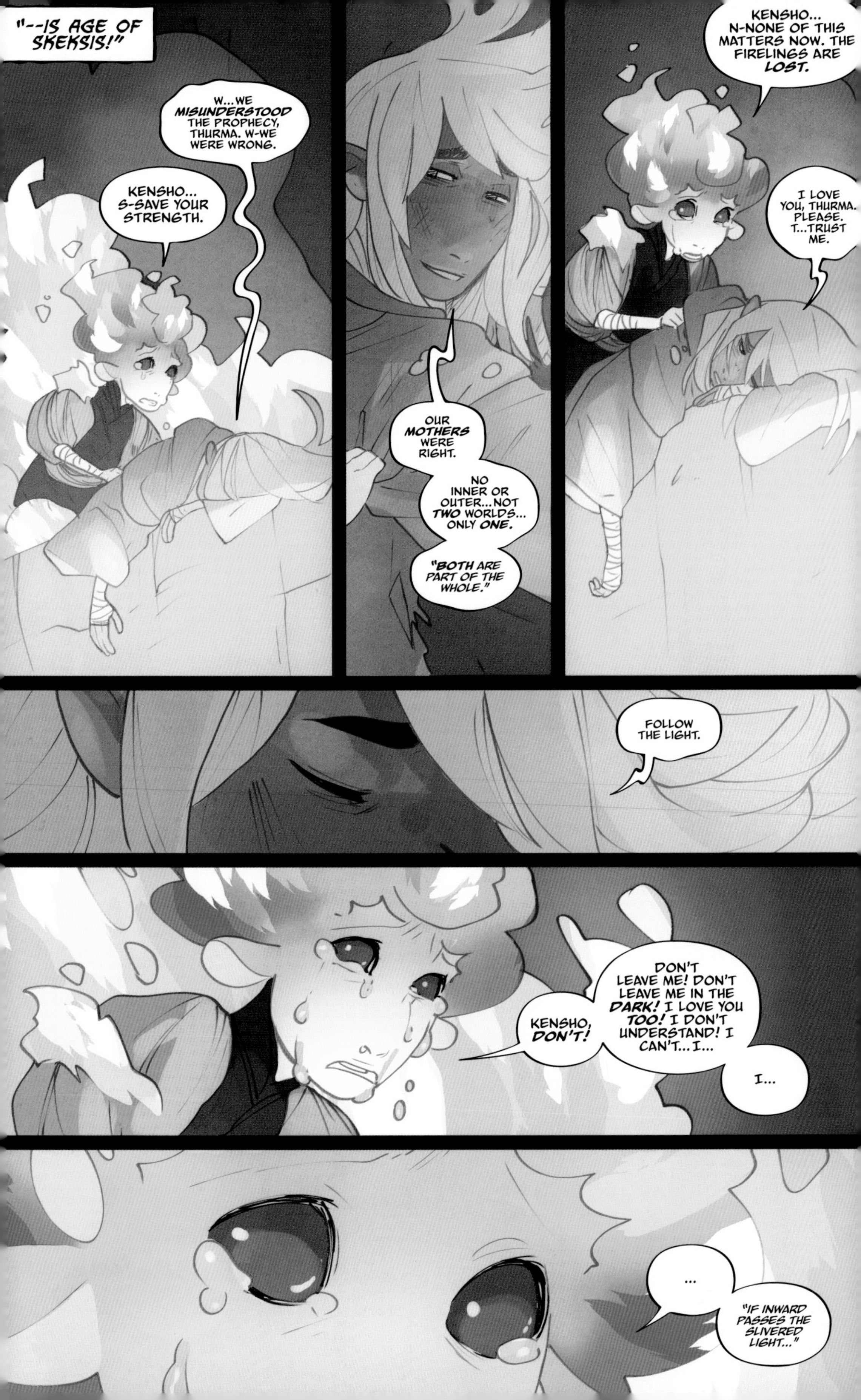
"--IS AGE OF SKEKSIS!"
W...WE MISUNDERSTOOD THE PROPHECY, THURMA. W-WE WERE WRONG.
KENSHO... S-SAVE YOUR STRENGTH.
OUR MOTHERS WERE RIGHT.
NO INNER OR OUTER...NOT TWO WORLDS... ONLY ONE.
"BOTH ARE PART OF THE WHOLE."
KENSHO... N-NONE OF THIS MATTERS NOW. THE FIRELINGS ARE LOST.
I LOVE YOU, THURMA. PLEASE. T...TRUST ME.
FOLLOW THE LIGHT.
KENSHO, DON'T!
DON'T LEAVE ME! DON'T LEAVE ME IN THE DARK! I LOVE YOU TOO! I DON'T UNDERSTAND! I CAN'T... I...
I...
...
"IF INWARD PASSES THE SLIVERED LIGHT..."

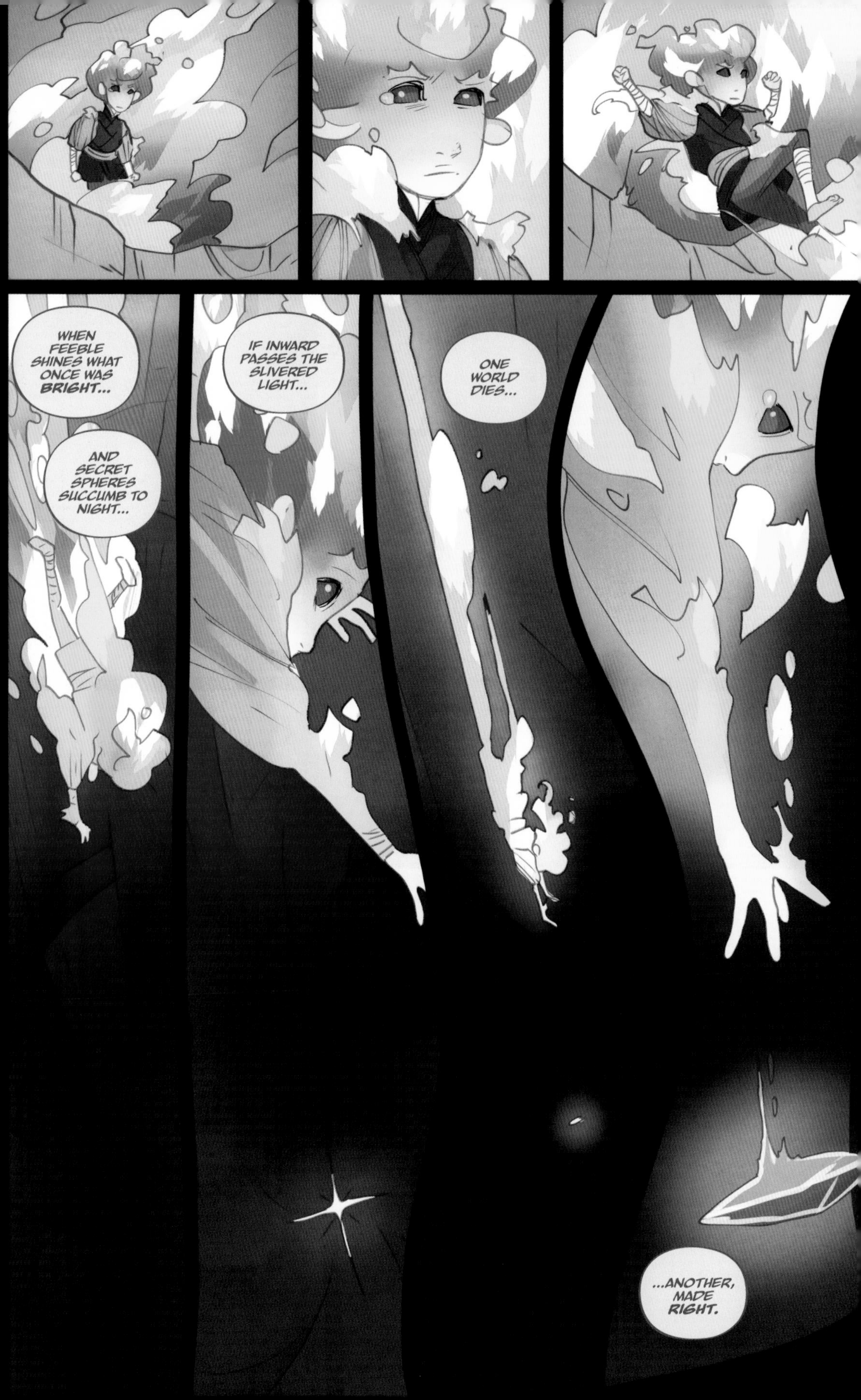
WHEN FEEBLE SHINES WHAT ONCE WAS BRIGHT...
AND SECRET SPHERES SUCCUMB TO NIGHT...
IF INWARD PASSES THE SLIVERED LIGHT...
ONE WORLD DIES...
...ANOTHER, MADE RIGHT.

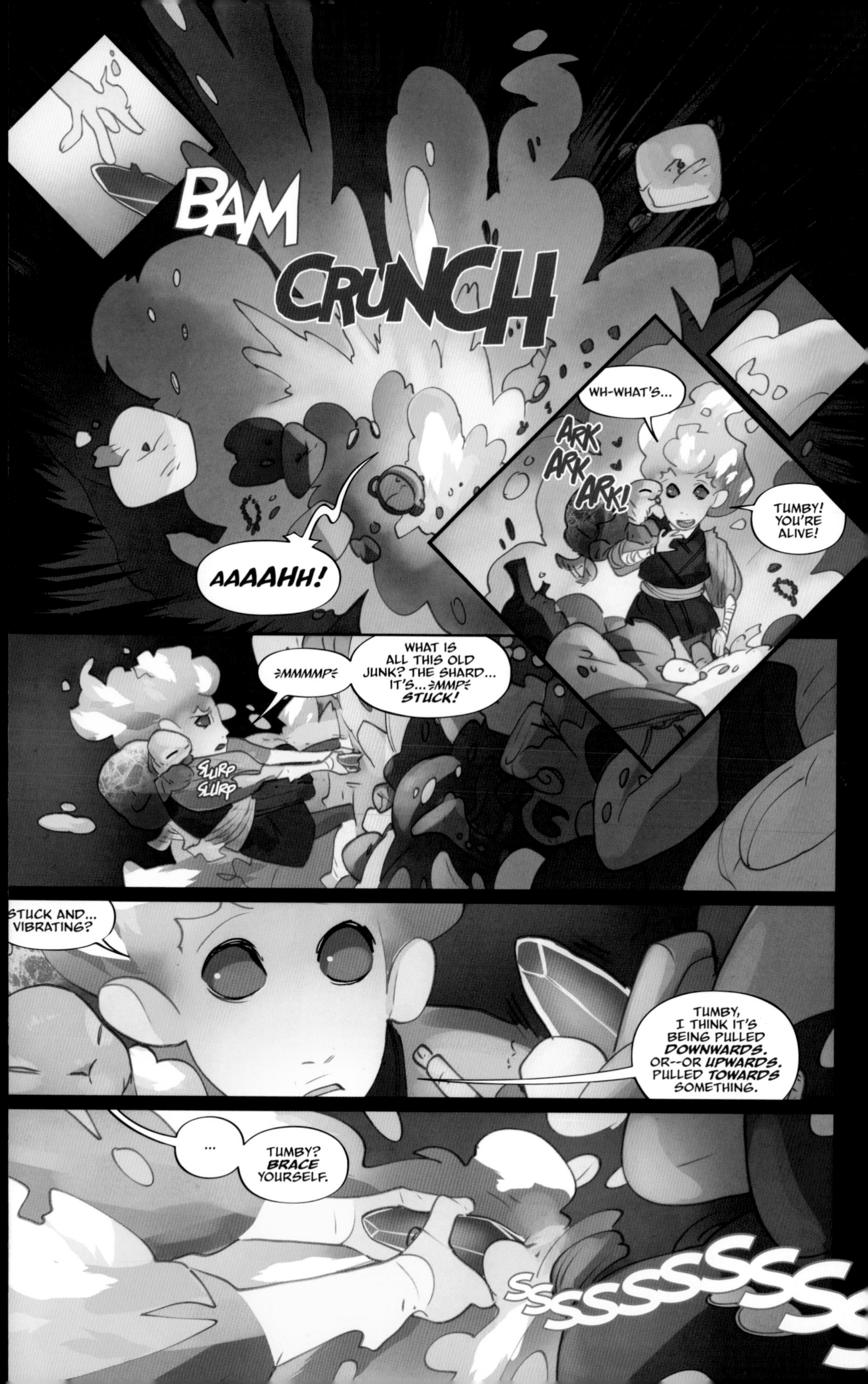

BAM
CRUNCH
AAAAHH!
WH-WHAT'S...
ARK ARK ARK!
TUMBY! YOU'RE ALIVE!
≥MMMMP≤
WHAT IS ALL THIS OLD JUNK? THE SHARD... IT'S... ≥MMP≤ STUCK!
SLURP SLURP
STUCK AND... VIBRATING?
TUMBY, I THINK IT'S BEING PULLED DOWNWARDS. OR--OR UPWARDS. PULLED TOWARDS SOMETHING.
...
TUMBY? BRACE YOURSELF.
SSSSSSSSSSSS

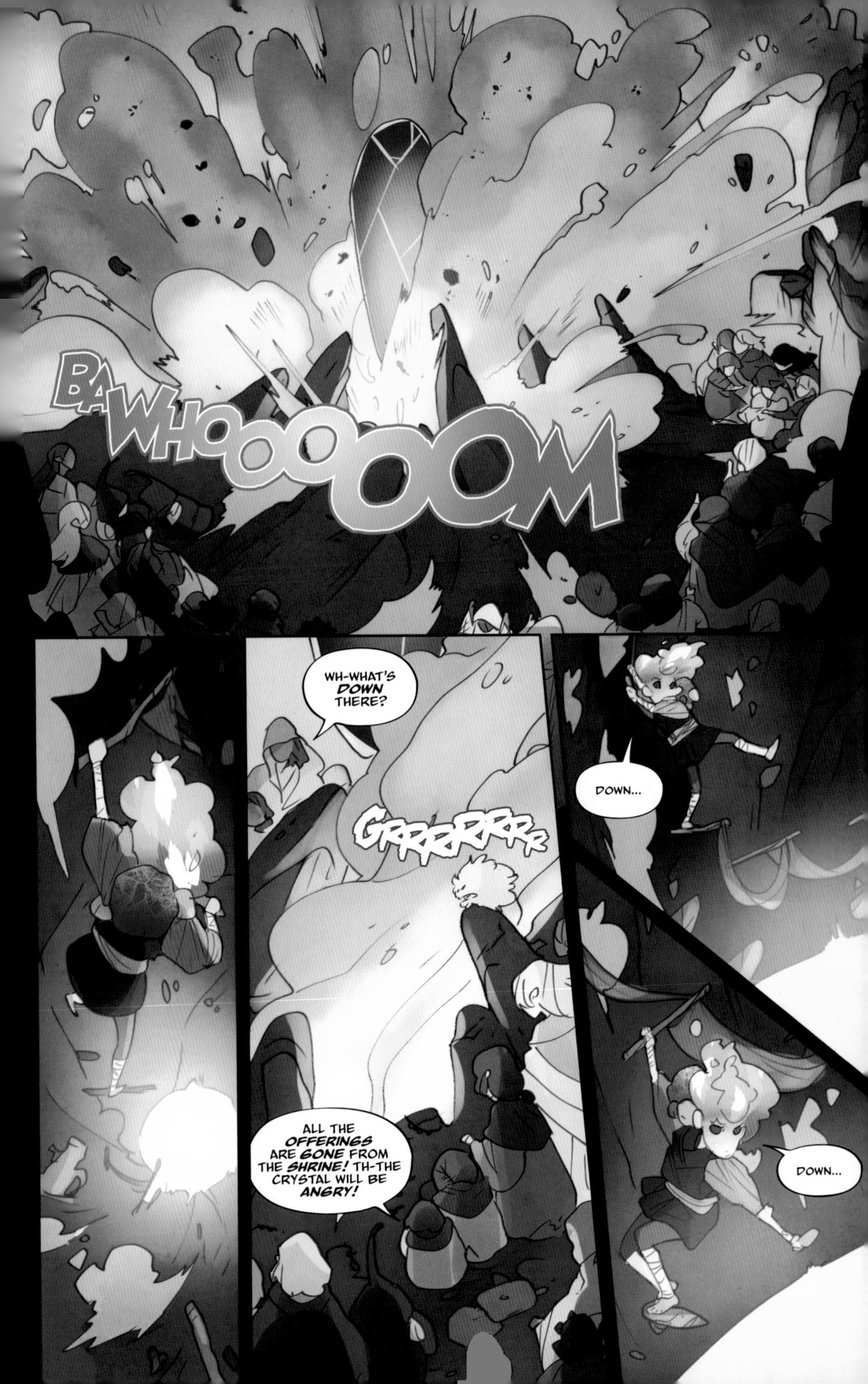
BAWHOOOOOOM
WH-WHAT'S DOWN THERE?
GRRRRRRRR
DOWN...
ALL THE OFFERINGS ARE GONE FROM THE SHRINE! TH-THE CRYSTAL WILL BE ANGRY!
DOWN...

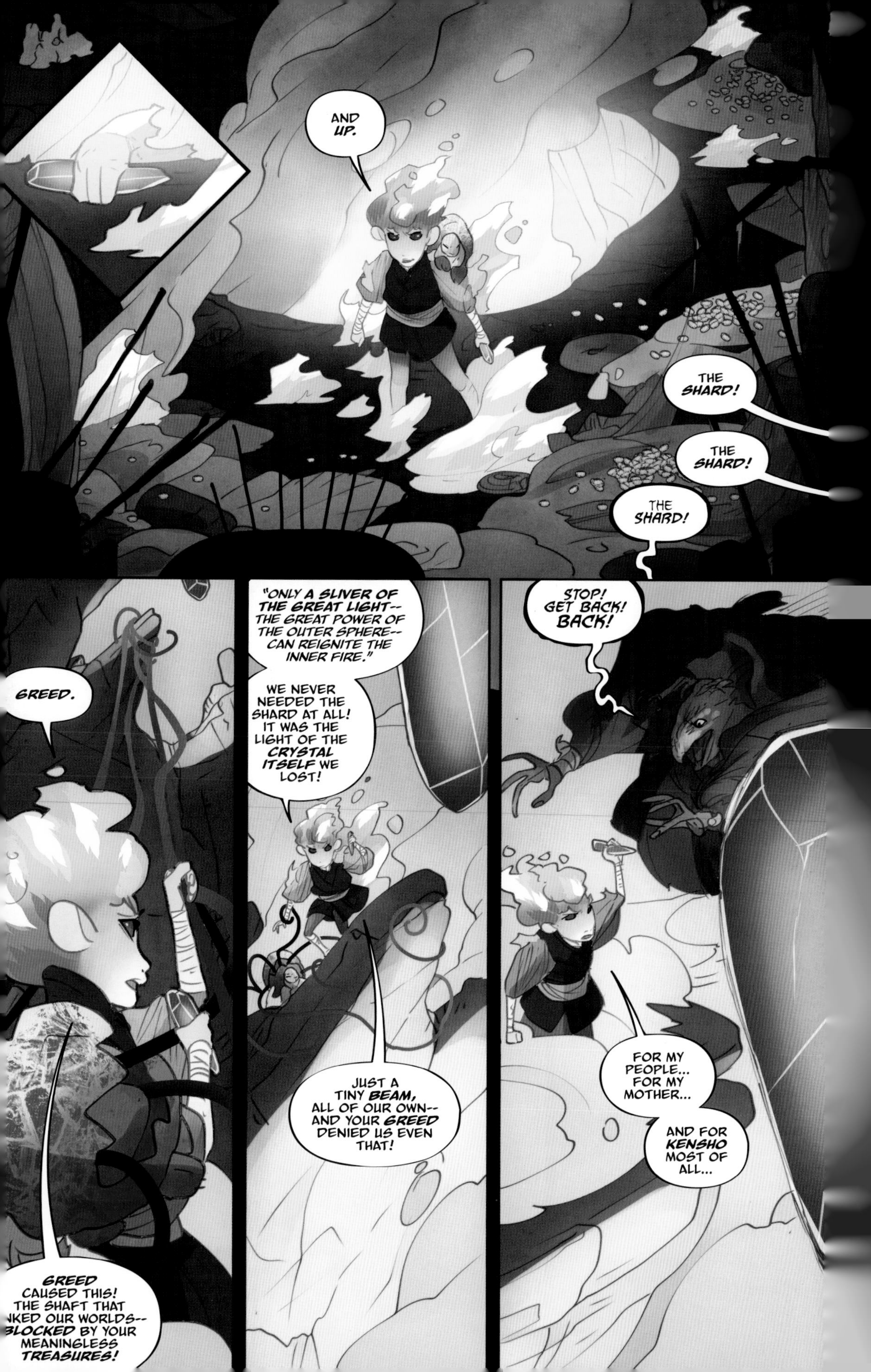
AND UP.
THE SHARD!
THE SHARD!
THE SHARD!
GREED.
GREED CAUSED THIS! THE SHAFT THAT NKED OUR WORLDS-- BLOCKED BY YOUR MEANINGLESS TREASURES!
"ONLY A SLIVER OF THE GREAT LIGHT-- THE GREAT POWER OF THE OUTER SPHERE-- CAN REIGNITE THE INNER FIRE."
WE NEVER NEEDED THE SHARD AT ALL! IT WAS THE LIGHT OF THE CRYSTAL ITSELF WE LOST!
JUST A TINY BEAM, ALL OF OUR OWN-- AND YOUR GREED DENIED US EVEN THAT!
STOP! GET BACK! BACK!
FOR MY PEOPLE... FOR MY MOTHER...
AND FOR KENSHO MOST OF ALL...

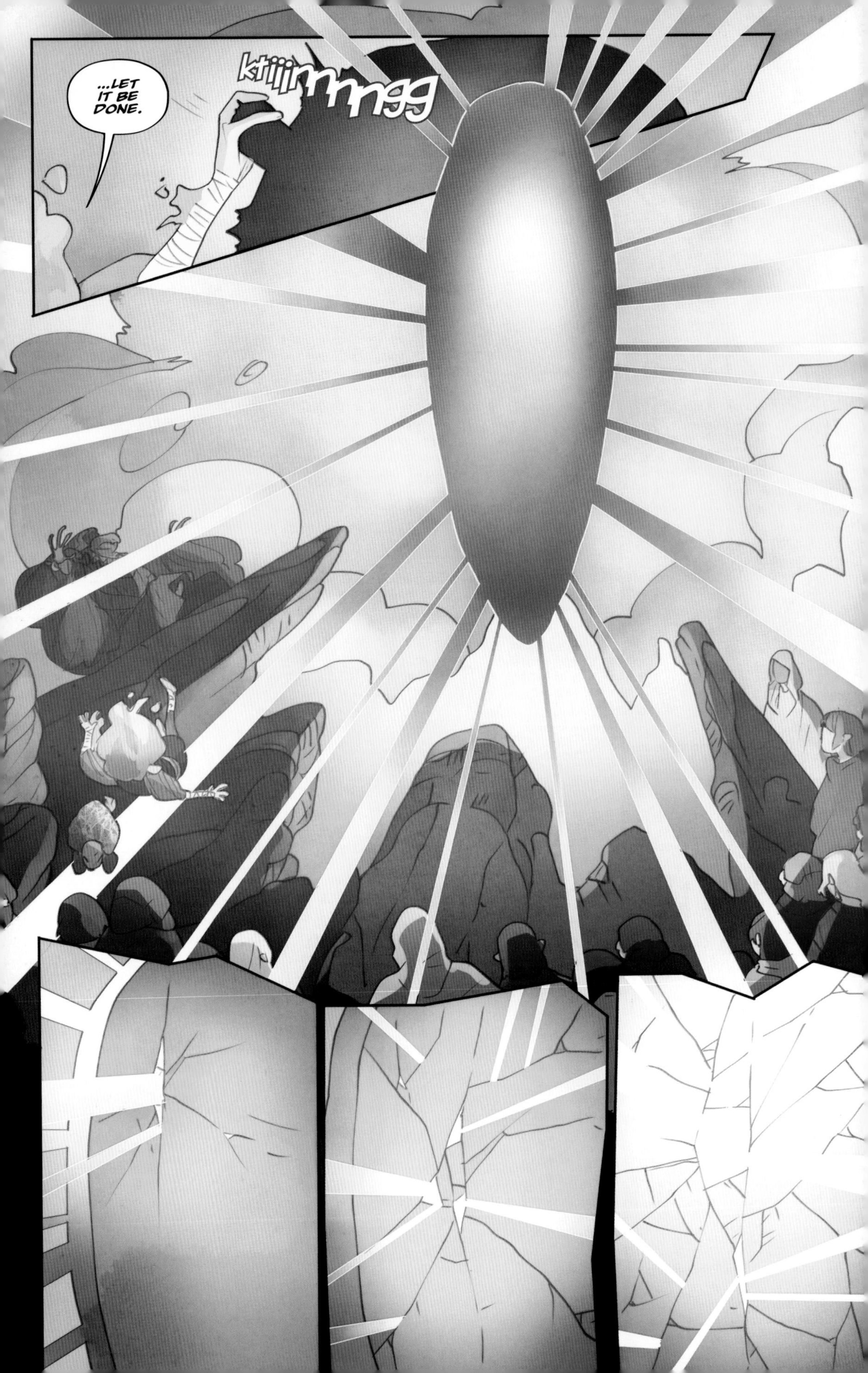
...LET IT BE DONE.
ktiiinnnngg

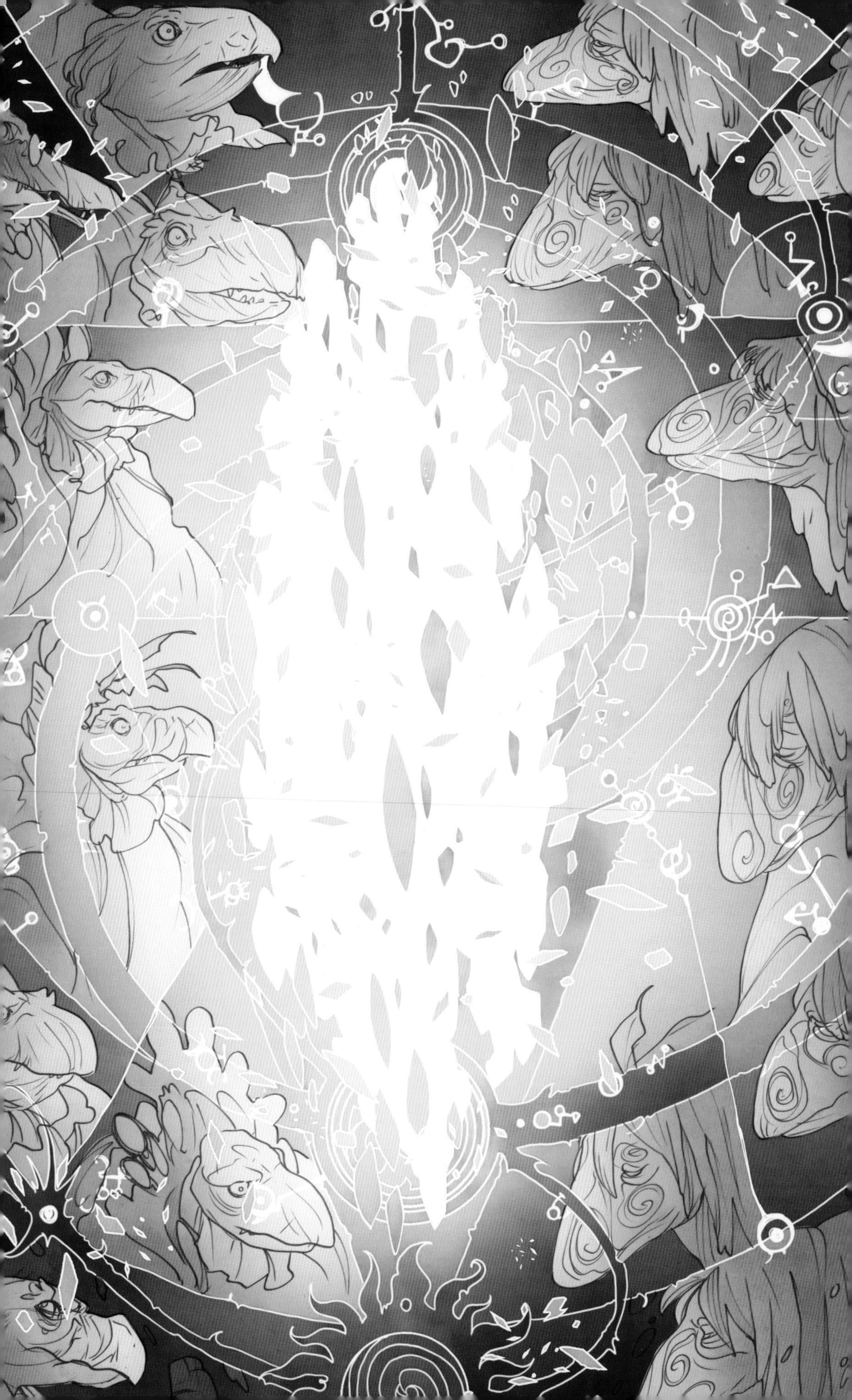

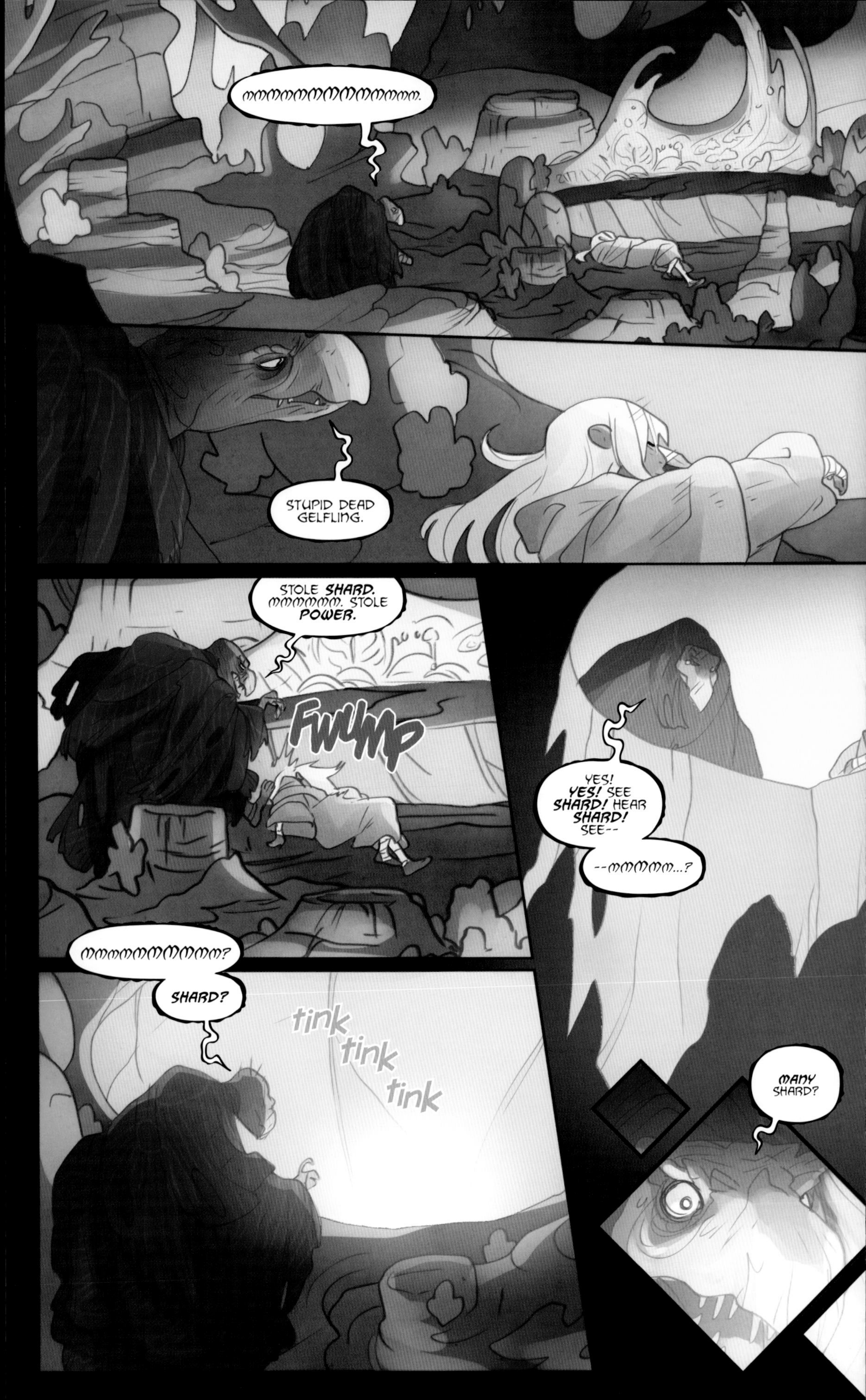
MMMMMMMMMMMMMM.
STUPID DEAD GELFLING.
STOLE **SHARD.** MMMMMM. STOLE **POWER.**
FWUMP
YES! **YES!** SEE **SHARD!** HEAR **SHARD!** SEE--
--MMMMM...?
MMMMMMMMMMM?
SHARD?
tink
tink
tink
MANY SHARD?

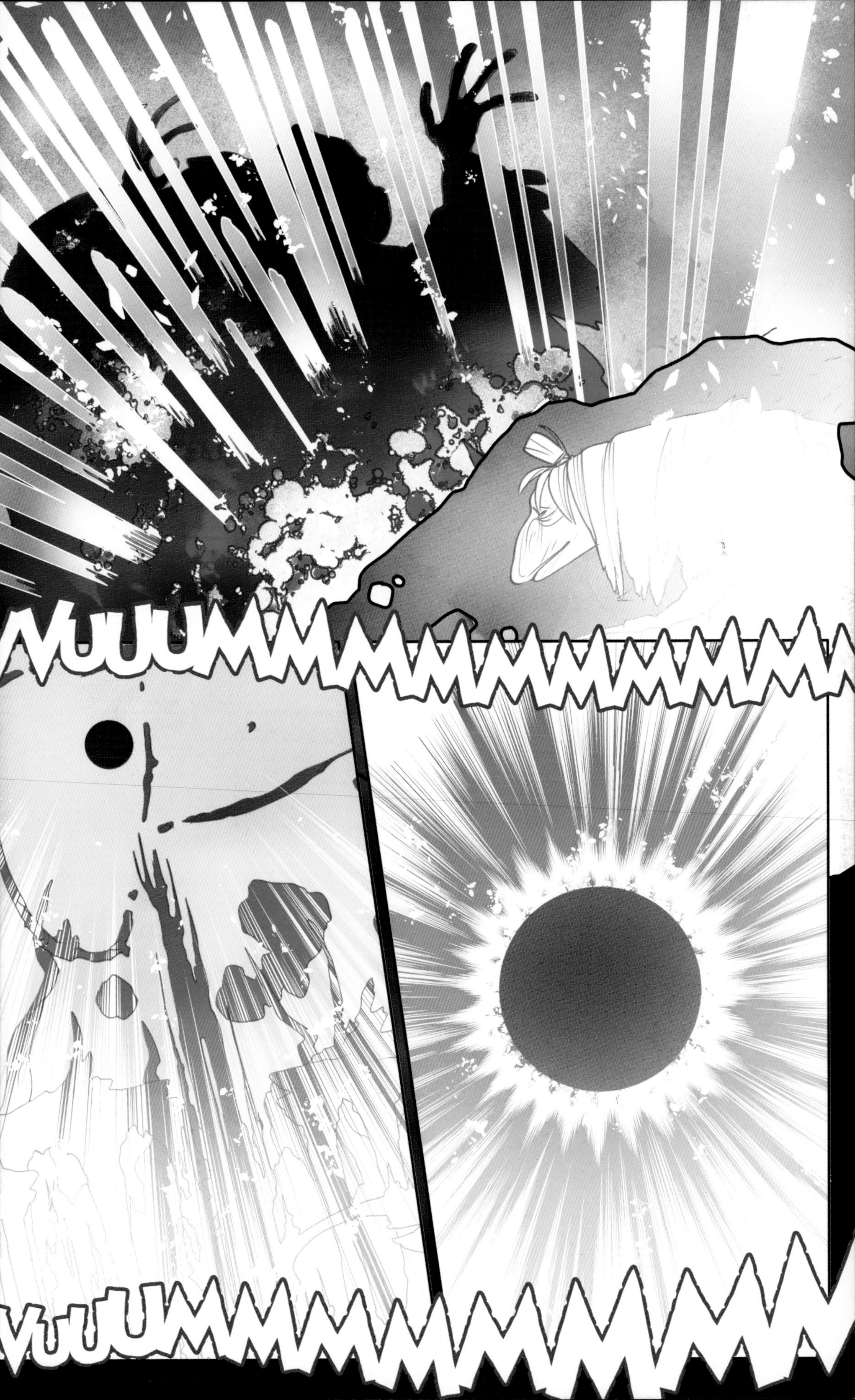
VUUUMMMMMMMMMMMMMM
VUUMMMMMMMMMMMMMM

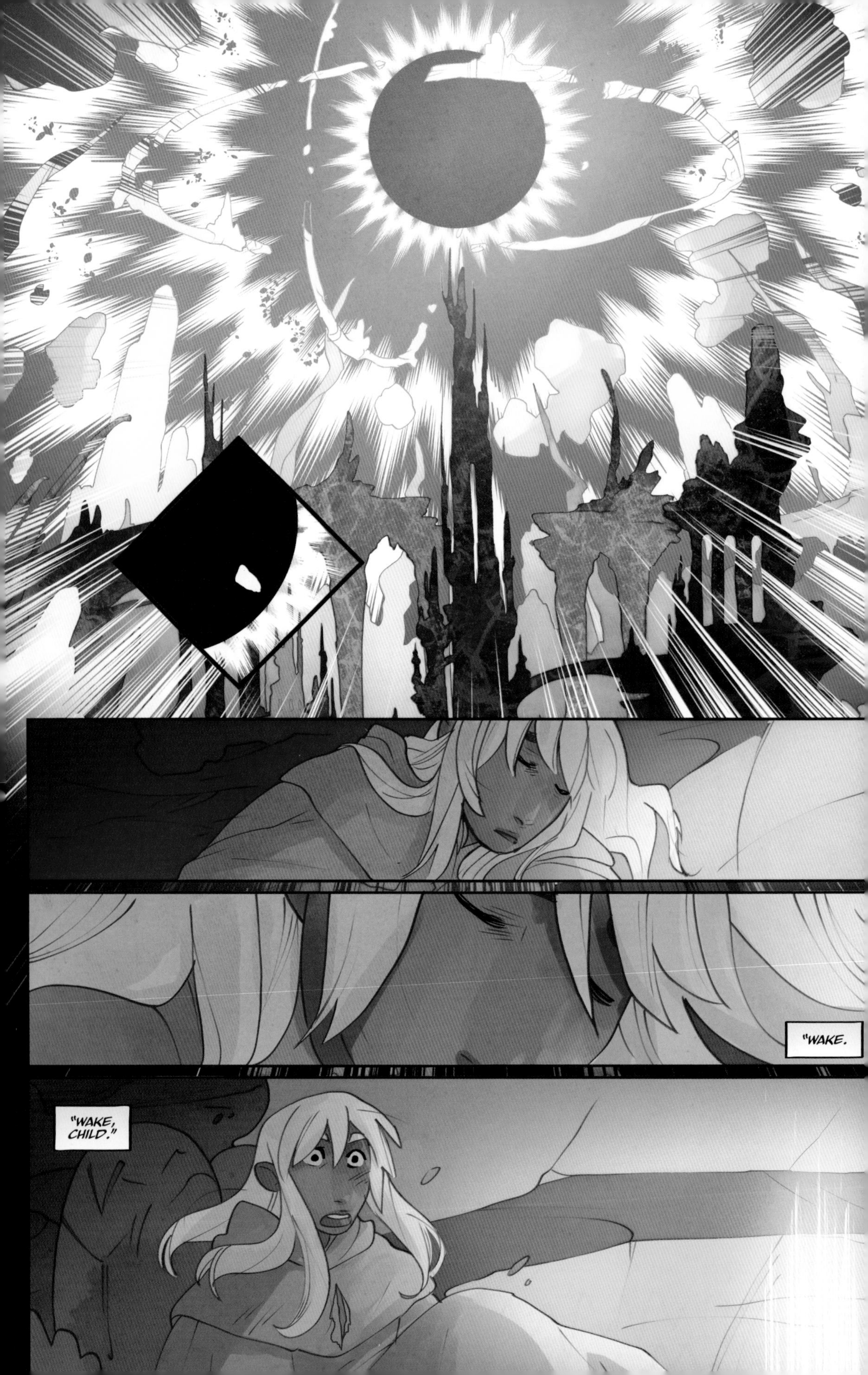
"WAKE.
"WAKE, CHILD."

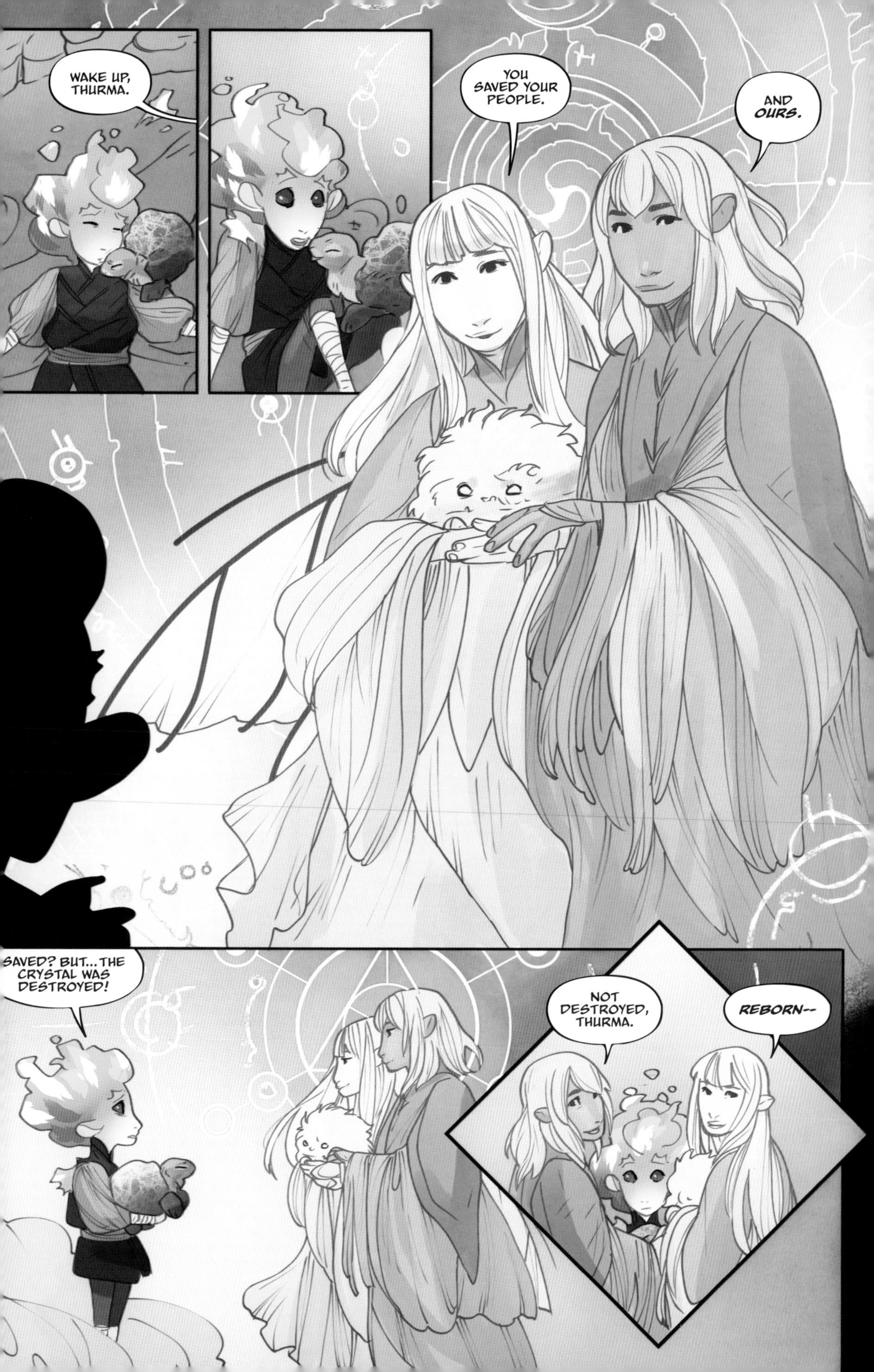
WAKE UP, THURMA.
YOU SAVED YOUR PEOPLE.
AND *OURS.*
SAVED? BUT... THE CRYSTAL WAS DESTROYED!
NOT DESTROYED, THURMA.
REBORN--

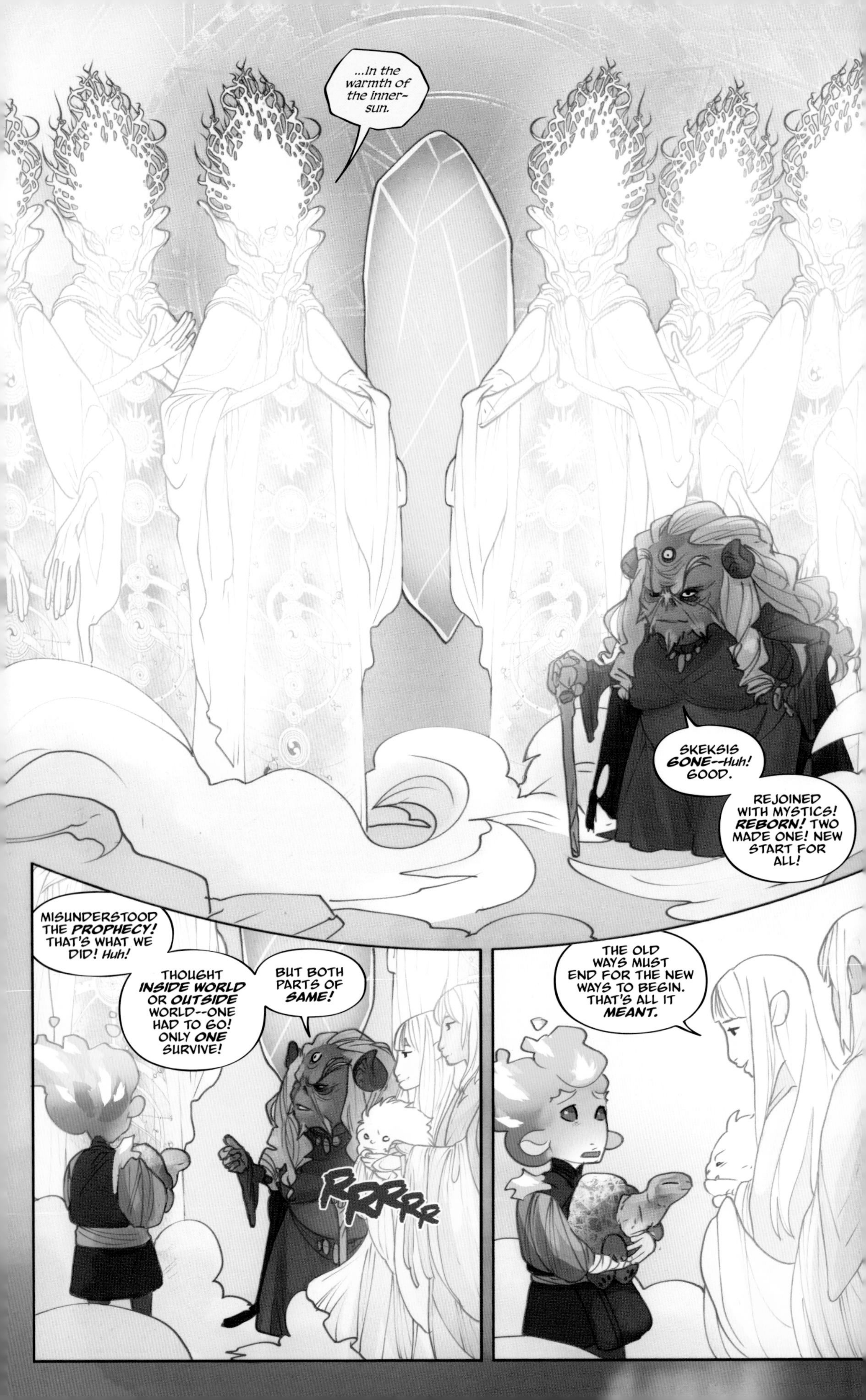
...In the warmth of the inner-sun.
SKEKSIS GONE--Huh! GOOD.
REJOINED WITH MYSTICS! REBORN! TWO MADE ONE! NEW START FOR ALL!
MISUNDERSTOOD THE PROPHECY! THAT'S WHAT WE DID! Huh!
THOUGHT INSIDE WORLD OR OUTSIDE WORLD--ONE HAD TO GO! ONLY ONE SURVIVE!
BUT BOTH PARTS OF SAME!
RRRRRR
THE OLD WAYS MUST END FOR THE NEW WAYS TO BEGIN. THAT'S ALL IT MEANT.

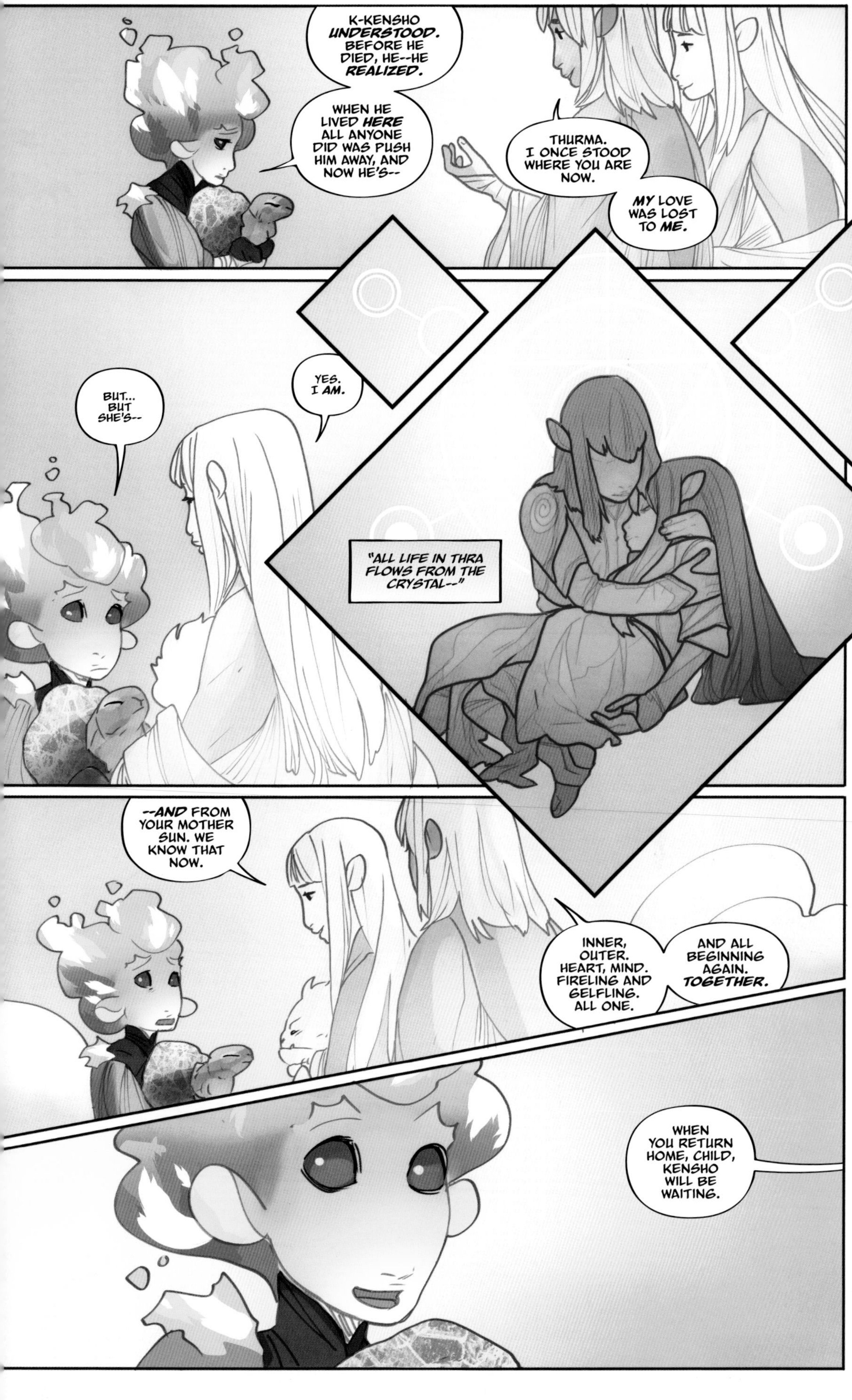
K-KENSHO UNDERSTOOD. BEFORE HE DIED, HE--HE REALIZED.
WHEN HE LIVED HERE ALL ANYONE DID WAS PUSH HIM AWAY, AND NOW HE'S--
THURMA. I ONCE STOOD WHERE YOU ARE NOW.
MY LOVE WAS LOST TO ME.
BUT... BUT SHE'S--
YES. I AM.
"ALL LIFE IN THRA FLOWS FROM THE CRYSTAL--"
--AND FROM YOUR MOTHER SUN. WE KNOW THAT NOW.
INNER, OUTER. HEART, MIND. FIRELING AND GELFLING. ALL ONE.
AND ALL BEGINNING AGAIN. TOGETHER.
WHEN YOU RETURN HOME, CHILD, KENSHO WILL BE WAITING.

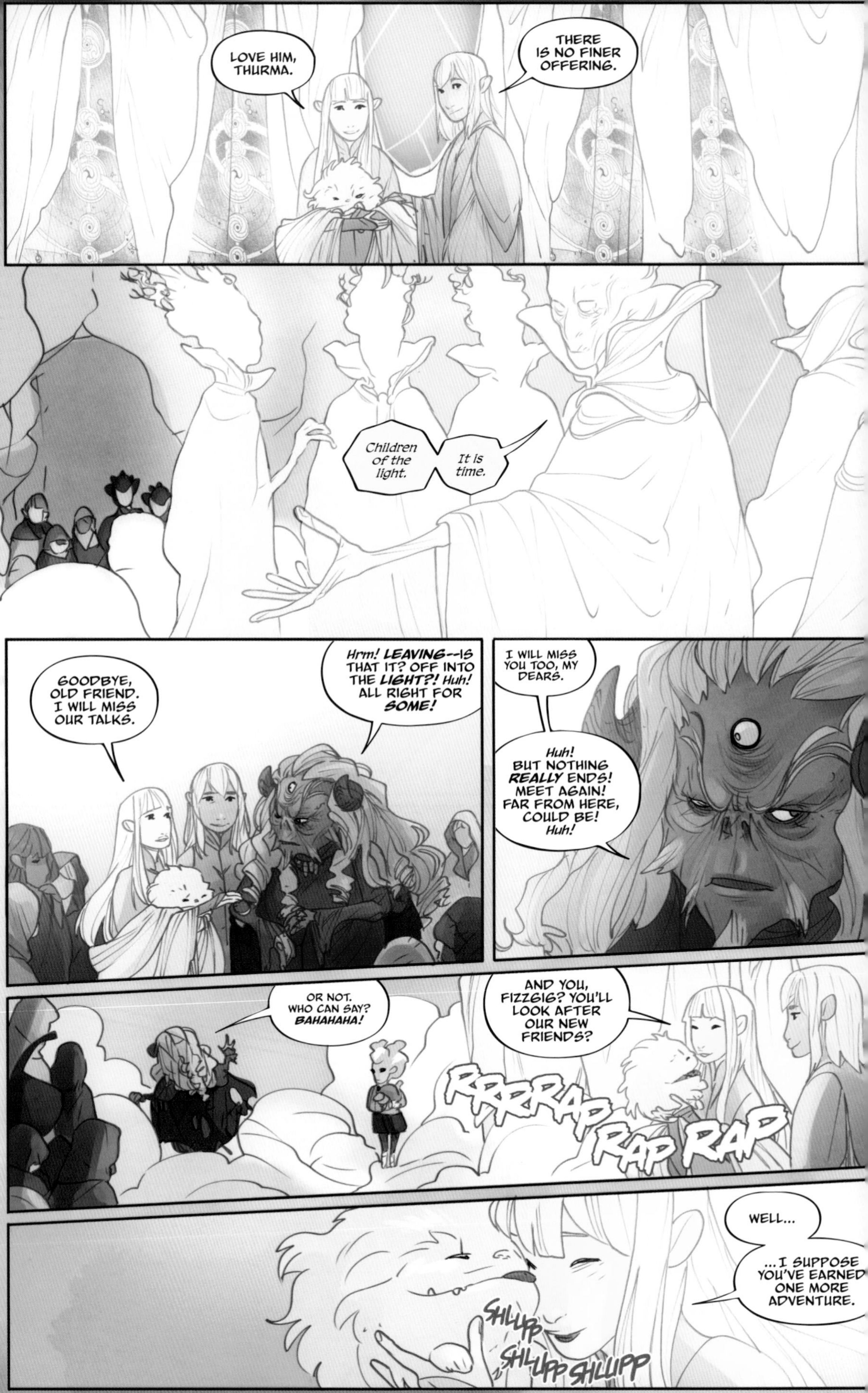
LOVE HIM, THURMA.
THERE IS NO FINER OFFERING.
Children of the light.
It is time.
GOODBYE, OLD FRIEND. I WILL MISS OUR TALKS.
Hrm! LEAVING--IS THAT IT? OFF INTO THE LIGHT?! Huh! ALL RIGHT FOR SOME!
I WILL MISS YOU TOO, MY DEARS.
Huh! BUT NOTHING REALLY ENDS! MEET AGAIN! FAR FROM HERE, COULD BE! Huh!
OR NOT. WHO CAN SAY? BAHAHAHA!
AND YOU, FIZZGIG? YOU'LL LOOK AFTER OUR NEW FRIENDS?
RRRRAP RAP RAP
WELL...
...I SUPPOSE YOU'VE EARNED ONE MORE ADVENTURE.
SHLUPP SHLUPP SHLUPP

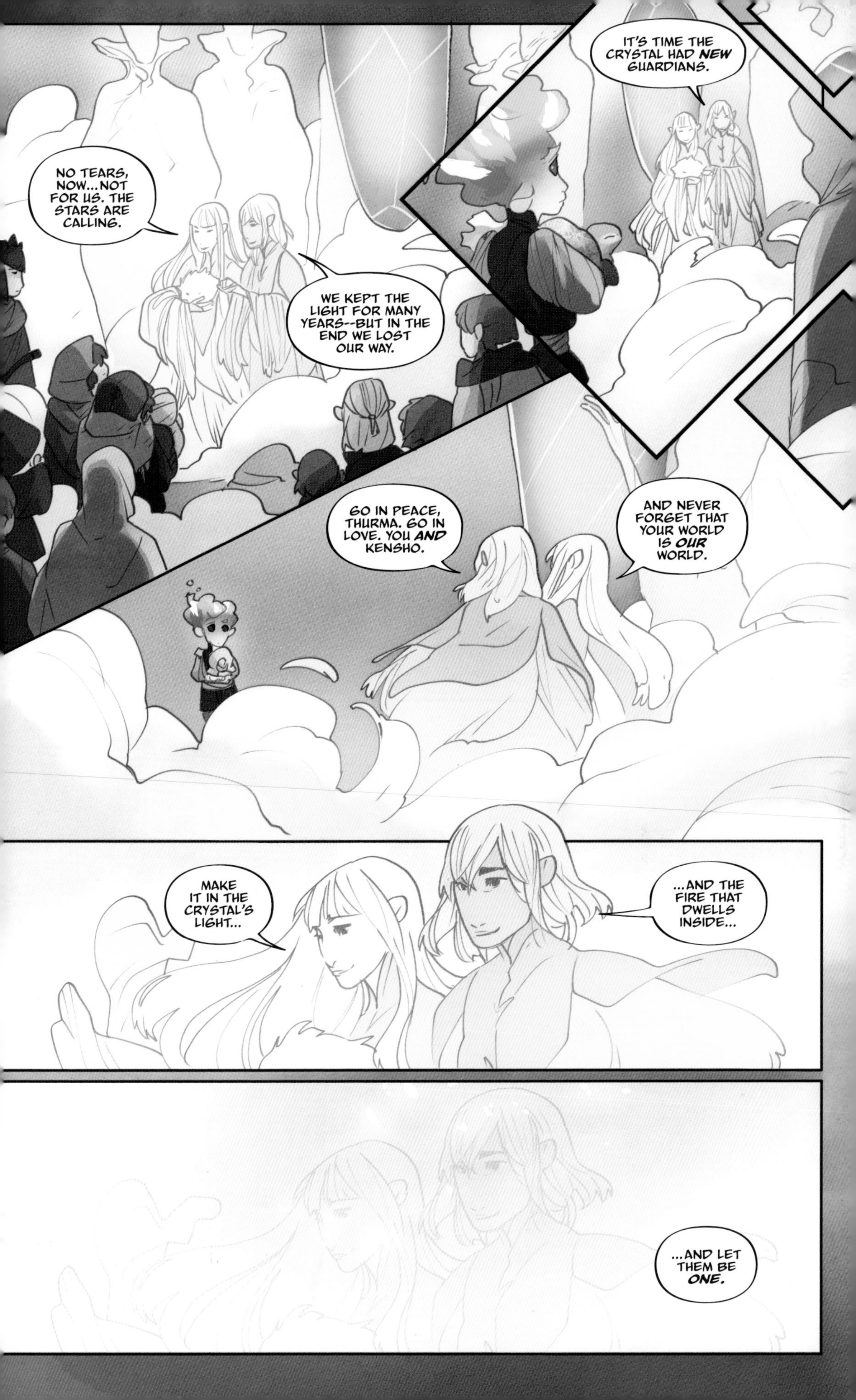
NO TEARS, NOW...NOT FOR US. THE STARS ARE CALLING.
WE KEPT THE LIGHT FOR MANY YEARS--BUT IN THE END WE LOST OUR WAY.
IT'S TIME THE CRYSTAL HAD *NEW* GUARDIANS.
GO IN PEACE, THURMA. GO IN LOVE. YOU *AND* KENSHO.
AND NEVER FORGET THAT YOUR WORLD IS *OUR* WORLD.
MAKE IT IN THE CRYSTAL'S LIGHT...
...AND THE FIRE THAT DWELLS INSIDE...
...AND LET THEM BE *ONE.*

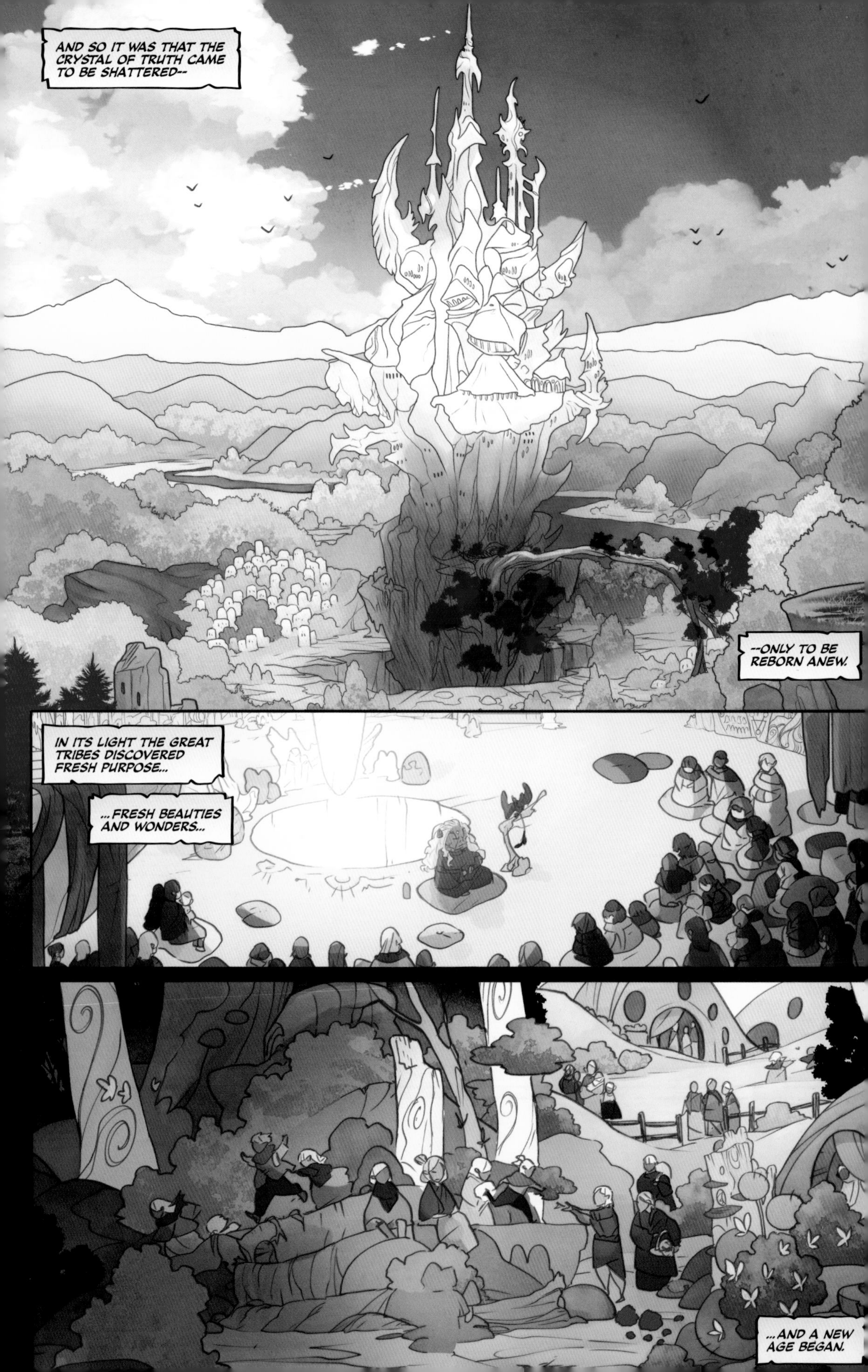
AND SO IT WAS THAT THE CRYSTAL OF TRUTH CAME TO BE SHATTERED--
--ONLY TO BE REBORN ANEW.
IN ITS LIGHT THE GREAT TRIBES DISCOVERED FRESH PURPOSE...
...FRESH BEAUTIES AND WONDERS...
...AND A NEW AGE BEGAN.

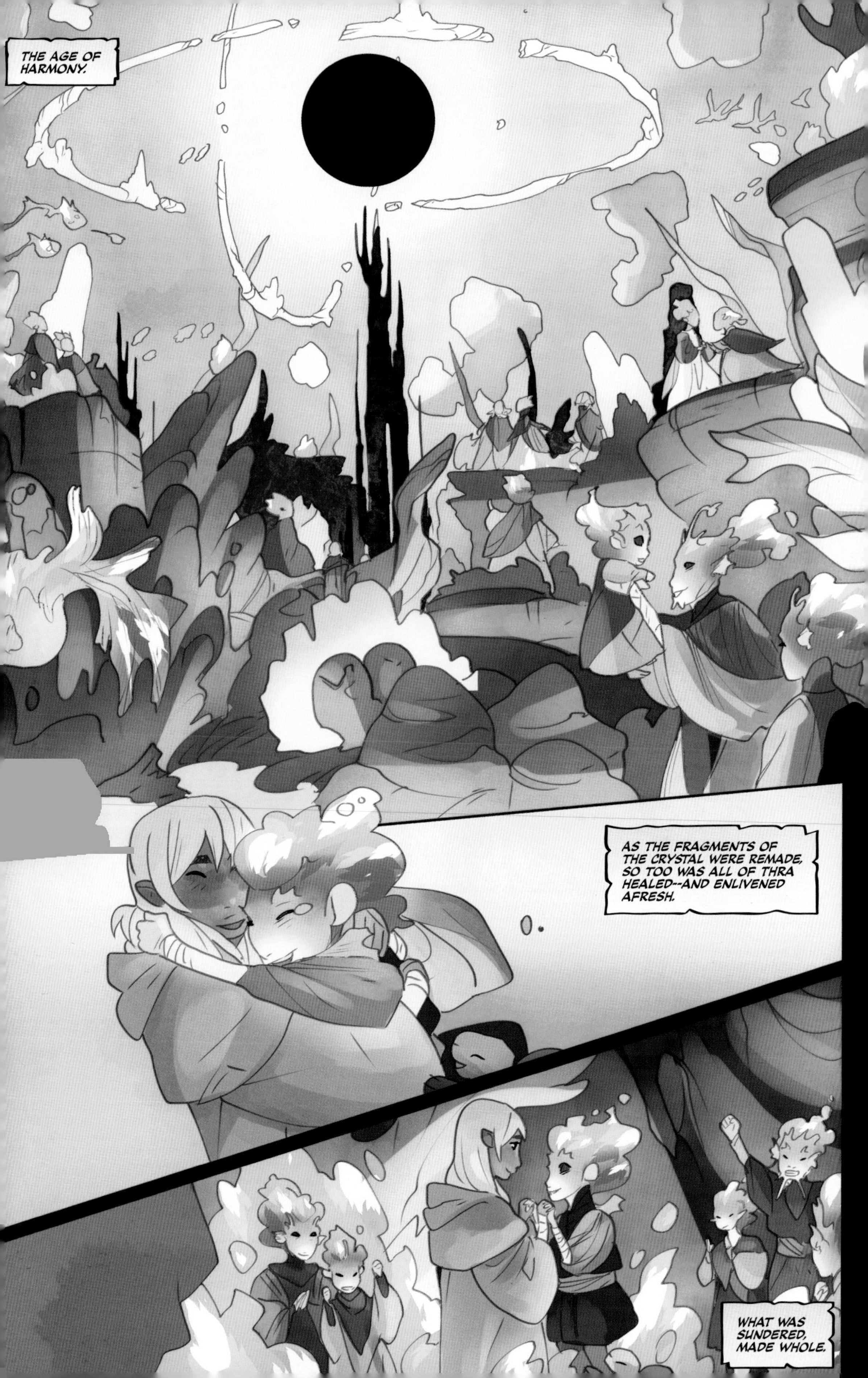
THE AGE OF HARMONY.
AS THE FRAGMENTS OF THE CRYSTAL WERE REMADE, SO TOO WAS ALL OF THRA HEALED--AND ENLIVENED AFRESH.
WHAT WAS SUNDERED, MADE WHOLE.

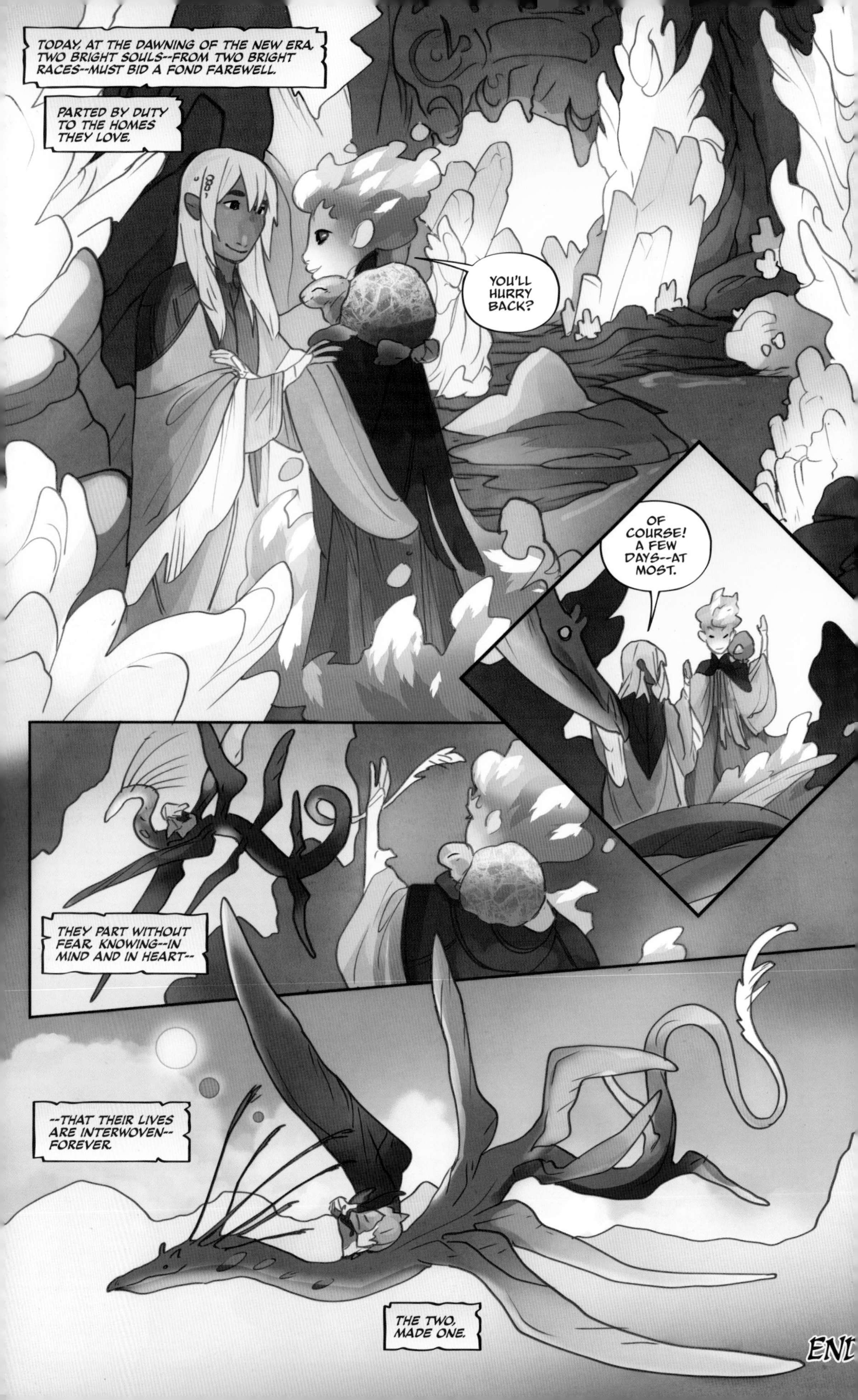
TODAY, AT THE DAWNING OF THE NEW ERA, TWO BRIGHT SOULS--FROM TWO BRIGHT RACES--MUST BID A FOND FAREWELL.
PARTED BY DUTY TO THE HOMES THEY LOVE.
YOU'LL HURRY BACK?
OF COURSE! A FEW DAYS--AT MOST.
THEY PART WITHOUT FEAR, KNOWING--IN MIND AND IN HEART--
--THAT THEIR LIVES ARE INTERWOVEN--FOREVER.
THE TWO, MADE ONE.

COVER GALLERY

Facing page: Issue #9 Cover by Mark Buckingham.
Following pages: Issues #10-#12 Covers by Mark Buckingham

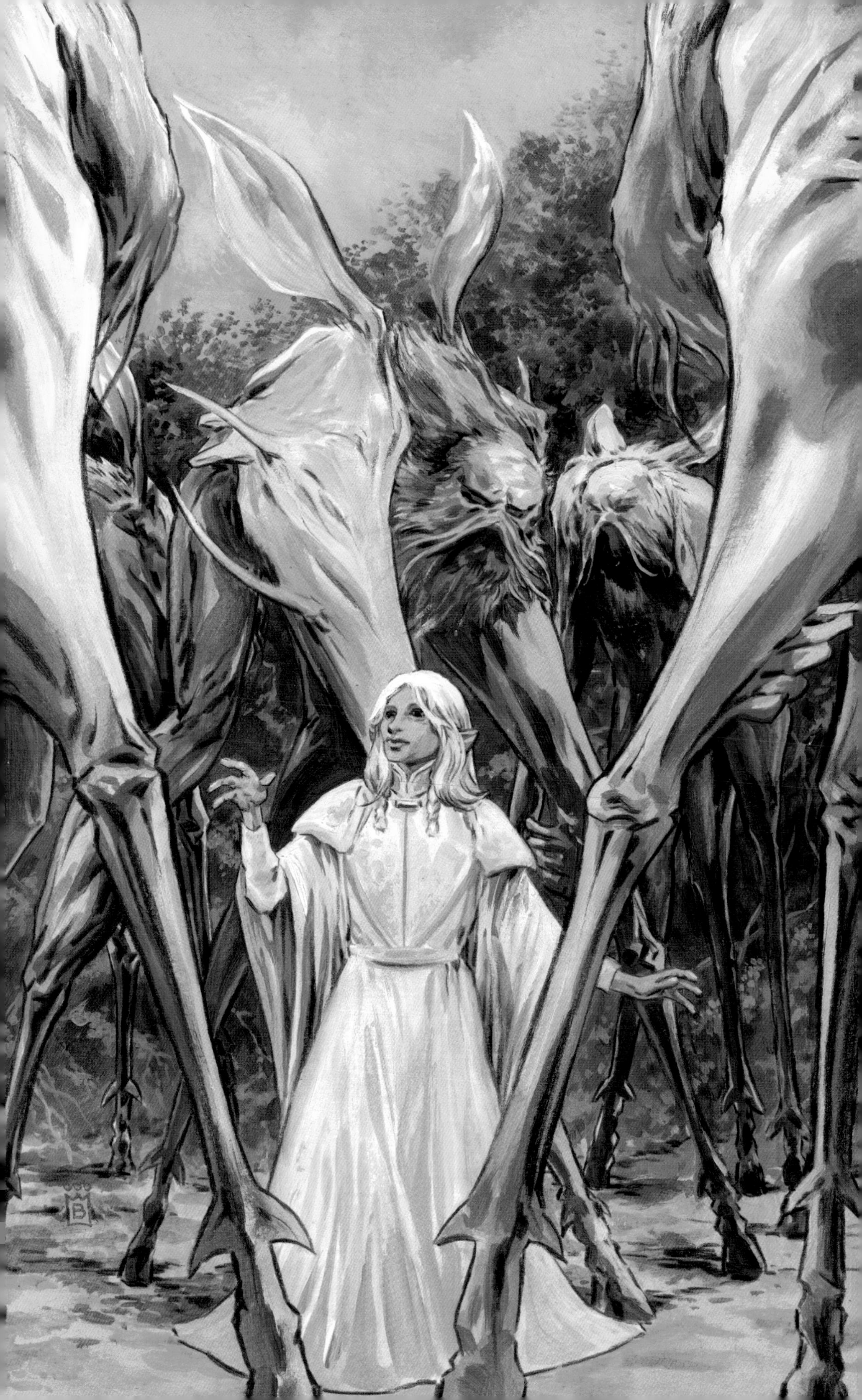

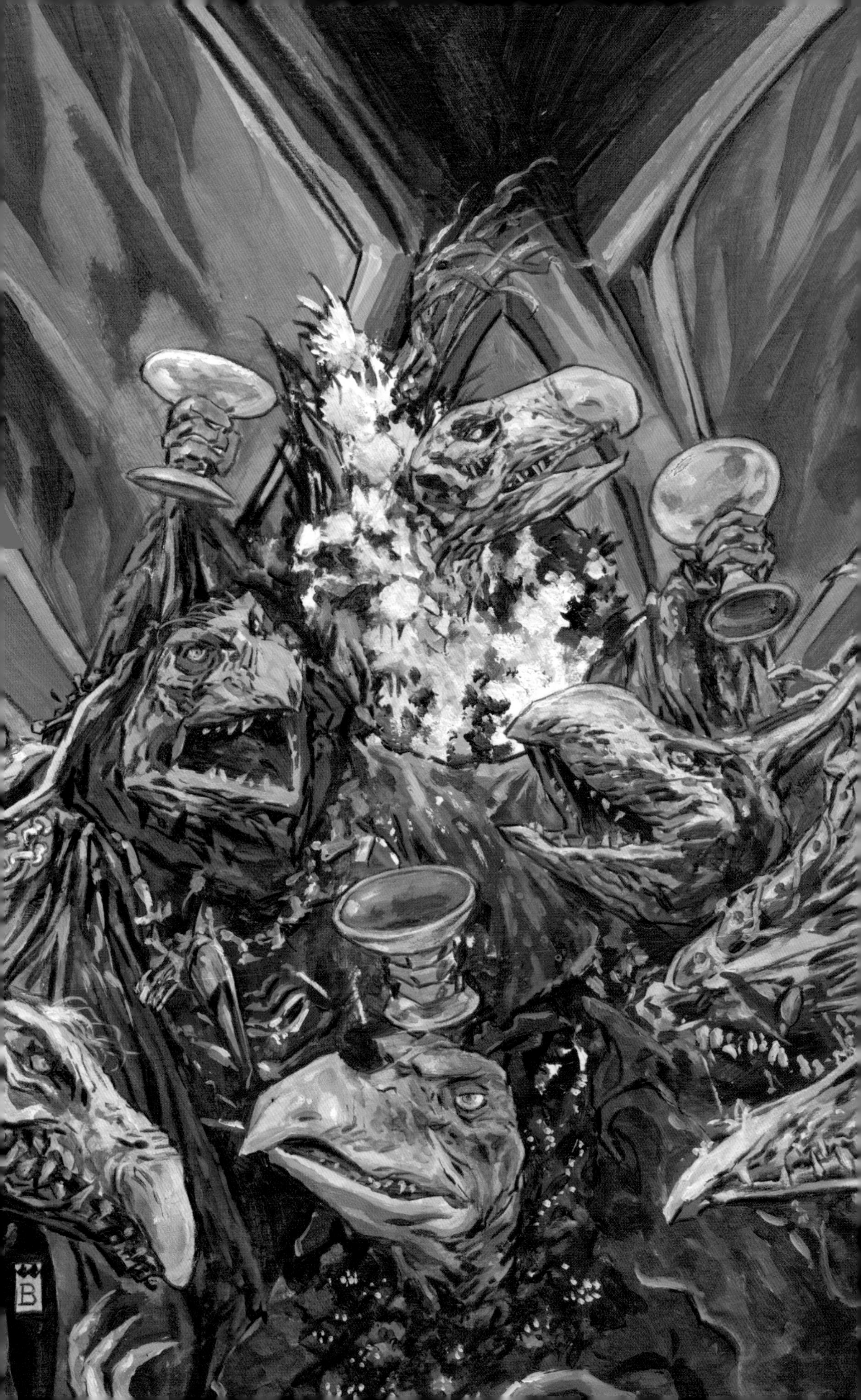

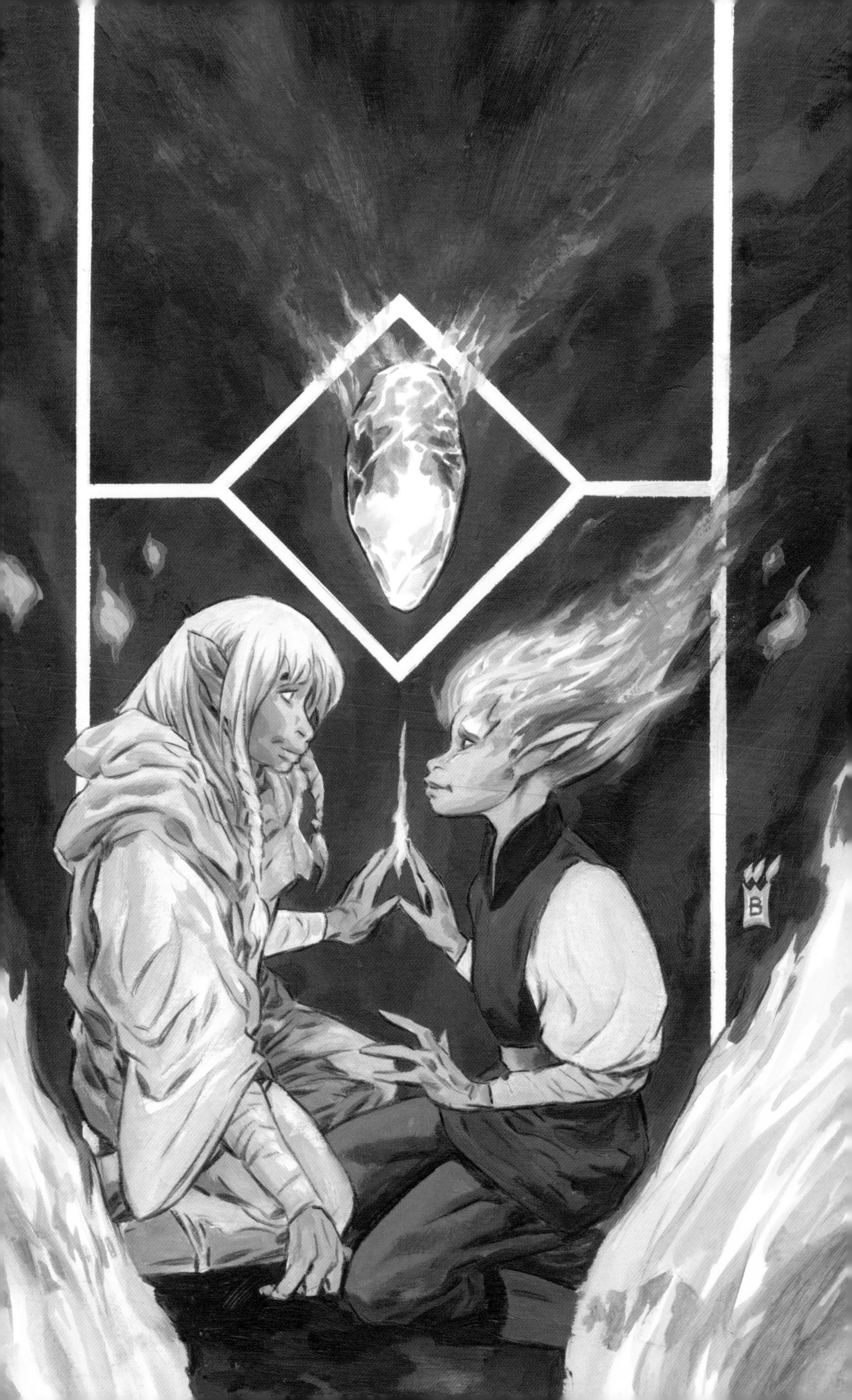

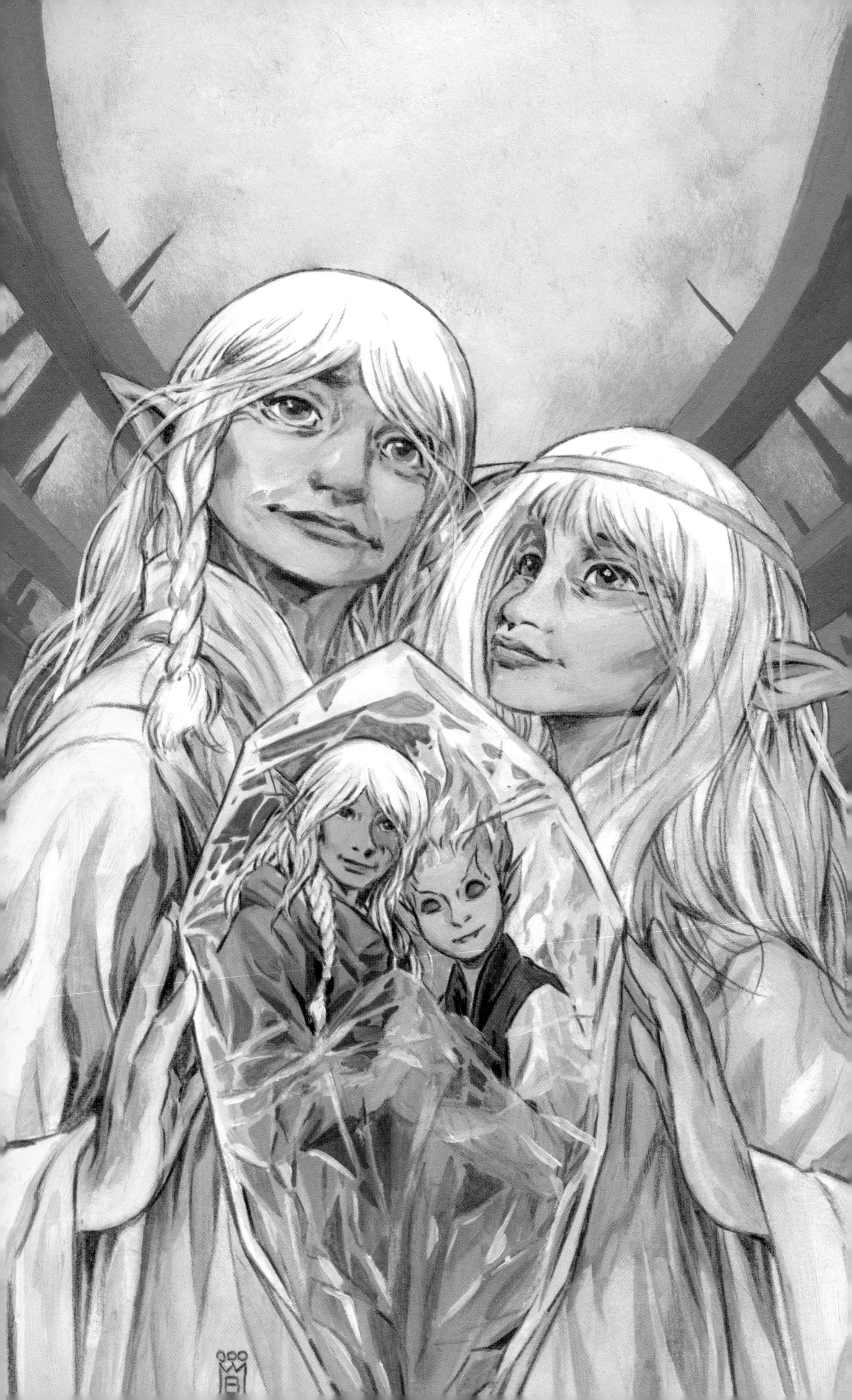

THE DARK CRYSTAL SKETCHBOOK

Under the guidance of The Jim Henson Company, Kelly and Nichole Matthews designed Thurma and the Firelings based on original concept art by Brian Froud. The following pages offer a behind-the-scenes look at the process.

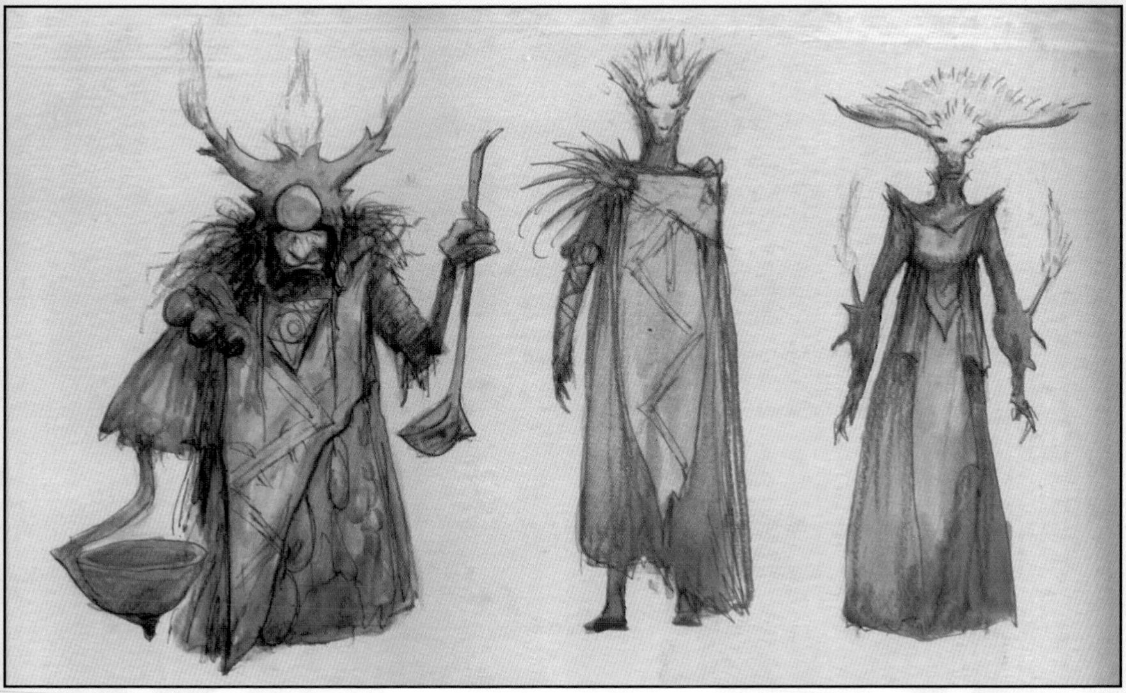

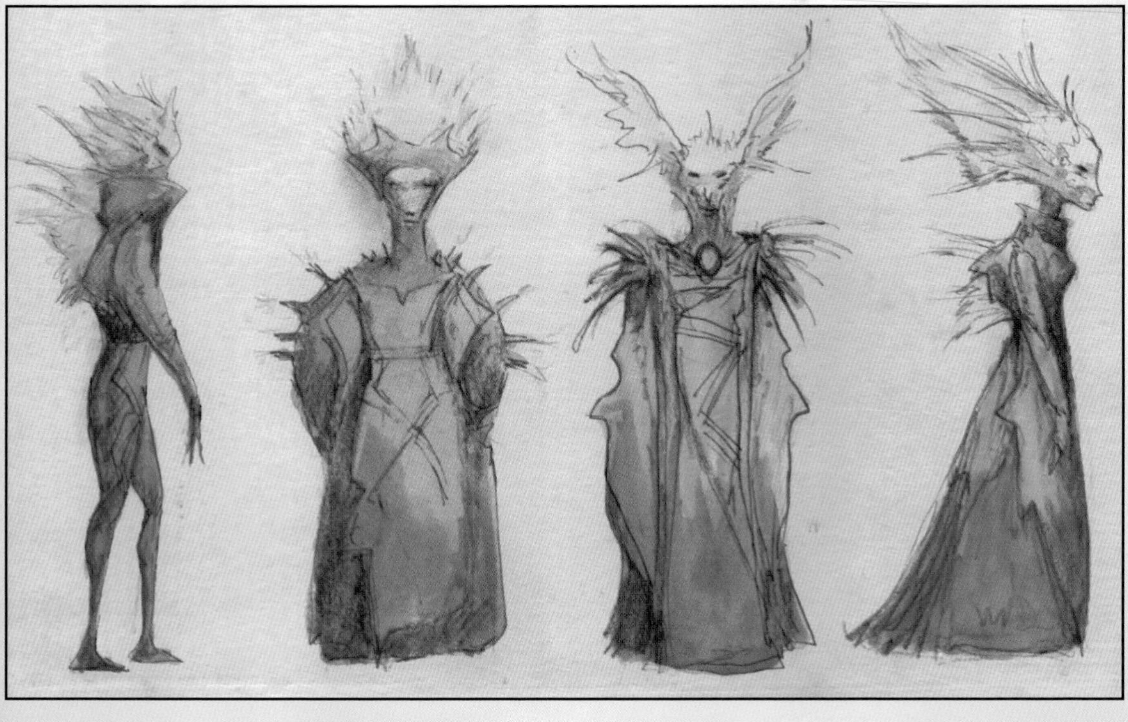

Original Fireling concept art by Brian Froud.

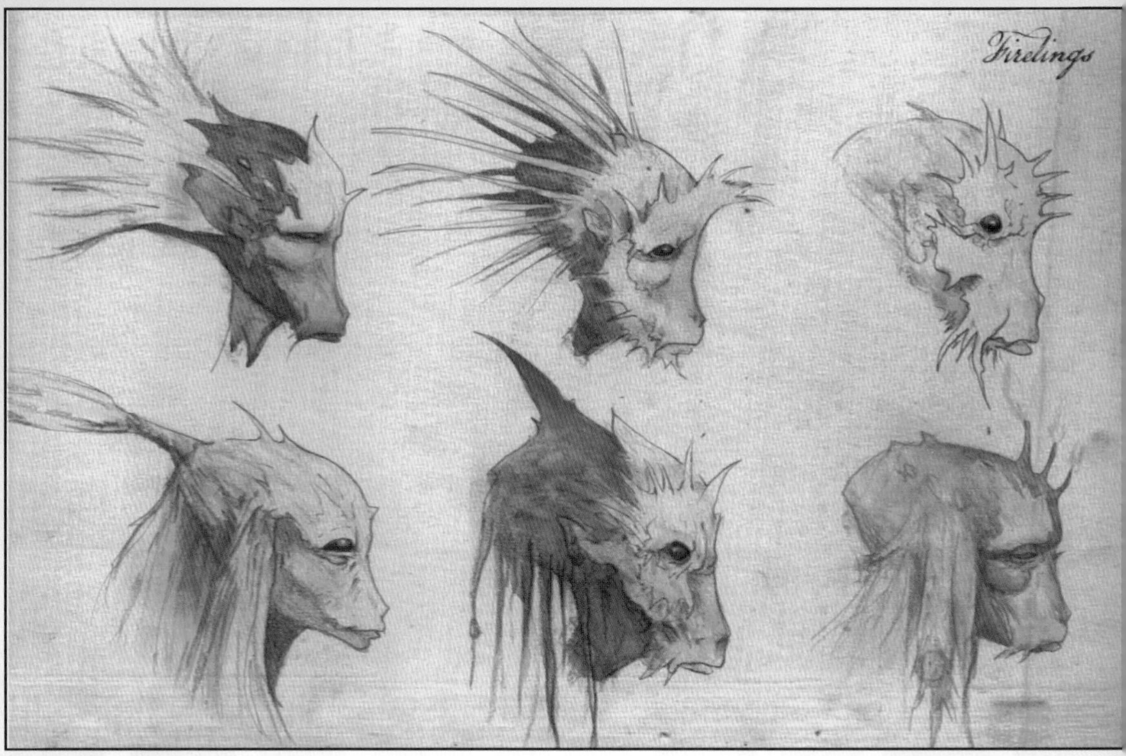
Firelings

Original Fireling headshot concept art by Brian Froud.

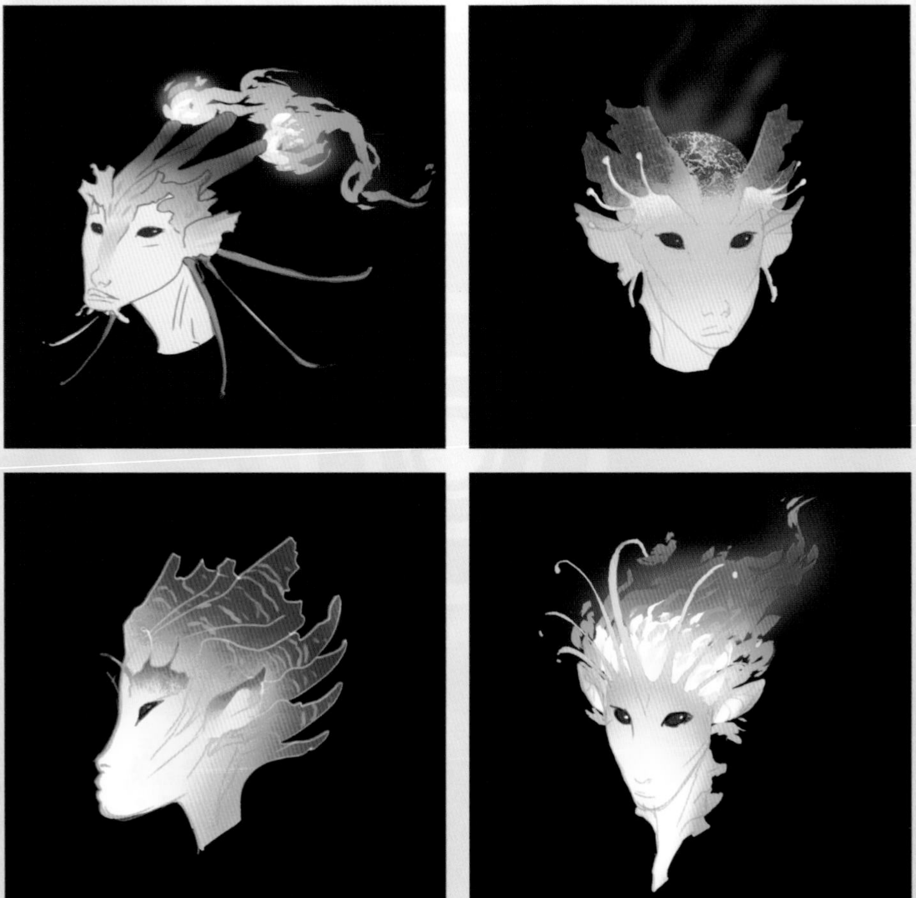

Fireling design process by Kelly and Nichole Matthews, based on Brian Froud's concept art.

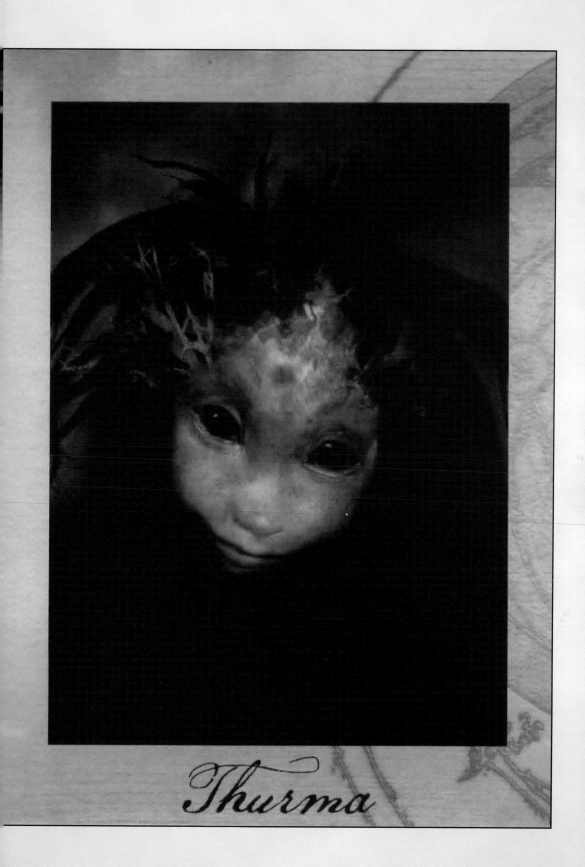

Thurma

Original Thurma concept art by Brian Froud and Wendy Froud.

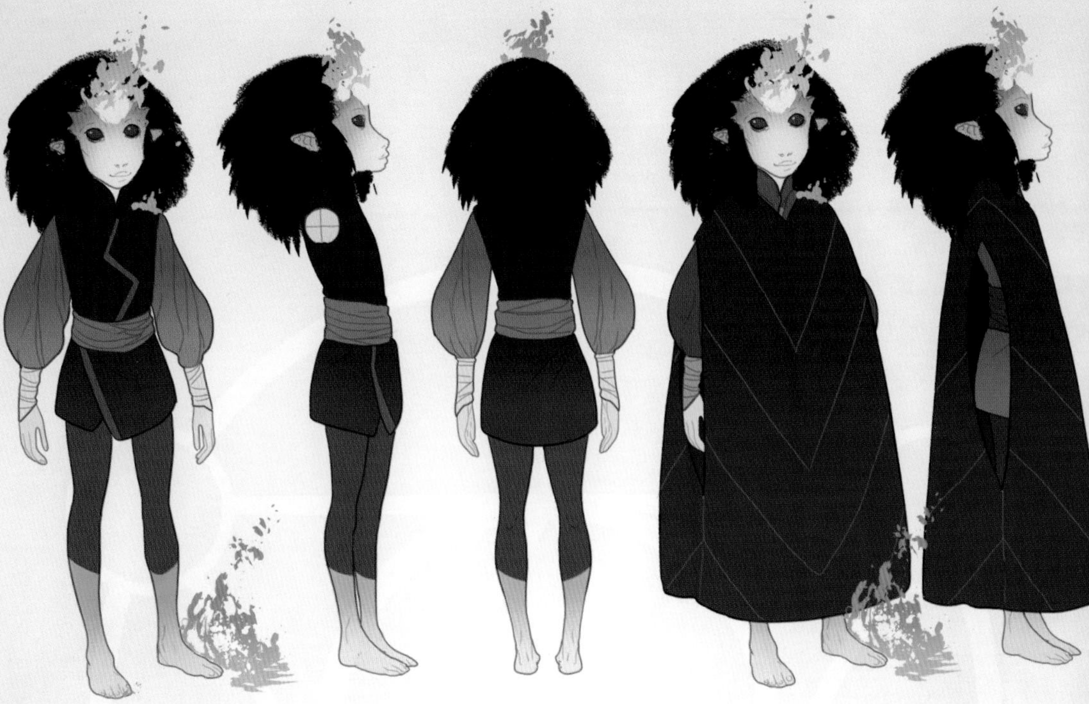

First pass on the Thurma character design by Kelly and Nichole Matthews.

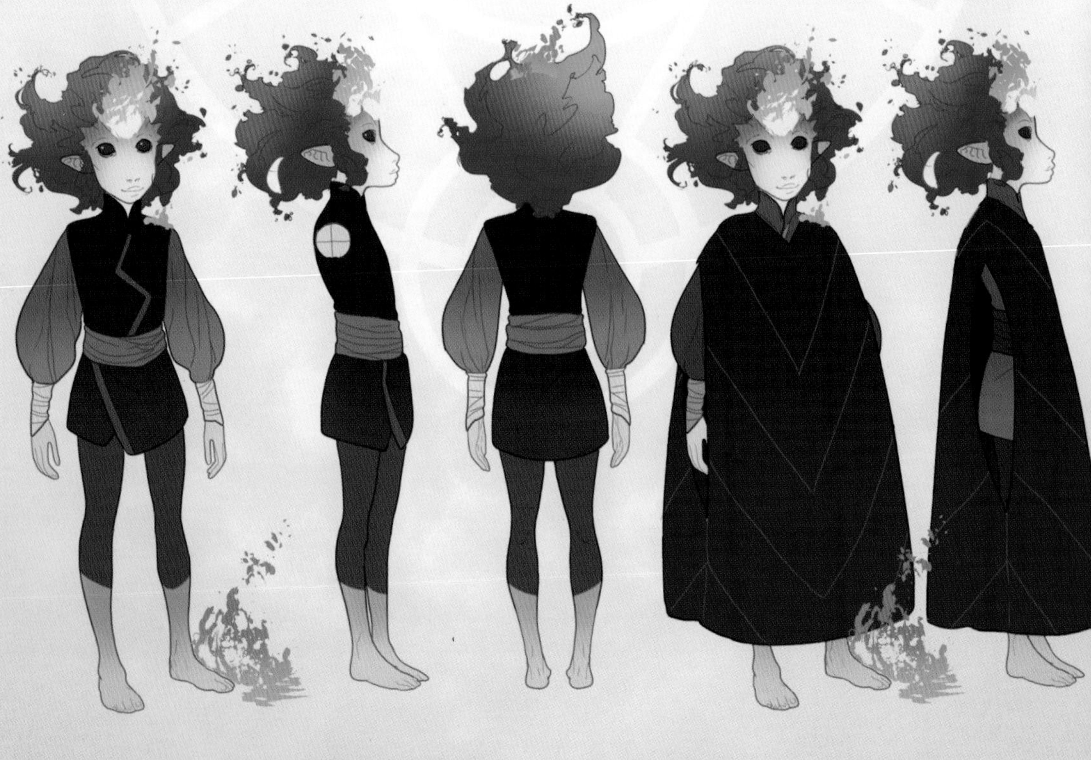

Second pass on the Thurma character design by Kelly and Nichole Matthews.

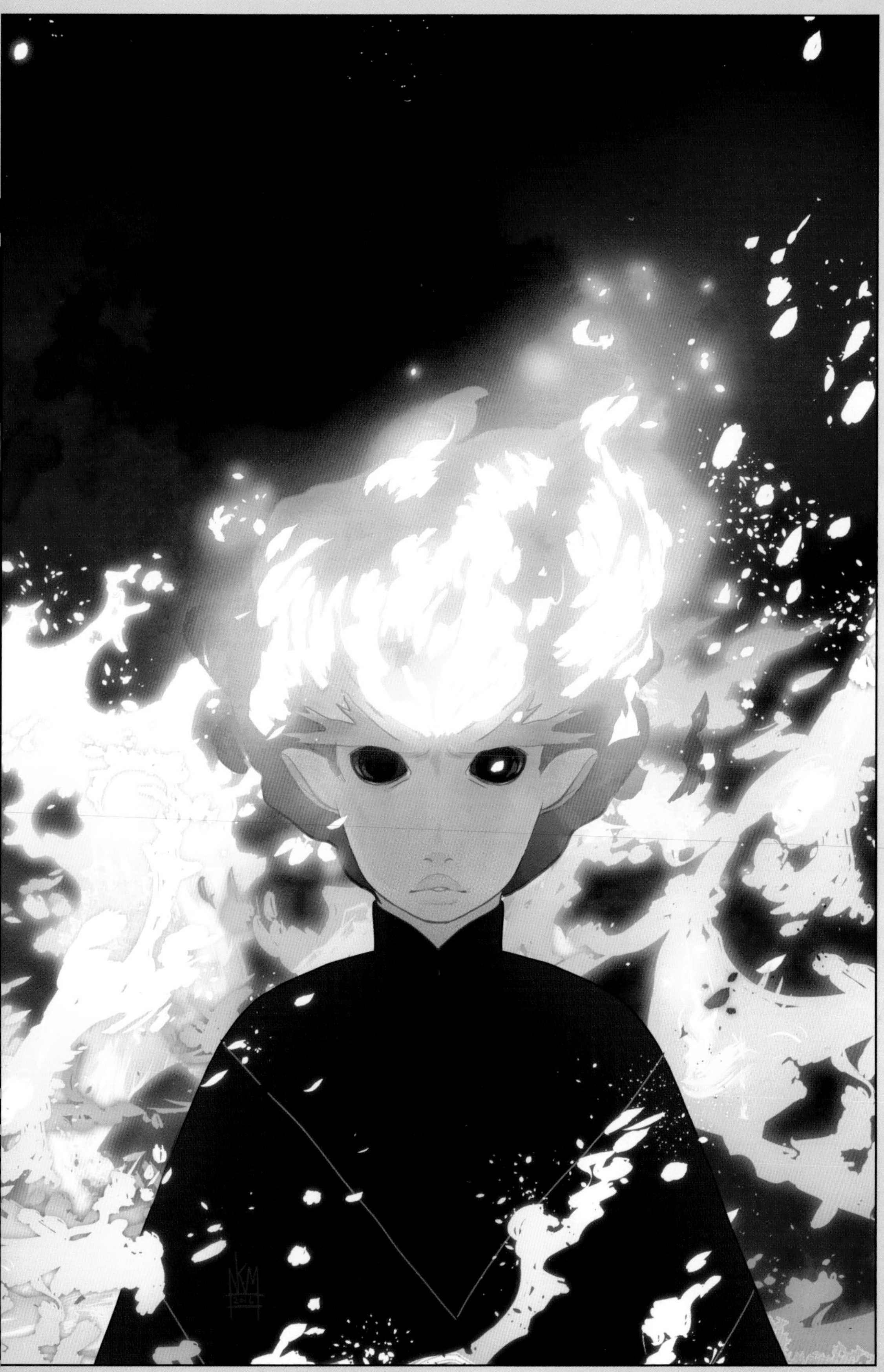

Final Thurma character design by Kelly and Nichole Matthews.

DISCOVER MORE FROM
THE DARK CRYSTAL

Jim Henson's
THE POWER OF THE
DARK CRYSTAL
SIMON SPURRIER
KELLY AND NICHOLE MATTHEWS

Jim Henson's
BENEATH THE
DARK CRYSTAL
ADAM SMITH
ALEXANDRIA HUNTINGTON
VOLUME ONE

JIM HENSON'S
THE DARK CRYSTAL
THE NOVELIZATION
Written by A.C.H. SMITH
with Illustrations from BRIAN FROUD
Jim Henson

Jim Henson's
THE DARK CRYSTAL
ARTIST TRIBUTE

THE DARK CRYSTAL
ADULT COLORING BOOK

Jim Henson's
THE DARK CRYSTAL
TALES

Jim Henson's The Power of the Dark Crystal
Simon Spurrier, Kelly and Nichole Matthews
Volume 1
ISBN: 978-1-68415-300-8 | $16.99 US
Volume 2
ISBN: 978-1-68415-457-9 | $16.99 US
Volume 3
ISBN: 978-1-68415-493-7 | $16.99 US

Jim Henson's Beneath the Dark Crystal
Adam Smith, Alexandria Huntington
Volume 1
ISBN: 978-1-68415-323-7 | $24.99 US
Volume 2
ISBN: 978-1-68415-396-1 | $24.99 US
Volume 3
ISBN: 978-1-68415-191-2 | $24.99 US

Jim Henson's The Dark Crystal: The Novelization
A.C.H. Smith, Brian Froud
ISBN: 978-1-68415-376-3 | $14.99 US

Jim Henson's The Dark Crystal Artist Tribute
Jae Lee, David Petersen, Mark Buckingham, Cory Godbey, and others
ISBN: 978-1-68415-182-0 | $24.99 US

Jim Henson's The Dark Crystal Adult Coloring Book
Dylan Burnett, Jorge Corona, Brandon Dayton, Jae Lee
ISBN: 978-1-68415-194-3 | $16.99 US

Jim Henson's The Dark Crystal Tales
Cory Godbey
ISBN: 978-1-60886-845-2 | $16.99 US

Jim Henson's The Dark Crystal: A Discovery Adventure
Laura Langston, Ann Marcellino
ISBN: 978-1-68415-169-1 | $14.99 US

ARCHAIA

AVAILABLE AT YOUR LOCAL COMICS SHOP AND BOOKSTORE
To find a comics shop in your area, visit www.comicshoplocator.com
WWW.**BOOM-STUDIOS**.COM

Jim Henson
THE JIM HENSON COMPANY

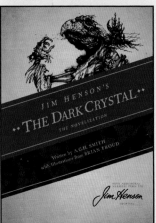